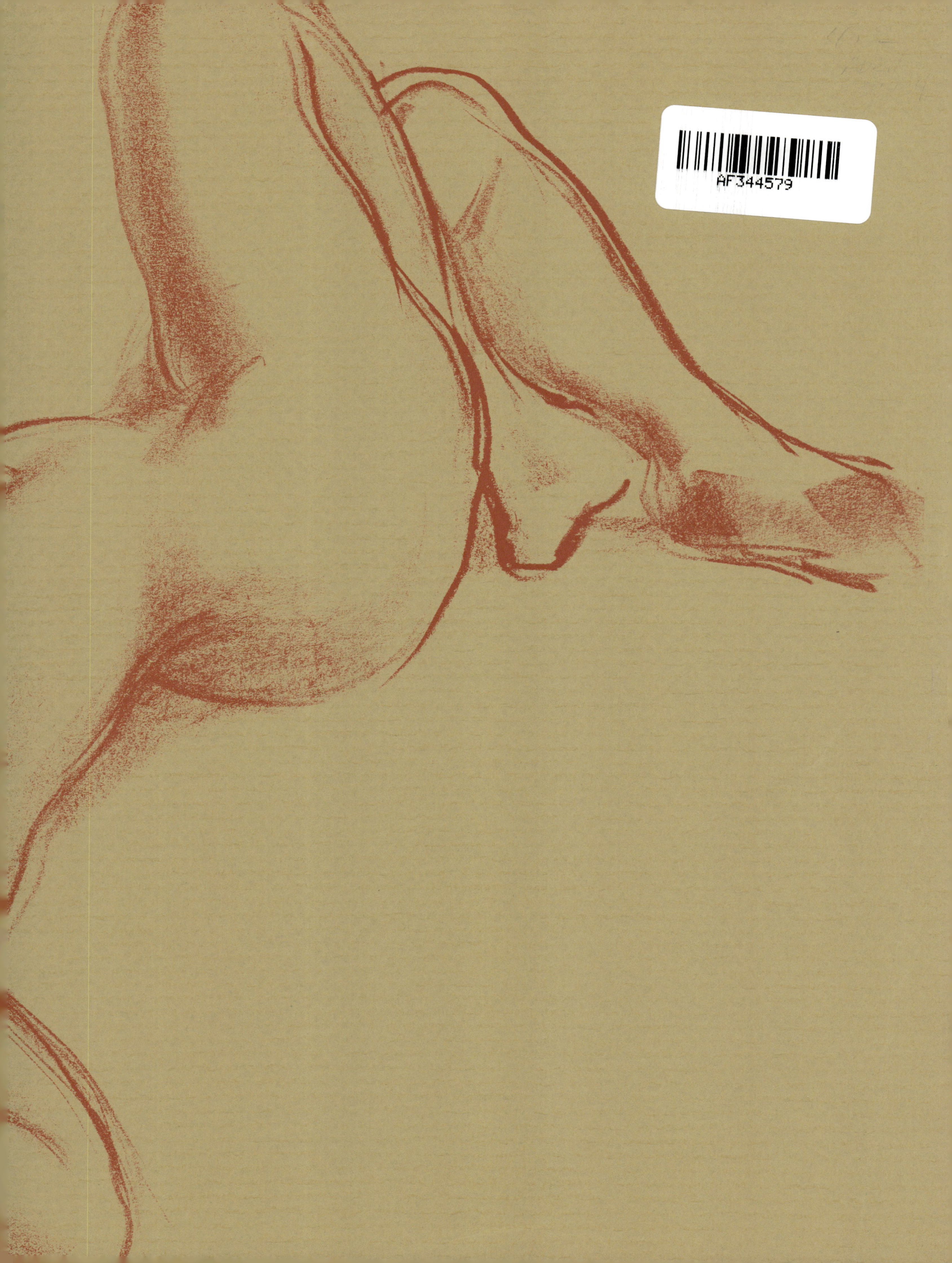

THE ART OF A. HENRY
NORDHAUSEN

THE ART OF A. HENRY
NORDHAUSEN

by

Laurence E. Schmeckebier

PHOENIX PUBLISHING

Canaan, New Hampshire

Schmeckebier, Laurence Eli, 1906-
    The Art of A. Henry Nordhausen.

    Includes index.
    1. Nordhausen, A. Henry, 1901-   2. Artists—
United States—Biography.   I.   Title.
N6537.N67S35   760'.092'4   [B]   80-20077
ISBN 0-914016-73-3

Contents

Acknowledgments   *vi*

Preface   *vii*

The Art of A. Henry Nordhausen   *1*

A Color Portfolio   *33*

Plates and Commentary   *65*

Figure Painting   *67*

Drawing   *98*

The Still Life   *106*

The Landscape   *108*

Prints and Monotypes   *114*

The Portrait   *122*

Appendices: Chronology   *150*

Permanent Collections   *152*

Plates and Illustrations   *153*

Index   *156*

The author wishes to express his special thanks to the following: to the artist for his complete and generous cooperation, to
the artist's wife, Ethel, for her assistance in assembling the
material, to the Archives of American Art for the privilege of
using the artists' papers in its collection, and to Mrs. Christine
Collins, Chief Librarian of the Parsons School of Design, for her
assistance in checking the early records of that institution.

Preface

WHY NORDHAUSEN?
The study of his art and career reveals
an important phase of American art in its dramatic transition from the period between the two World
Wars and the second half of the twentieth century. It is one that has either been taken for granted
or ignored altogether, or indeed flatly condemned as non-art by protagonists of special interests in
the promotion of their own aesthetic, financial, or patriotic points of view.

That the transition represented a fundamental change from a relatively limited and provincial art form
to one of international prominence there can be no argument. However, the complex and universal
character of that art form as it evolved in such a transition has yet to be fully understood. Therefore the
necessity for the study of specific artists, each within its own context and objectives—the archive
approach if you will—with the purpose of building a broader foundation for further interpretative study.

Through a lifelong and highly productive career, Nordhausen was motivated by certain fundamental
concepts: he believed in sound craftsmanship; he believed in the human figure as having the greatest
possibilities for artistic expression; he believed in the value of a recognizable subject as an enhancement
rather than a detriment to the expressive character of a work of art; and he believed that
the artist, the unique and distinctive individualist that he must be, must also accept his responsibility
as a functioning member of society.

There are a number of historic problems which are associated with this discussion but reach
far beyond the purposes of this study. One is the increasing recognition of the importance of Munich
along with that of Paris and Rome as significant influences on the development of American art.
A second is the persistence of realism and representational art from the early twenties through the second
and third quarters of this century when the abstract and other non-representational styles became
the dominant form of artistic expression.

While as a historian I find these challenging and important, I must confess my basic interest
in this study is Nordhausen as an artist and personality. Having known him since student days
in Munich I have had the opportunity to follow his work and ideas through the many years since then
and have always found them sound, consistent, and inspiring. Because of his natural reticence as well

as independence, the published articles about his work have been few: those by Leo da Vinci in *Artists and Models,* September 1925; Boyland Fitz-gerald in *The Artist,* April 1960; Ernest W. Watson's article on Nordhausen's monotypes in *American Artist,* June 1947; and my own article on Nordhausen's figure paintings in *American Artist,* February 1965.

My purpose, therefore, is to present the artist and his work, largely from his point of view, in as clear and straightforward a manner as possible. Questions of aesthetic judgment and the ultimate critical evaluation of his achievement I leave to the reader. Indeed, one cannot escape the feeling that the traditional position of the art critic as both arbiter and tastemaker has long been outmoded and that the current tendency among so many of our museums and galleries to present the work of contemporary artists of varied viewpoints, supported by scholarly catalogues, opens vast new vistas for both the artists and patrons of the future.

Finally, a word of praise and gratitude to the distinguished members of Phoenix Publishing, particularly A. L. Morris as publisher and designer, and Adrian A. Paradis as editor. With all due respect to the large achievements of the metropolitan art press, here is a small, regional operation dedicated to the old-fashioned idea that a well-designed book can be as much a work of art as the finest museum painting.

The design is not intended as a weighty decoration for the cocktail table, but rather as an organic development of the intellectual and aesthetic content of the text. The illustrations are kept in scale with adequate space to provide clarity and continuity in the flow of the content rather than being dramatized for a sensational effect which is often at variance with the quality of the original work represented. The integration of form and content—what the graphic designer calls "structure"—is therefore as essential in the design of the book as it is in any of the other arts.

Laurence E. Schmeckebier

Lyme, New Hampshire
May 15, 1980

viii

I

THE ART OF A. HENRY NORDHAUSEN

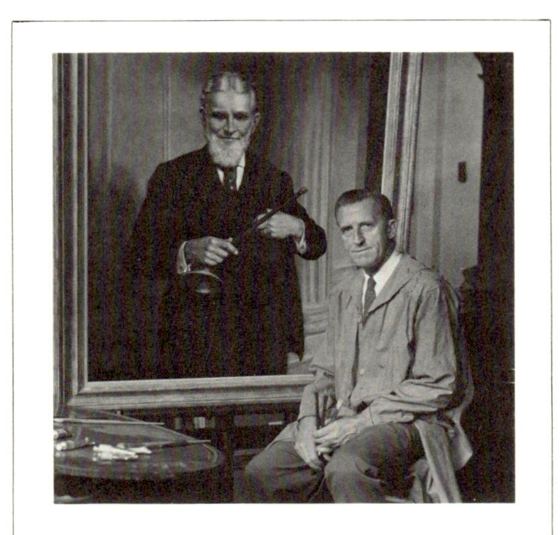

Early Life

"I believe a lot of hard work in drawing and painting has to be performed until the art becomes an unconscious and easy one," Nordhausen has often said. "The full rhythm of a musical phrase can only be expressed when familiarity with the instrument and the art of reading have made it unnecessary to concentrate on each note. Good and varied instruction is essential. One cannot simplify, distort, suggest, or abstract in painting unless one has a complete and thorough knowledge of one's craft. In this way one can give oneself over more effectively to the excitement of the genuinely creative."

Such a credo is a matter of faith and working habit that has its roots in a closely knit family background. It has characterized Nordhausen's sixty-year career as an artist through a fantastically varied period of depression, war, prosperity, and cultural reevaluation. The artistic product of that career does not necessarily reflect the "events of his times," as the cliché would have it, but rather the stubborn independence of one artist in his lifelong struggle to maintain his own creative expression against a historical panorama of incredibly rich artistic resources, opportunities, pressures, and frustrations.

AUGUST HENRY NORDHAUSEN was born in Hoboken, New Jersey, on January 25, 1901. His parents had migrated from the Hannover district of Germany in the late 1880s. His father's family originally came from the historic medieval town of Nordhausen in Lower Saxony. Henry was the youngest of four children (a fifth, Henry's twin brother, died at the age of two). His family moved to the Bronx in New York City and a short time thereafter to the resort town of Lake Huntington, Sullivan County, in the Catskill Mountains of New York, where they established a boardinghouse popular with summer vacationists escaping the oppressive heat of metropolitan New York.

Henry's education began in a one-room schoolhouse in Lake Huntington, then Public School No. 27 in the Bronx, and continued for a short time at Morris High School until he dropped out to go to work to help with the family finances. The two years' work, first as an office boy in a Wall Street law firm and then as a clerk in an insurance office, convinced him of the need for an education. In the fall of 1917 he entered Stuyvesant Technical High School, which a New York newspaper at the time praised as one of the outstanding high schools in the American public school system. At Stuyvesant he was a good student and completed the required four-year academic program in three years. He excelled in mathematics and science, but his major interest developed in art under the influence of a German art teacher, Henry Fritz. On evenings, weekends, and holidays he delivered newspapers for the *Bronx Home News* and worked in a neighborhood grocery store.

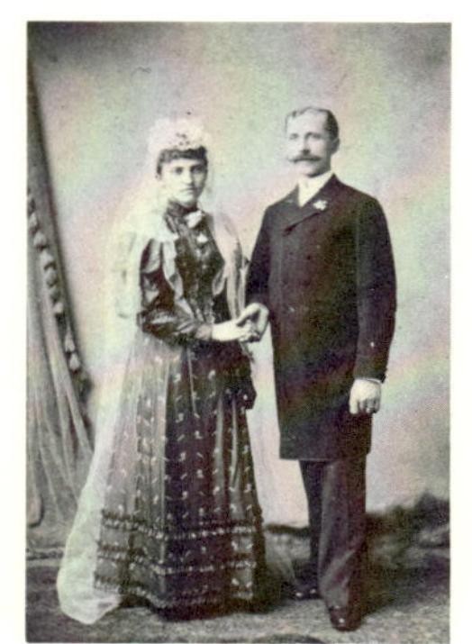

*Henry and
Katherine Nordhausen's
wedding photograph,
Hoboken, New Jersey, 1890.*

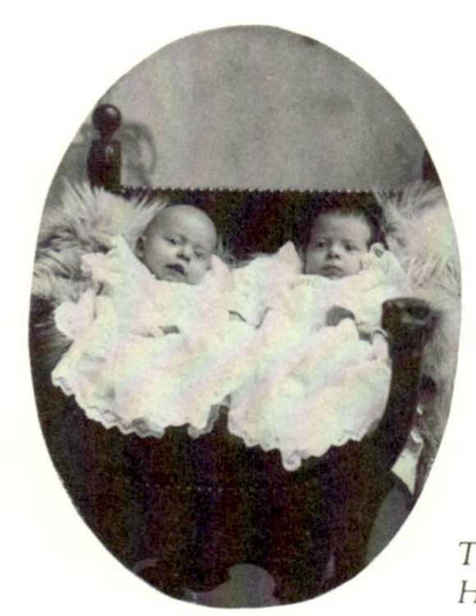

*The twins,
Henry and John, at six months.*

In the student records he is listed as the gold medal winner of the competition for the 1919 Christmas cover of a student publication, *The Caliper*; a winner of a poster contest in 1920; and a member of the sketch club. In his senior year he was art editor for the school annual, *The Indicator*, for which he did most of the art and layout work, and he was a regular member of the baseball team. What finally determined his future as an artist was the award in 1920 of a scholarship in a citywide competition sponsored by the New York School Art League.

The definition of character in an artist's early work is an elusive problem. The romantic concept of the child as father of the man compels the observer to search beyond the surface patterns and technical skills for more deeply rooted attitudes which may or may not determine the subsequent development of the mature artist.

The selection of examples given here reveals two facets of the artist's abilities. First, the young artist was able to handle the standard assignments of the class in commercial illustration with ease and facility; second, his later work is distinguished by his remarkable capacity for observation of essential detail combined with a gentle and prevailing sense of humor. The casual but not accidental association of the rounded form of the static still life and boxers in action suggested in quick sketches on the back of a watercolor indicate again a characteristic that persists throughout the artist's later work.

Studies In New York

IN 1920 Henry Nordhausen enrolled as a scholarship student in the New York School of Fine and Applied Arts (now the Parsons School of Design), then located at 2239 Broadway. The program included courses in poster advertising, commercial art, and stage design—all of them prefaced by courses in life drawing and painting from nature.* Frank Alvah Parsons taught the courses in art history and interpretation; other instructors included Guido Rosa and Frank Fiore. In the 1922 catalogue, the young Nordhausen is listed as "Assistant in Life Drawing and Illustration." The courses he liked best were those on figure drawing with Harry B. Baker and painting with Howard Giles. He considered Giles no giant as an artist but a great teacher: sincere, articulate, a good draftsman, and an artist able to demonstrate on the canvas or drawing board the idea or theory he sought to present.

Howard Giles was well known as an illustrator in the 1920s; he had been a frequent lecturer on art at various colleges and universities such as Harvard, Yale, Wellesley, and the Carnegie Art Institute; and he was later dean of the fine arts department of the Master Institute of the Roerich Museum in New York. Although he was fully aware of the necessity of intuition and the creative independence of the individual, his teaching stressed knowledge and the intellectual mastery of

---

* Marjorie F. Jones, *A History of the Parsons School of Design, 1896-1966* (Ann Arbor, Mich.; University Microfilms, 1969).

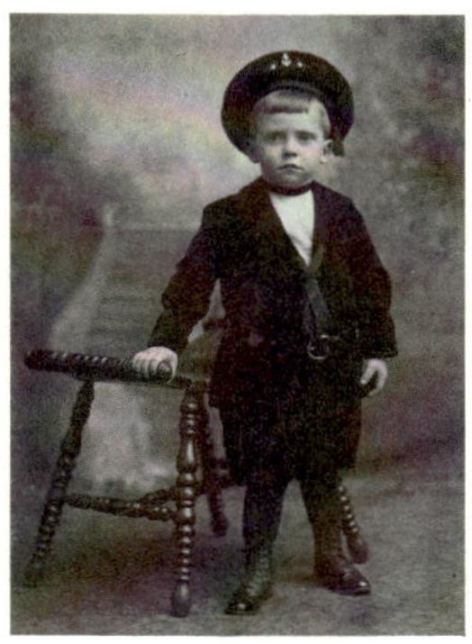

Henry, age four.

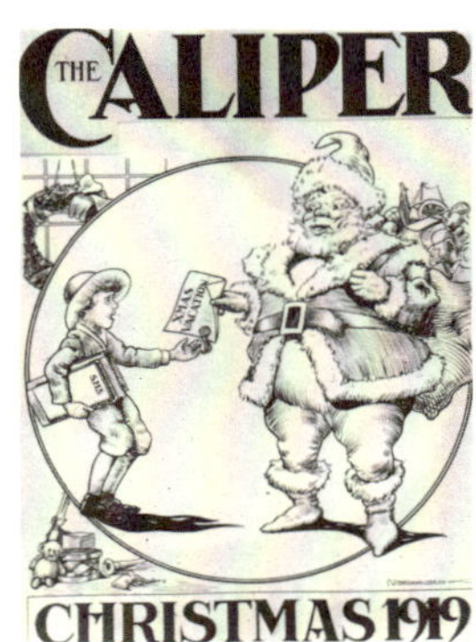

*Cover design
for the Christmas
issue of* The Caliper, *1919.*

artistic means. He was interested in anatomy, not strictly in the facts of bone and muscle structure, but in how it worked as a functioning organism. He applied this approach to the total structure of the figure, but he also stressed the details: how the ear, hand, ankle, and foot operate as moving mechanisms. The same process could be observed in the study of drawings and compositions of the old masters.

Such analysis could often be justified through the use of mathematics, and it is in this respect that Giles became intrigued with the design theories of Jay Hambridge, who began to lecture and publish in 1916 and had considerable influence on many of the artists of the 1920s. Indeed, the 1921 catalogue of the New York School of Fine and Applied Arts lists a course called "Hambridge Research," which was devoted to the "Jay Hambridge Discovery," that is, dynamic symmetry.* Giles was well aware that theory and mechanical formulas could make design formal and rigid, but for the artist he used to say, "it all depends on whether he uses it or it

uses him." "Our generation is passing," he is quoted as saying. "The intimate personal affectations pass with us. But the impersonal knowledge accumulated over the years can and must be transmitted to oncoming youth."

Although he felt that he was getting a good foundation at the New York School of Fine Arts, the young Nordhausen became restless. With his German background and awareness of the Munich tradition that had been kept alive in New York for so many years by William Merritt Chase, he decided to go to Munich for further study.

To that end he worked at whatever odd jobs he could find during the year and drove a taxi during summers at Lake Huntington. "Hacking," he said, "was good business at the time and I was making an average of fifty dollars a day." With the money he had saved he set sail for Europe in the fall of the year 1922.

---

* "Dynamic symmetry is a system of notation in areas and like the natural notation of numbers, a series or a scheme adaptable to any particular purpose may be selected." (Jay Hambridge, *Dynamic Symmetry in Composition as Used by Artists,* New York, 1923, p. 31). Its chief concern is the proportioning of areas from the design point of view, with the square as its basic unit whose equal sides form a 1:1 ratio, which Hambridge called a root 1 rectangle. By placing the diagonal of this square on the baseline, a second rectangle is formed, which he called a root 2 rectangle. The process can go on indefinitely in a series of continuing proportions which include such standard concepts as the golden section and the whirling square. In the book Hambridge also describes the procedure as used by a number of artists including George Bellows, Robert Henri, Howard Giles, Leon Kroll, Denman Ross, and others.

A retrospective exhibition devoted to the principles and use of dynamic symmetry was organized by the Museum of Art, Rhode Island School of Design, Providence, Rhode Island, in 1961 with a catalogue by David G. Carter and an extensive bibliography.

With his interest in mathematics Nordhausen had always been intrigued by the Hambridge theories of dynamic symmetry. His copy of the Hambridge *Dynamic Symmetry in Composition* is full of his notes and diagrams based on his study of the various procedures. He often cited the deep impression made in these early years when he learned that the great Shakespearean actor, Walter Hampden, used this method of design in determining his position on the stage at a given dramatic moment.

Munich

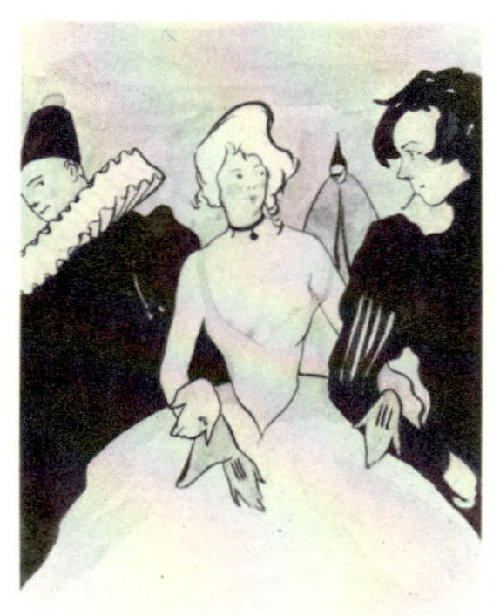

Carnival watercolor, 1919.

MUNICH during the early 1920s was in the throes of postwar reconstruction, political turmoil, and disastrous inflation, so that conditions there were difficult. But Americans were well received. They had the advantage of possessing solid dollars, and living for them was comfortable and indeed abundant. Studies at the university and art schools were intense and thorough in the prewar tradition. After the usual preliminary examination involving two days of drawing from the figure, Nordhausen was accepted into the class of Hugo Freiherr von Habermann at the Munich Academy of Fine Arts.

Along with Dresden and Berlin during the 1920s, Munich was one of the most vital and active art centers in Germany. The outstanding painters at the academy were Hugo von Habermann and Franz von Stuck, both of whose classes were considered the most competitive and prestigious in the school. Stuck represented the more progressive traditions of the *Münchener Sezession* and the *Jugendstil,** with his rather heavy, dark, and allegorically charged decorative style; Habermann was more of a realist, emphasizing genre, animal, figure, and portrait studies. Habermann was considered an inspiring and genial local old master, having originally studied with Piloty and Wilhelm von Diez and developed under the influence of Wilhelm Leibl and the Impressionists in Paris, especially Whistler.

Whereas Munich at the time was considered politically and socially conservative, in the realm of stylistic and aesthetic ideas it remained open to all aspects of contemporary movements with a consistent emphasis on local masters and traditions. These go back to the mid-nineteenth-century historical painter Karl von Piloty, the portrait painter Franz von Lenbach, the figure painter Hans von Marées, and the animal painter Heinrich von Zügel. The interest in bright color and the freer handling of paint evident in the work of Zügel became more specifically Impressionist in the work of Max Liebermann, who had lived in Munich from 1878 to 1884, and more expressive and dynamically personal in the work of the younger Lovis Corinth and Max Slevogt.

Of particular attraction at the time was the work of Wilhelm Leibl and Arnold Böcklin. Böcklin was of Swiss origin and had developed a combination of romantic allegory with luminous color and strong figure drawing. Leibl had studied in Munich and Paris under Courbet's influence and became well known for his realistic and factual studies of Upper Bavarian peasants and genre scenes with their brilliant color and solid, sensitive drawing. Indeed, the earthy realism of Gustave Courbet had been a strong element of Munich's artistic tradition since the famous exhibition of his work in the Glaspalast in 1869, which first established him as an international influence.

---

* In Munich as well as Berlin and Vienna there were numerous groups of progressive artists who seceded (hence, *Sezession*) from the established organizations to promote their own ideas and work through publicity and special exhibitions. The Munich group, known as the *Münchener Sezession,* was organized in 1892 by Stuck, Fritz von Uhde, and Wilhelm Trübner and continued as a stimulating artistic force for many years. The *Jugendstil* was a broader-based decorative style related to French *Art Noveau* and the English Arts and Crafts movement (William Morris) and promoted largely by the art review *Jugend* (Youth), founded in 1896.

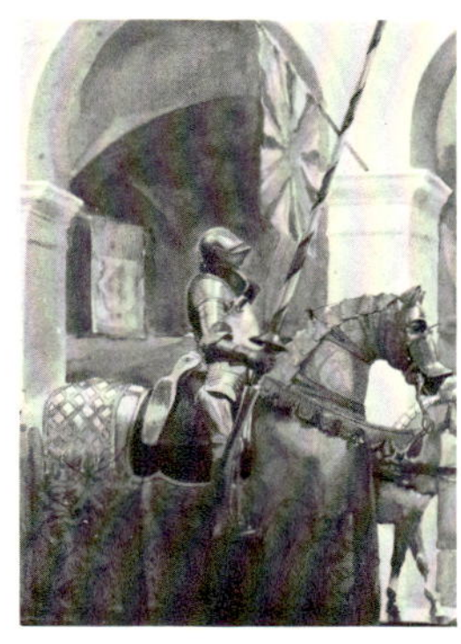

*Watercolor of knights
in armor in the Metropolitan
Museum's Medieval Hall, 1919.*

Sketch of Harry B. Baker, 1921.

There were still memories of the American artists who had studied and taught in Munich during the 1870s, notably Frank Duveneck, William Merritt Chase, and Frank Currier. The Americans had little influence on the Germans at the time, but they did provide leadership and encouragement to a considerable number of younger Americans during that decade and became a major factor in the development of American art of the later nineteenth century.*

In contrast to these more realistic and nature-oriented approaches, the modern movement in Munich, with its Post-Impressionist background in the work of Cézanne, Van Gogh, Gauguin, Ferdinand Hodler and especially Edvard Munch, had its own *Blaue Reiter* (Blue Rider) group (especially Wassily Kandinski, August Macke, Franz Marc, and Paul Klee) of prewar days. These artists gradually became identified as Expressionists parallel to the active groups in Dresden and Berlin (notably Max Pechstein, Emil Nolde, Karl Schmidt-Rottluff, Ernst Ludwig Kirchner, Erich Heckel, Karl Hofer, and Max Beckmann), with their emphasis on a deeper spiritual content and a more personal dynamic and expressive form.

In the spirit of continued and lively competition of *Der Blaue Reiter* artists organized themselves into another and even more vocal progressive group, the *Neuekünstlervereinigung* (New Artists' Federation), which felt itself more in tune with the international abstract movements.

Along with the works of the old masters in the magnificent collection of the Alte Pinakothek, all of these artists were represented in the official museums such as the Neue Staatsgalerie, the Neue Pinakothek, the Schackgalerie, and the Lenbach Museum. There were also regular exhibitions by local artists in Munich's gigantic iron-and-glass exhibition hall built in 1854 as its version of the famous London Crystal Palace and devoted to the annual shows of local artists since 1888. Local as well as internationally recognized artists were also shown at the Münchener Künstlergenossenschaft (Munich Artists Association) as well as at the private commercial galleries such as Hanfstaengl's, Heinemann's, Thannhauser's, and Caspari's.

This was the artistic scene in Munich during the early 1920s. For a young man of twenty-one with little more than the foundation for a professional artist's training, the educational opportunities thus presented were unlimited. His objectives were clear: he wanted to learn how to draw and paint so that he could earn a living, but he also wanted to become an artist like those whose work he saw in the museums and art galleries.

* In 1978 an exhibition entitled "Munich and American Realism in the 19th Century," with a comprehensive and scholarly catalogue, was organized by the E. B. Crocker Art Gallery in Sacramento, California, to celebrate the hundredth anniversary of the first exhibition of the "Munich Men," held in 1878 and sponsored by the Society of American Artists to honor the young American artists who had studied in the Bavarian capital.

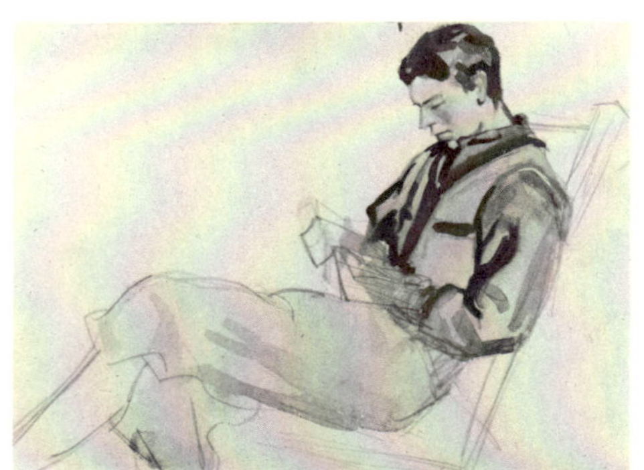

Seated figure, 1921.

Study at the Academy

HIS ROUTINE was quickly established. No English was spoken then except in the major hotels, and although Henry had heard his parents speak in German among themselves, the family spoke only English at home. Thanks to his natural aptitude and habitual enthusiasm, the young artist learned German quickly, and in his daily communications he could always draw a picture of what he wanted when his vocabulary failed.

The class program at the academy was well-established but not rigid: alternately drawing and painting from the model, mostly life-sized, six to eight hours a day, five days a week. No attendance records were kept, but the class was always full. The urbane and much respected Professor von Habermann, known affectionately as "The Baron" by his students, appeared two or three times a week, during which he made his rounds to deliver individual critiques and occasionally to engage in group discussions.

Max Doerner's class in painting techniques was held in his studio on the top floor of the academy building. Through lectures, demonstrations, and actual practice, one learned to grind one's own colors, prepare canvases, and follow the procedures employed by the masters in building a painting from the first sketches to the final product.

Anatomy classes were conducted by Professor Mollier in the circular auditorium of the university's medical school, where the entire system of bone, tendon, and muscle structure of the human body was studied from actual cadavers. Regular lectures on the history of art were available at the university on an audit basis, but for the most part study of the old masters was based on the original work in the Alte Pinakothek and discussions in the studio. Nordhausen's visits to museums and galleries became habitual, usually taking place at noon and on weekends, with a constant shifting of attention to specific painters and problems that became an extension of the practical problems dealt with each day at the student's own easel.

For relaxation and practice the evenings were spent in sketch classes where a model was available in successive poses. There was no instruction, but opportunity was provided for drawing and experimenting. There was a regular sketch class at the academy, but there were also *Abendakt* (evening figure drawing) sessions at two private schools popular among students who were preparing to take the entrance exams at the academy. The more conservative of these was Heymann's; the more liberal and progressive was Hans Hofmann's, which was particularly favored by the Americans.

During the spring of 1923 Henry attended a number of courses in commercial layout and graphic design at the Munich Kunstgewerbe-schule, particularly one with Olaf Gulbransson, the great Norwegian graphic artist and painter, whose drawings in *Simplicissimus* made him one of the most famous and feared caricaturists in Germany. Gulbransson's penetrating analysis of character, his superb drawing, and his uncanny economy of line had a profound influence on the

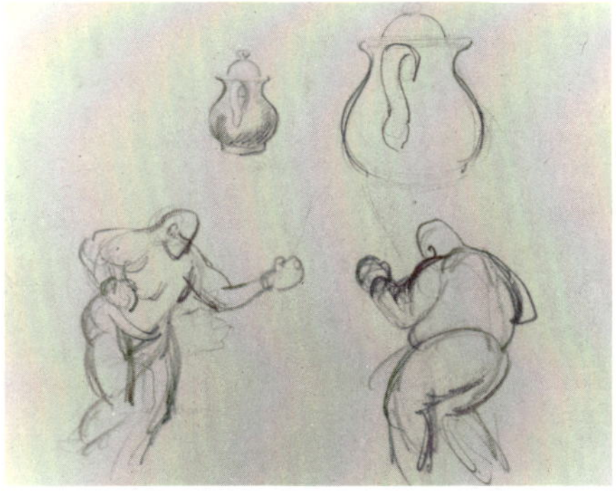

Sketchbook exercise, 1921.

young artist.

It was at one of these sketch classes that Nord-hausen made the acquaintance of Lyle W. Funk, a young American art student who later became a prominent advertising designer in New York. Funk was then living in Munich with his uncle, Wilhelm Funk, a distinguished painter and personality who became a close friend, teacher, and advisor to Nordhausen both during those early years and when he returned later in 1928 for continued study. He maintained an elegant studio with house and garden on Georgenstrasse in fashionable Schwabing, where the young Americans were frequently entertained.

In this connection the art and career of Wilhelm Heinrich Funk have more than a casual relationship, not only as an influence and inspiration for Nordhausen, but also as a continuing link between Munich and American art during the years just before and after World War I. Funk, born in Hannover, Germany, had attended the Munich Academy for several years before emigrating to New York in 1885 where he continued his studies at the Art Students League. He became a successful portrait painter in New York and exhibited in the Carnegie Institute shows in Pittsburgh in 1904 and 1905 as well as the Paris Société des Arts Françaises. He returned to take up permanent residence in Munich well before the outbreak of the war, had taught for a time at the Munich Academy, and continued to exhibit in the annual Glaspalast shows from 1914 on. Both before the war and after, even during the difficult years of the 1920s, Funk had been a highly successful artist, painting portraits of the Bavarian royal family and many of the

socially prominent Munich residents at prices comparable to the best in London and New York.

Compared with the teeming excitement of metropolitan New York, Munich in the 1920s was a quiet, reserved, congenial Bavarian town, but it had cultural advantages unrivaled in any of the great metropolitan centers of Europe. Opera flourished in the National Theatre and in the Residenz (now Cuvilliés) and the Prinz Regenten theaters. Superb symphony programs were conducted at the Odeon by Bruno Walter and Hans Knappertsbusch, and the museums provided some of the finest examples of both contemporary and historical works of art, with of course a strong emphasis on the city's own local tradition. All of these were within walking distance of the center of town, or at least a short ride on the convenient and ever present streetcar. And with a student identity card these were available at a less than nominal fee.

The Search for Identity

FOR NORDHAUSEN'S artistic development the change was dramatic, swift, and consistent. The ideal he had followed as a young student in New York was that of the more commercially oriented working artists such as J. C. Leydendecker, H. P. Raleigh, Walter Briggs, and N. C. Wyeth. Here in Munich the artist seemed to have a more independent standing and was considered a social and cultural asset, with the annual exhibitions of the Glaspalast and the per-

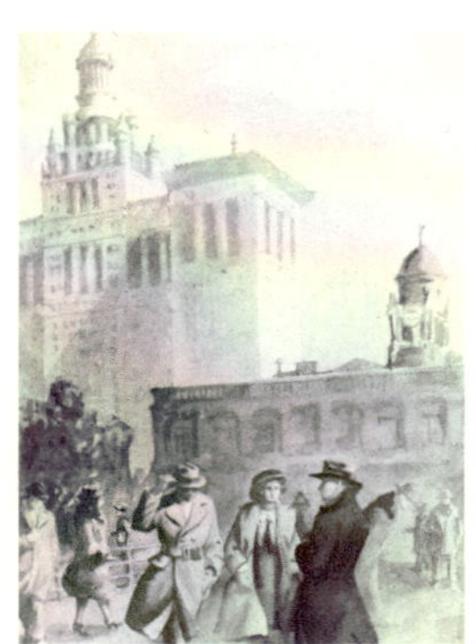

Project for advertising design class, 1921.

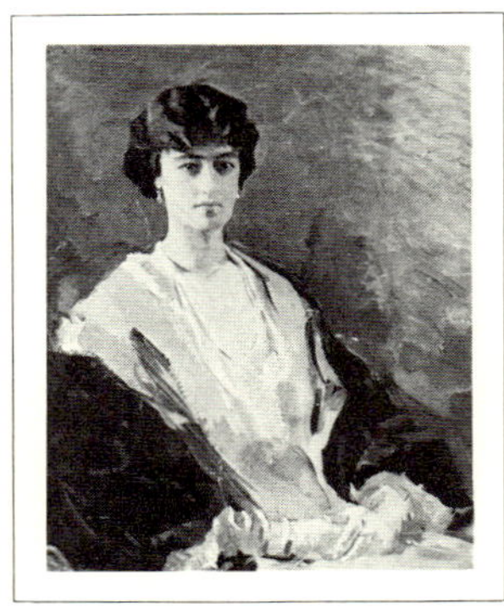

Wilhelm Funk's "HRH the Crown Princess of Bavaria," painted in 1921.

manent status of the museum as the ultimate goal. This is not to say that such an ideal had not existed in New York, but in Nordhausen's experience and development in the new cultural environment of the German city he discovered that the importance and the possibilities of the artist were considerably different, the horizons broader, and the challenges much more demanding.

His art was essentially realist in attitude. It was not encumbered by the elaborate allegory and symbolism characteristic of Franz von Stuck and Arnold Böcklin but insisted on the direct adherence to nature as advocated by Habermann, Leibl, and Lenbach, with the international influence of Courbet in the immediate background. The artist's effort was concentrated on the medium and the eternal struggle for control of his own means of expression. One does not invent ideas out of the air or one's inner self but works from the object in nature; ideas develop out of this integral creative process.

The modern point of view, with its infinite stylistic variations, was vital and very much in evidence at the time. It was not "taught" as such at the academy but was available in superb examples in the Neue Staatsgalerie and the commerical galleries. Although Hans Hofmann advocated good drawing and worked from models in his school, he encouraged each of his students to probe and experiment with any and all problems of color and form so as to develop his own sense of freedom, individuality, and confidence.

In the studio, the *Bierstube* or the café, the issue of the academic-conservative versus the progressive-modern was a subject of constant and lively discussion. Among Nordhausen's American friends were Carl Holty and Vaclav Vytlacil, two young men from Hofmann's school who later developed a considerable reputation in the United States. For a time, Nordhausen shared a studio with Vytlacil, who had been painting in a strictly academic manner and was now experimenting with more abstract forms. Both of his friends were enthusiastic and vociferous about the modern abstract point of view, understanding and respectful of Nordhausen's drawing and painting ability, but benignly condescending in their comments that he had not yet seen the light.

Nordhausen's reply was that whereas he appreciated the specialized commitment to the problems of color, design, and form, as well as the sometimes exotic or personal subject matter that have made up the panorama of isms in the modern movement, the limitation to a specific abstract concept suited neither his personality nor his purpose. He admired the fantasy and deep psychological insight of Paul Klee and Edvard Munch, and the vigor and brute force of Oskar Kokoschka and Max Beckmann but refused to be overwhelmed by the power of their character and presentation. Stimulating as they were, the study of the modern work of art for him invariably led to a renewed understanding and appreciation of the old masters, from Renoir and Degas to Rubens, Rembrandt, and Franz Hals.

This background suggests not only the technical training at the academy but also the atmosphere, the ideas, and the attitudes which existed in Munich at that time and set the pattern of Nordhausen's career for the next fifty years. His was a genial, enthusiastic, and outgoing personality; he was always interested in people, from the

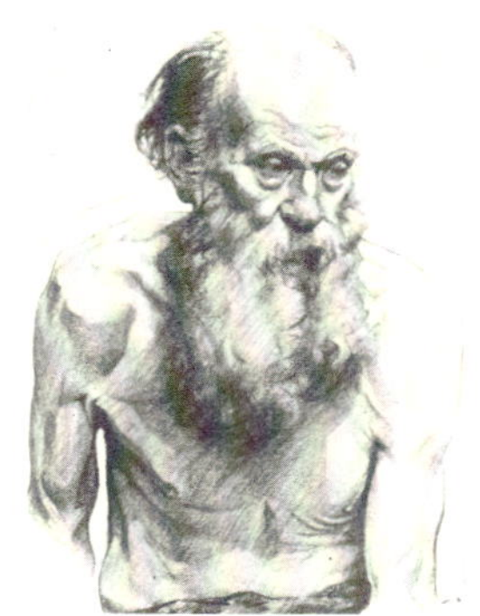
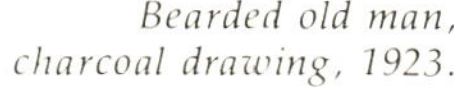

*Bearded old man,
charcoal drawing, 1923.*

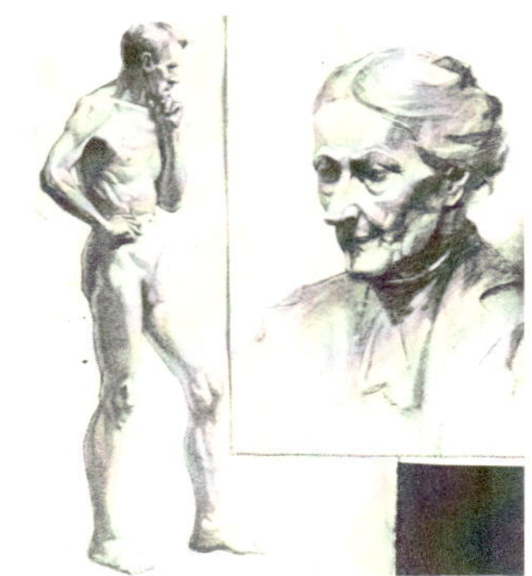

Charcoal studies, 1923.

jovial Bavarian peasants and barmaids in the *Bierstube* to the exuberant crowds of the annual *Fasching* (the famous winter Mardi Gras) and *Oktoberfest* (the great outdoor fall beer festival) celebrations, to the superb, distinctly Bavarian performances of Munich's theater and opera.

The mood is perhaps best expressed by Nordhausen himself just after his return to New York in an article with illustrations, "Aus Meiner Münchener Mappe" (From My Munich Portfolio),* in which he described the beauty of the city and the cultural advantages of Munich for the young American artist. He was impressed by the easygoing, good-natured *Gemütlichkeit* of the Bavarians; by their love and respect for their local traditions; and by the friendly, devoted concern of his teachers, particularly Wilhelm Funk and Hugo von Habermann: "If you want to live in a city filled with art and the spirit of the artist," he concluded, "go to Munich!"

The romantic reminiscences of student life in Munich had a realistic side, however, which left a profound impression on the young artist. For an American student with even the most modest resources, life in Germany during those years of disastrous inflation was indeed luxurious, whereas for the Germans it was increasingly difficult and often tragic. The story was told of an elderly peasant from one of the mountain villages in Oberbayern who had come to the big city to celebrate *Fasching* with his life savings in his pocket. Between the inflation and the drunken melée of the famous carnival he lost every cent he had and

shot himself in despair. What shocked Nordhausen was the realization that a couple of American dollars could have saved the man's life.

A second episode, much more frightening in its implications, is Nordhausen's eyewitness account of the abortive Munich Putsch of Adolf Hitler and some two thousand followers. Wilhelm Funk's elegant studio on the Georgenstrasse had been the frequent meeting place of the chief Nazi conspirators during the turbulent days of the summer and fall of 1923, and it was on one of these occasions, while Nordhausen was painting in the garden in the rear of the studio, that he was introduced to Hitler, Ludendorff, Hess, Roehm, and Putzi Hanfstaengel. It was only a short time afterward on that fateful November day that he watched the motley crowd of would-be revolutionaries headed by Hitler and Ludendorff marching triumphantly toward the center of the city in the mistaken belief that the government was already in their hands. There at the Kriegsminsterium they were opposed by General Commissioner von Kahr and Police Colonel von Seisser, who had been in on the conspiracy but had felt double-crossed and now stood firm with loyal troops and machine guns. In the ensuing battle at Odeonsplatz, sixteen Nazis were killed. Their bodies were loaded into police trucks and carted around the city as a warning against further violence. Hitler was quick to escape but was arrested, tried for treason, and imprisoned, which gave him the opportunity to write *Mein Kampf*. In telling the story Nordhausen has often repeated the obvious and ironic comment that if only Hitler had been one of the so-called martyrs, how different the course of modern history would have been.

* *Deutsch-Amerika,* May 9, 1925 (a German-language illustrated weekly newspaper published in New York).

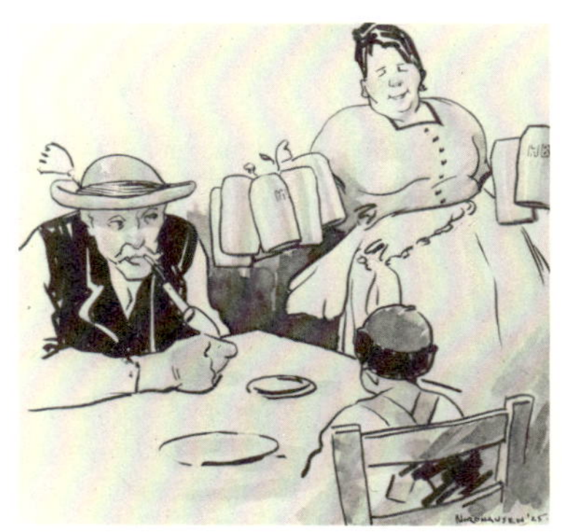

Hofbrau sketch, 1925.

1923
22"x 20"
Oil on canvas

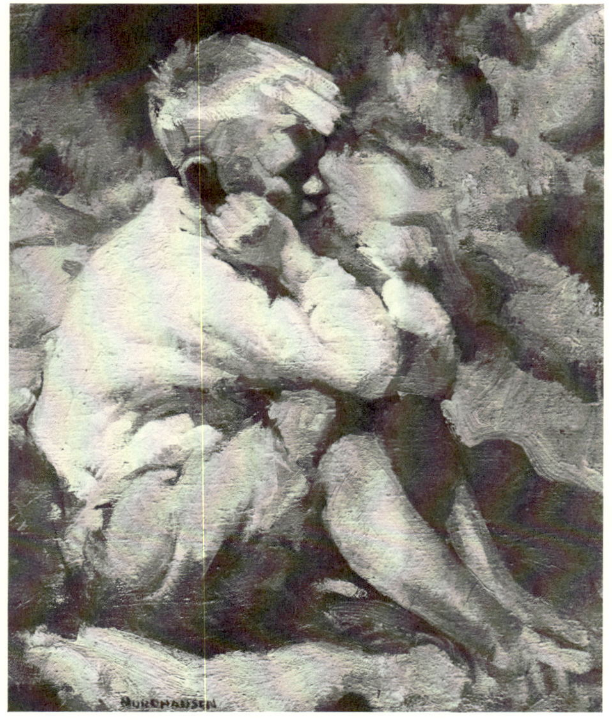

1. Boy in the Sun

The Munich Work

P UBLIC RECOGNITION of Nordhausen's work during the Munich years was modest but positive. A number of his paintings were reproduced in successive issues of *Jugend*. He painted portraits of various prominent people, including Else Thieme, which were reproduced in color on the cover of *Jugend*. His work was accepted in the annual juried shows of the Glaspalast, which on one occasion caught the interest of a reporter for the *Münchener Neuste Nachrichten* who commented on their fresh and lively character: "Eine frische, flotte Note bringen die Bilder von Nordhausen."*

The two and one half years of study in Munich produced hundreds of paintings, drawings, and watercolors. Some of them were destroyed or the canvases painted over and a few were sold, but many survived and were used in successive exhibitions.

The drawings include an endless variety of local people and street scenes, landscapes, and a large volume of models in the studio. Some of the models were young and attractive, but his tendency was to concentrate on the older types, peasant men and women in native costumes or nude, in which the character of both head and figure provided a more formidable challenge to the artist's perceptive skill.

The paintings of female nudes tend toward the more contemplative, closed composition, em-

* September 21, 1924.

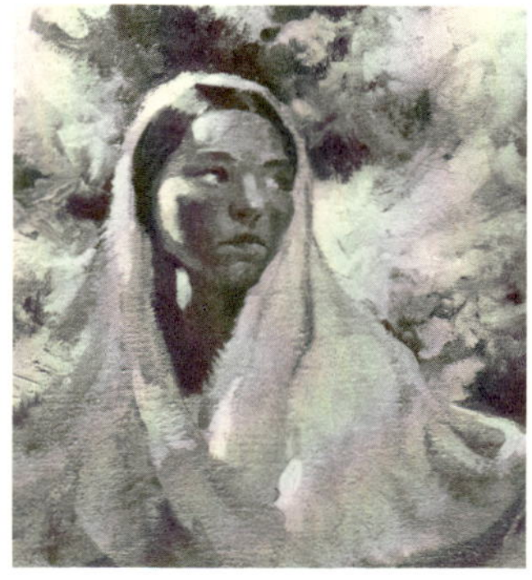

2. Girl in White Shawl

phasizing the total form rather than details. The head studies stress the solid structure, beginning with the skeletal form and building the successive values and planes through the underpainting in tempera and various glazes in subdued but luminous color. This direct and elemental simplicity of form has much of the solid realism of Duveneck and the Lenbach tradition, which was still alive and valid in the Munich Academy, especially in Habermann's classes.

The historic contrast between the dark confinement of the studio and the bright atmosphere and freedom of the outdoors which had become such an issue in late nineteenth-century painting was a logical development in Nordhausen's case. The solid, almost geometrically built head of the *Girl in White Shawl* (2) is enveloped by the flowing drapery and direct sunlight, with vigorous brushstrokes, and brilliant color in yellow, blue, and green—all of which have the character of contemporary Expressionists. *Boy in the Sun* (1), a bold conception of a figure in nature under the direct light of the sun, produced a form solidly built into the light and space without being dissolved in an Impressionist atmosphere.

A succession of character studies, mostly of Bavarians in peasant dress, reveals this combination of solid form, brilliant color, bright sunlight, and a vigorous brushstroke that suggest the artist's interest in both Wilhelm Leibl and Franz Hals, as is seen in the *Bavarian Peasant in Sunshine* (158).

Through these student years the problem of establishing himself as a formal portrait painter was very much a part of the artist's effort. For the most part he was accorded not official commis-sions but courtesy sittings by generous friends. One of the earliest was that of Madam Leander, a leading soprano at the Munich opera during the early 1920s, which has much of the strength and individual character interpretations of his studio studies. The protrait of Else Thieme has a more formal character and composition with its modish coiffure and enveloping robelike coat. The drawing of Irene Bordoni, a distinguished musical comedy star performing in Munich at the time, shows both the relaxed spontaneity and promise of the young professional artist.

Besides these, there are numerous drawings and oil sketches which had no purpose other than to record an idea or everyday scene. One of these is a wash drawing of a typical Bavarian peasant in the Hofbräuhaus with one of the husky waitresses, famous for their skill in toting as many as six full *Masskrüge*—liter-sized ceramic beer mugs—in each hand as they sweep through the crowded aisles of the massive beer hall. Another is a free interpretation of the traditional reclining Venus composition, with a lecherous horned devil substituted for the adoring Cupid and a pipe-playing Bacchus silhouetted in the background.

Return to New York

HIS FUNDS EXHAUSTED, Nordhausen returned to New York in the spring of 1925 and was obliged to face new problems of readjustment. The art scene in New York had remained fairly consistent through the inter-

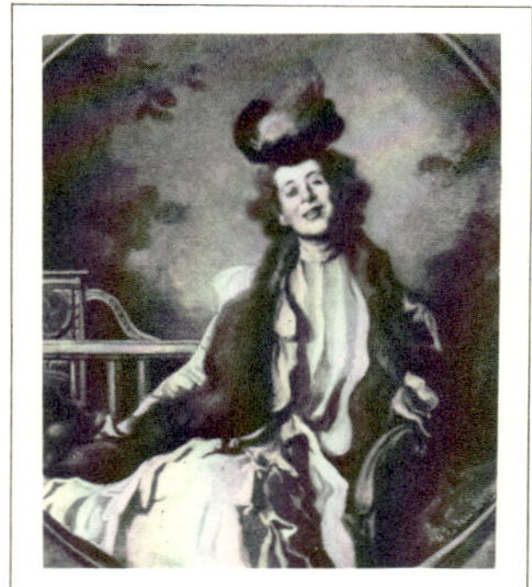

1923
30"x 24"
Oil on canvas
Private collection

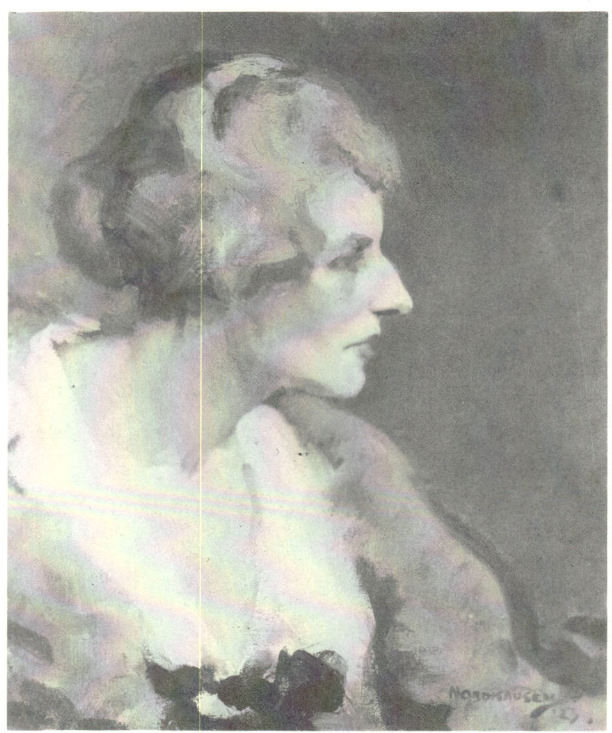

3. *Madam Leander*

vening years, but Nordhausen's taste and perception had undergone a considerable change. The ideal of Leyendecker, Wyeth, and the commercial illustrators was no longer the sole criterion except as a sure means of livelihood. Now he felt a deeper affinity with, and appreciation for, the work of Robert Henri, George Luks, and George Bellows, as well as indeed, Thomas Eakins. It was not necessarily the obviously realistic respect for the model that attracted him in the work of these artists but the solid drawing and sense of form, the luminosity and richness of color, and the vitality of the brushstroke. The emphasis on means, again, was not as an end in itself but as an expression of human character.

He was able to exhibit his Munich work in a number of shows and received some recognition as a promising young artist. "The Art of Henry Nordhausen" was the title of an article by Leo da Vinci that same year,* which led off with the comment that "painting in this country has become so academic that it is a pleasure to review the fresher, freer work of American students." Characterizing Nordhausen's teachers—Wilhelm Funk as a great portrait painter and Habermann as "the only survivor of the famous student trio: Habermann, Chase and Duveneck" (Habermann had been a fellow student with Chase and Duveneck at the Munich Academy in the early 1870s)—da Vinci praised Nordhausen's "masterful wielding of the brush, the modeling and texture of his nude studies, and his mastery of light and shadow. He is one of the best of a group of young American artists whose work shows much promise."

* *Artists and Models,* Vol. 1, no. 6 (September 1925), p. 150.

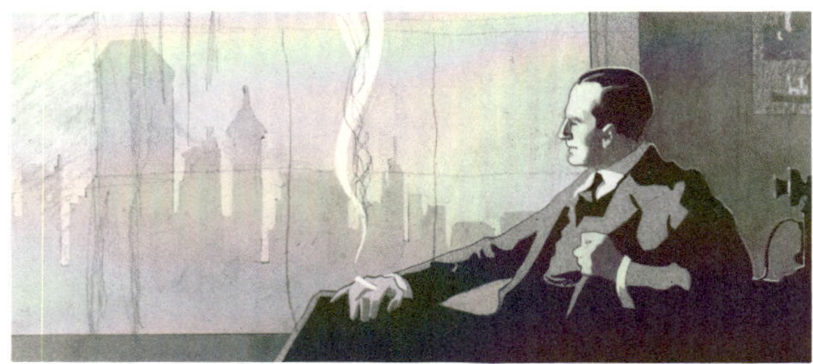

Gouache study,
"The Executive," 1926.

Nordhausen soon discovered that New York and the business of earning a living was an entirely different world from the studio atmosphere of Munich. He lived in Greenwich Village and for a time shared a studio with Alexander Calder, who was then (1925) studying at the Art Students League and painting circus scenes. Nordhausen continued to paint, but his progress was slow. A number of costumed figure studies like the *Girl in Costume* (7) recall the efforts of the previous year but appear stiff and tentative, lacking the earthy vitality of the Bavarian peasant models.

He managed to earn a living through free-lance commercial work, taking on anything that would come his way—posters, display cards, lettering, advertising layouts and illustrations, even stage designs. Here again it was his superb drawing, skilled craftsmanship, and inventive enthusiasm that brought him considerable success. The small gouache study of "The Executive" reveals something of the suave manner and sophistication characteristic of the acceptable commercial style of this period. It was during this time that he began to do design work for the Flora Mir candy shops.

Among the more ambitious commercial projects was a "Hall of Fame" for aviators, commissioned in 1927 shortly after Charles Lindbergh's famous transatlantic flight to Paris. This was designed as a special feature for the opening of *Wings,* a Paramount motion picture of war in the air, at the Criterion Theater in New York. There were some seventeen portraits of leading heroes of aviation, including French aces (Georges Guynemer, René Fonck, and Charles Nungesser), German (Manfred von Richtofen, Oswald Boelcke), English (William Bishop), Italian (Fran-

cesco Baracca), and American (Eddie Rickenbacker). Included, too, were those of more recent transatlantic fame: Clarence Chamberlin, Richard Byrd, and of course Charles Lindbergh. This latter portrait was based on the famous photograph of the young flyer with "the boyish smile that first greeted Paris and has captivated millions in Europe and America."

Artistic Maturity

DESPITE his commercial work, Nordhausen maintained a consistent schedule of painting in his studio. Genuine progress and readjustment are revealed in a number of portraits which begin as early as the fall of 1925 such as that of Queenie Smith, with its voluminous drapery encasing its figure and the smooth texture of the brushstroke defining the forms of both the figure and the folds. This concept is somewhat subdued in the portrait of Betty Hunner with the soft texture of the fur coat, but it was used with remarkable effect to enhance the personal dignity and detachment of the sitter in the portrait of Dr. Hunner.

In 1926 an exhibition of modern portraits held in the Maryland Institute of Art in Baltimore included this portrait, along with others by Robert Henri, John C. Johansen, and a number of local artists. A review in the *Baltimore Sun* criticized the show "as not 'modern' at all, since it contained no Sloan, Bellows or Matisse . . ."* On the whole, the

* December 5, 1926.

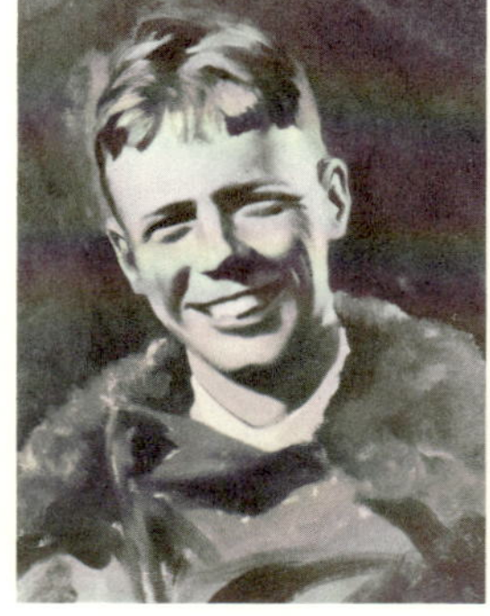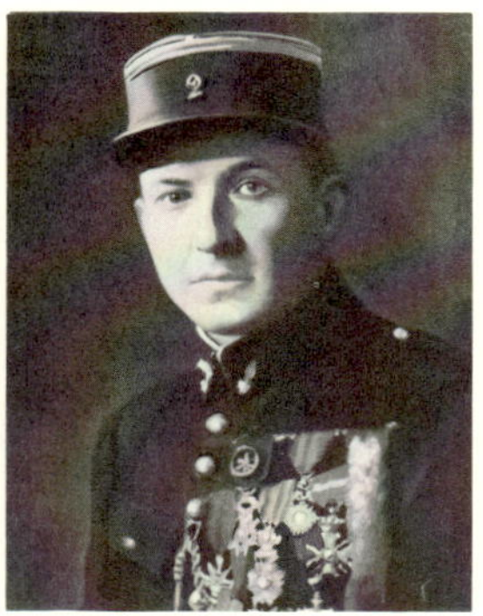

1924
30" x 24"
Oil on canvas
Private collection

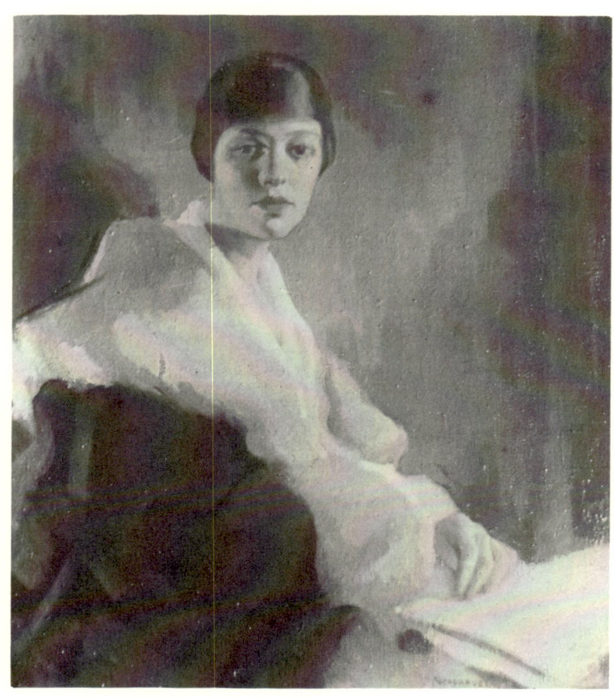

4. *Miss Else Thieme*

show was considered Victorian and depressing, except the portraits by Henri and Nordhausen. The reviewer singled out that of Dr. Hunner as "about the only genuinely modern portrait in the room" and commented that there was "something reminiscent of El Greco in the way the academic robes were treated." Actually the relationship is less with El Greco than with the established portrait tradition of Sargent then flourishing in New York and with which the young Nordhausen now felt he could compete. In his adjustment of color and design to the character of the sitter, somehow he knew he could do it better than Sargent, and the reviewer's comment seemed to justify his own conviction.

The portraits he painted of his mother and father in 1926, particularly that of his father, showed the simplicity of means and modest reserve which produced a work of great dignity and character. In the portrait of Frank Alvah Parsons the problems and uncertainties seem to be resolved, and the artist appeared confident of his future.

In 1927 he was elected to membership in the Salmagundi Club, an event which marked the beginning of a long and distinguished relationship that involved a succession of prizes and awards for his work, which was shown in annual exhibitions, as well as his activity in the charitable and educational program of the club.

Recognition of another sort came the following year when he was awarded a summer fellowship by the Louis Comfort Tiffany Foundation at Oyster Bay, Long Island. Among the critics and instructors there was Gifford Beal, whose work he admired and whose criticism he felt was particularly

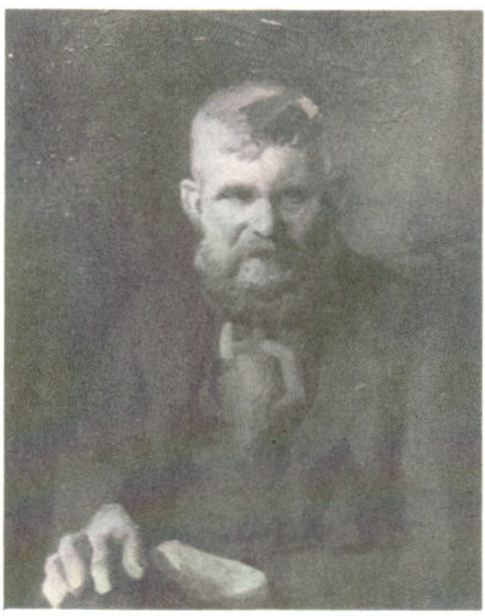

1924
32''x 26''
Oil on canvas

5. *Man with Red Beard*

useful to him at the time because of Beal's emphasis on rational analysis and the necessity for the artist to think as well as to react emotionally.

Munich, 1928-1929

NORDHAUSEN thus returned to Munich in the fall of 1928 not as a student but as a professional artist determined to use this year of freedom for solid work in the studio. A request from the editor of *Jugend* magazine produced the pastel "Portrait of a Lady," which shows the thorough confidence and technical skill of the commercial artist. Some of the first figure studies of this period have the compact, carefully drawn, and well-modeled form of his earlier work, but they also have the luminous and iridescent color of Peter Paul Rubens, particularly the earlier work of the Flemish master in the Alte Pinakothek. This interest in light and color, with the paint handled freely in many glazes and a vigorous brushstroke, reflects Nordhausen's study of Rubens's early and later figure painting as well as that of both Franz Hals and Velásquez.

There are many variations, often depending on the character of the model that happened to be available. Frequently these would develop into a series of studies of the same model. The good humor and thoughtful manner revealed in the *Man with a Cane* (167) could be interpreted in another painting as that of a genial poet. The carefree independence of a Bavarian *Bierstube* character stimu-lates a kind of painterly exuberance in the *Bavarian with Newspaper* (168). The same combination of expressive freedom and control appears in the studies of peasant women, especially the *Bavarian Peasant* (166), with its rich black costume and bright color of embroidery decoration, and the *Woman with Jug* (169).

Another series of studies, particularly of younger women, concentrates on light and color as they affect the form and texture of materials. Thus, the yellow-ocher highlights of the silken folds of *The Gold Shawl* (170) about the head and shoulders provide the framework for an easy, relaxed composition. In the *Girl in Costume* (171) the concentration of the drapery around the central form of the figure from the knees to the torso, arms, and turbaned head, combined with an ample space around the figure, produces a kind of quiet and modest dignity.

Nordhausen had always been interested in children and was particularly fascinated by the child studies of Robert Henri and George Luks as well as those of Franz Hals. The *Little Girl with Doll* (9) has much of the bright color, luminosity, and vigorous brushstroke of his painting style that year, but it also has a kind of freshness and naïveté not found in the other work. This is essentially the character of the subject, but it also reflects much of the kindly criticism and encouragement of Wilhelm Funk, whose masterful composition of brilliant color planes that seem to hover in space as well as build solid forms had considerable influence on Nordhausen's development during the year spent in Munich.

Nordhausen had a rather spacious studio with a beautiful north light on Rambergstrasse, just a

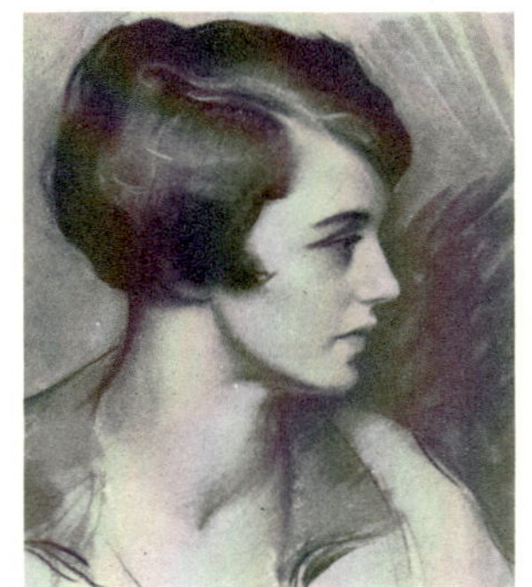

short distance from the Academy of Fine Arts and a few blocks from Wilhelm Funk's home on Georgenstrasse. As was his habit in earlier years, Funk made frequent visits to see how the young artist was getting along. On one of these occasions Nordhausen had about completed a portrait of a male model. Funk came in—a tall Edwardian figure with an elegantly trimmed goatee, English tweeds, and bamboo cane—studied the painting for a few minutes, and shook his head.

"No, that's not right," he said, and he proceeded to scrape off the entire painting with the palette knife down to the canvas and the base coat. Nordhausen was horrified and almost writhing in anguish as he watched the weeks of hard work in building the many-layered foundation, modeling, and glazes of paint come rolling off in gravy-colored globs. But he dared not complain or protest, first of all because Funk, the kind and fatherly type of artist-professor that he was, was not one to be contradicted, and also because Nordhausen realized that the problem involved the art of painting, not personality.

So he watched and listened. Funk had no objection to the concept or the basic composition but simply with the way it was executed. He then proceeded to lay in the light and color areas of the hands and head, the various planes in the modeling of the forms, and the succeeding steps in building up the different colors of the composition. After more than an hour's work he put down the brushes, exclaiming, "Now you can go on from there!"

Actually, Nordhausen did not "go on from there" with that painting, and though his professional pride was somewhat bruised, he kept it for many years as a hard-earned lesson and inspiration. In the art of criticism this was quite a different procedure from what he had experienced with an artist-critic like Gifford Beal. In his critique Beal did not touch the canvas but tried to sharpen and clarify the student's thinking process by means of analysis and discussion. Genial personality that he was, Funk's method was the craftsman's practical demonstration, where the logic of thinking is an integral part of the visual and manual execution.

New York, Marriage, and the Depression

THE RETURN TO NEW YORK in the summer of 1929 brought no shock of readjustment as it had in 1925 but steady progress along the lines of the year's work. This progress is shown in his portraits of Edwin Malone and "Uncle Heinie," which maintain the process of building solid, luminous forms of the head and shoulders as he had done in the portrait of Laurence Schmeckebier in Munich the previous spring. The *Baby Gwenn* (12), *Girl in Peasant Costume* (53), and the *Girl with the Red Shawl* (54) in like manner reveal the ease and confidence as well as the painterly bravura in the handling of the brushstroke, which maintained a consistent quality he carried on for the next twenty years.

For a young artist at the beginning of a professional career things seemed to be going very well indeed. He established himself in a large and ele-

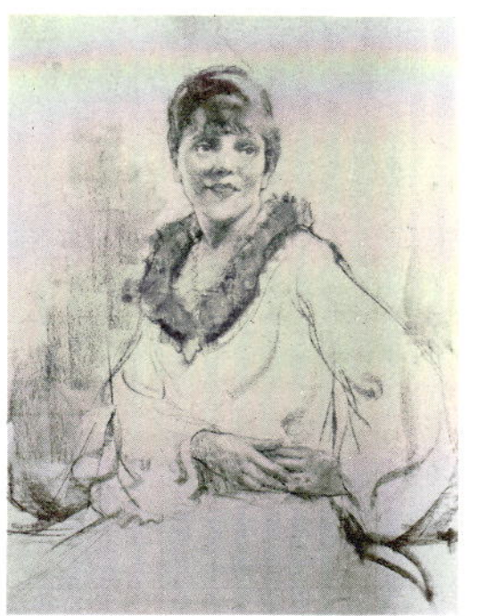

1925
30" x 24"
Conte crayon
Private collection

6. Miss Irene Bordoni

gant studio in the fashionable Gainsborough Studio building on Central Park South. He married Miriam Bernstein, one of the founders of the successful Flora Mir candy shops, and he was honored by an extensive exhibition of more than fifty of his paintings, drawings, prints, and watercolors at the High Museum of Art in Atlanta, Georgia. His work was exhibited by the prestigious Macbeth's and Grand Central galleries, and was consistently exposed to a growing and knowledgeable public.

The point of view of a number of progressive galleries and patrons regarding the search for new artistic talent at the time was perhaps best expressed by Robert Macbeth, whose famous gallery on Fifty-seventh Street had been the original sponsor of "The Eight" and still maintained the tradition of creative realism of the older generation. In his foreword to the pamphlet announcing an exhibition of paintings in May 1932 by a group of younger artists (Gerald Foster, Henry Nordhausen, C. G. Nelson, and Paul Sample), Macbeth wrote:

"What we look for in the work of younger painters is promise rather than fulfillment. . . . Inness in his forties was painting what are now known as very early examples, negligible except as stepping stones in his development. Even our own George Bellows, had he lived, would probably have developed far beyond the splendid canvases that represent him today. [We show these four young painters because] we like their point of view; we like their respect for the traditions which they have respectfully followed; and we shall be glad if the encouragement that should come from this showing, will spur them on to the future that we believe is in store for them."

In the following years such prizes and fellowship awards as the Spencer Trask Foundation (Yaddo) and MacDowell Colony fellowships, provided encouragement, some cash, and the occasional opportunity to devote his full time to independent work in the studio.

Through the 1930s he continued to participate in most of the important national competitive exhibitions, including those of the National Academy of Design, the Art Institute of Chicago, the Metropolitan Museum of New York, the Corcoran Gallery in Washington, D.C., the Pennsylvania Academy in Philadelphia, the Baltimore Institute of Art, Allied Artists of America, Audubon Artists, and the American Watercolor Society, as well as local competitions and the regular annual shows of the Salmagundi Club.

The financial reality of the Great Depression, however, struck Nordhausen as it did every artist in the early 1930s. He gave up his impressive studio on Central Park South and moved to a small studio-apartment in Greenwich Village on East Ninth Street. Survival was difficult, but he was not one to complain. The reality of the situation is suggested by a set of notes for a lecture found among his papers written on the back of a 1933 letter from his landlord threatening legal action if he did not pay his rent.

He did not participate in any of the many government-sponsored WPA art programs but made his own way as best he could by teaching classes of all types, from poster design and commercial art to regular drawing and painting in such institutions as the Roerich Museum, the Morris High School, and the New York School of Industrial Art. He gave frequent lectures and painting

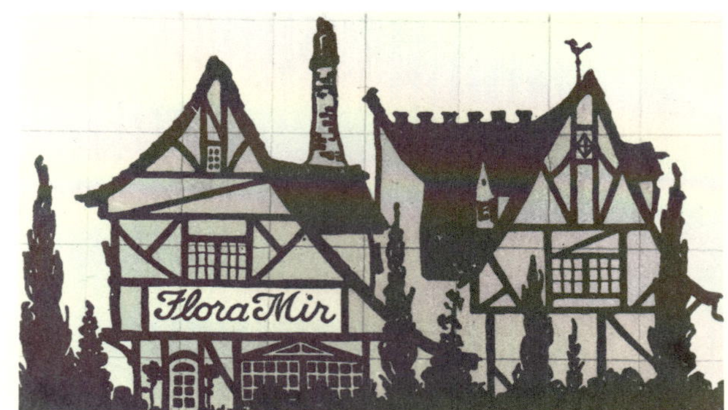

Flora Mir trademark, 1927.

demonstrations, such as those at the Metropolitan Museum and the School Art League, and he continued doing free-lance commercial work, including stage designs for the Metropolitan Opera and the Globe Theater.

Among the various commercial projects two may be of interest in suggesting both the scale and character of this enterprising artist at that time. The Flora Mir candy shops began in 1927 in the family kitchen of Mir (Miriam) Bernstein and her two cousins, Flora and Jessie Shane. From a small store in Brooklyn where production was maintained in the back room of the shop, the business developed in the late 1930s into a prosperous chain of twelve shops and an independent factory until it was sold to a large corporation in 1947.

The success of the enterprise was due not only to a good product and to the imagination and enterprise of three dedicated and hardworking young women but also in large part to Nordhausen's design work. With his marriage to Mir he had become virtually a working member of the firm. He designed the factory with an extensive assembly-line, as well as the firm's trademark, the packaging, all the advertising, and the stores themselves. Some of these store designs were based on sets he had prepared for a French film at the Globe Theater in 1932. Others used stylized versions of late medieval street scenes, many of them based on his watercolors of picturesque Rothenburg and Dinkelsbühl. He developed an integrated system of display units that included the front show window, the display counters, the windows in the building facades, and the vistas provided by the illusionary winding streets. In

keeping with the economic restrictions of the time, the artist built and painted most of them by hand.

Historians have only begun the study of the fascinating decade of the Great Depression, with its complex issues involving problems of political, economic, and social dislocation; war, nationalism, and mechanization; and a host of other active forces which threatened the very existence of the artist. In 1936 a group of American artists of all types—academicians, modernists, purists and Social Realists—with Stuart Davis acting as national secretary, called a meeting billed as the First American Artists' Congress in Town Hall in New York City. As the conference developed, the general trend of the discussions veered toward an increasingly radical left-wing political stance, but a number of artists revealed more balanced ideas of intelligence and concern. Nordhausen did not attend the congress but knew most of the participants and followed their discussions with considerable interest.

In the opening address, Louis Mumford made an impassioned appeal to face the two catastrophes: (1) the economic depression that was "marked for the artist not merely by his usually meager diet, but sometimes by the inability to get so much as the bare food necessary for life"; and (2) fascism and the threat of war. Rockwell Kent appealed in his usual militant way to the artists to be active in the movement against war: "It is by virtue of their love of life in all its manifestations . . . that men are artists."

Somewhat later in the discussion Arnold Blanche observed that "Wherever artists have gathered, it is their differences they have made

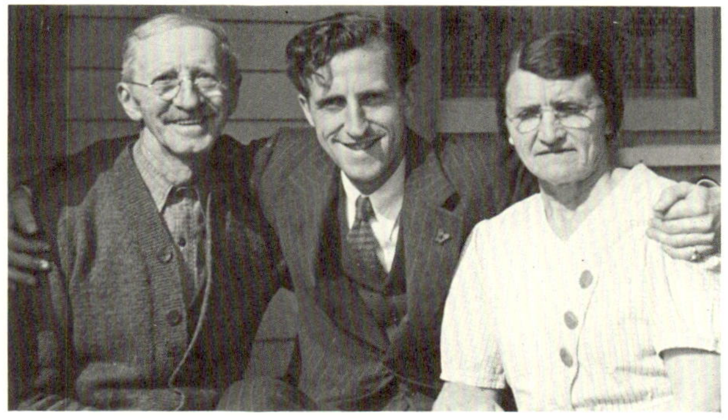

important. But now—we are faced with greater dangers than our dissimilarities. I do not want to emphasize our variations but I want to defend them. I feel that only by a collective solidarity may real individuality be preserved."

The Struggle for Artistic Integrity

INDIVIDUALITY had been the theme of many of the comments on Nordhausen's work since his Munich days. It appeared again in Ruth Hinman Carter's three-column review of his one-man show at the High Museum in Atlanta, Georgia. She wrote: "The exhibition gives the immediate impression of marked strength and individuality. . . . [the work is] executed with fresh vigor of thought . . . without sentimentality."*

By coincidence there appeared alongside this review an extensive report from New York by William B. McCormick of Universal Service on the establishment of the new Whitney Museum of American Art. Quoting an article by William M. Ivins, Jr., in the January bulletin of the Metropolitan Museum, the report featured comments on the fashionable and wholly inexplicable revival of interest in modern French art bought only by Americans and considered outmoded by the French themselves. From the founding of the Whitney and Mr. Ivin's comments, the author suggested that

* Art Page of the *Atlanta American*, January 12, 1930.

"one may easily pluck a strong feeling of revulsion against the current craze for Gallic pictorial art." Whether it was due to the depression, the widespread destruction of the cotton crop in the South owing to the recent ravages of the boll weevil, or the "current craze" for French art, the only sale from Nordhausen's show was the small but beautiful watercolor, *Child in Garden* (10).

It was not that he did not try. In later years the artist recalled this Atlanta exhibition as his first great opportunity to enter the museum world as a major artist. Virtually all of his best paintings were on display. He gave lectures and demonstrations, was given interviews by press and radio, and was lavishly entertained by the various social groups active in the museum. But still there was only the one sale.

Such was the mood of the times, and to Nordhausen the issues were very real indeed. He had seen the brutality of Nazi fascism at first hand during the early days in Munich as well as hunger, the breadlines, and the restless crowds of the jobless he had lived with in Munich and again in Brooklyn and lower Manhattan. The issue of an "American" art was equally real, both because of his own affinity for Henri, Luks, and the tradition of the American Realists, and because of sheer economic necessity. The interrelationship of these issues and their opposition to the growing trend toward French modernism were problems facing artists long before they became prominent in the popular press of the 1930s.

Nordhausen's position in these matters was as positive as it was predictable. He was fully in sympathy with the experimental point of view and the

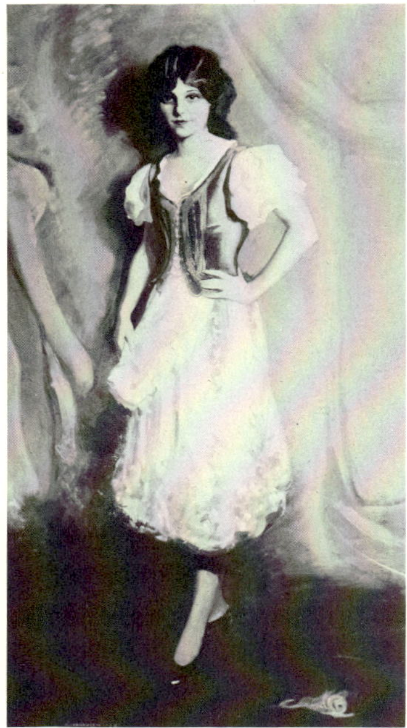

7. *Girl in Costume (Lillian Bliss)*

succession of artistic problems with their resultant styles that characterized the development of modern art in America since the Armory Show of 1913, which many art critics look to as the beginning of the modern movement in this country or indeed as the source of a genuinely ''American'' art. But he saw each of these styles as artistic ''problems,'' a means to an end rather than an end in itself. Political, social, and economic problems, as well as the inner psychological aspects of the individual and his society remained outside the range of his artistic interests.

For him, what was basically important about art was artistic integrity itself. ''I don't like a faker,'' he has frequently said, ''but that's not the point. The fact is that others have different approaches which have something to do with taste but are primarily differences in character. As an artist I simply am not interested in painting the seamy side of life, the emotional disturbance nor, for that matter, the social conscience.''

It was thus characteristic that Nordhausen somehow managed to maintain his own consistent course. As has been noted, he did not become involved with WPA or with the many other government programs; and he did not embrace each

new style or ism for the sake of the publicity and recognition that might result. And though he had high ideals of the professional artist in his studio, he was not adverse to taking on the menial labor of a commercial job when it was necessary. With his natural flexibility and designer's skill he was able to undertake each project as it came but was strong enough not to let the commercial requirements of the trade infect the aesthetic quality of his own independent work.

Thus he was also able to demonstrate that real individuality can indeed be preserved without the ''collective solidarity'' proposed by Arnold Blanche. This is not to say that Nordhausen was an artistic recluse or isolationist. On the contrary, he was well aware of an artist's social and educational responsibilities, and was consistently involved with various art organizations, not only for the companionship of art-minded people, but for the opportunity of generally contributing whatever he could for the benefit of the artistic community. The venerable Salmagundi Club was one of his first loves, but he was also a member of the School Art League (serving on its board of directors for many years), the Artists' Fellowship, the Allied Artists of America, the Audubon Artists, the American Watercolor Society, the Explorers' Club, and other organizations. Although he had participated in many of the National Academy of Design exhibitions and won awards from independent juries, he refused to submit his name for membership, since he did not want to be judged by what he considered then to be inferior artists. In the same way, the collective solidarity offered by the militant groups of politically minded artists was not for him.

World War II
and Readjustment

THE IMPACT of World War II on the American artist and its contribution to the artistic character of the period is another historical phenomenon worth studying. One thinks of Picasso and the siege of Guernica, Orozco and Siqueiros and the revolution in Mexico, George Grosz and Otto Dix in the Germany of World War I. During World War II many Americans were recruited as artist-reporters and combat artists and served successfully as pictorial historians in the European and Pacific theaters. Nordhausen, long incensed by the Hitler terror and shocked by the Japanese surprise attack, was forty years old but enlisted as a private in the U.S. Army two days after the attack on Pearl Harbor. He was sent to Camp Croft for basic training in the infantry; from there he went to Fort Belvoir to study camouflage with the army engineers. After graduation from officers' training as a second lieutenant, he underwent specialized training in radar at the Massachusetts Institute of Technology where he studied with the distinguished physicist, Professor William Schockley (later a Nobel Prize winner), as well as other scientists from Bell Laboratories and General Electric. After being promoted to the rank of captain, he was transferred to the Air Force and became chief of radar intelligence of the Twentieth Air Force under Gen. Curtis LeMay in the China-Burma-India and South Pacific theaters.

Drawing on his early training in mathematics together with his experience as a designer, he developed a system of relief maps and precisely calibrated three-dimensional models of bombing targets for the training and final briefing of pilots. He also developed a new type of map of the target area that was an exact duplicate of the radar picture as it appeared on the screen, which provided greater accuracy. In designing these models it was his duty to participate in many of the preliminary flights to take high-altitude aerial photographs of prospective targets. From the angle of the sun at a given time of day it was possible to determine the height of the structures and then to build models of them to scale. To check on the effectiveness of his design program he was obliged to participate in many bombing missions. Thus, he and his group of seventeen trained specialists were responsible for planning the radar approaches to the bombing of most of the Japanese targets of the entire war, including those in which atomic bombs were dropped. He was awarded many citations and eight battle stars.

Civilian life after four years in the service, during which time there had been few opportunities for drawing or painting, presented new problems. The first painting executed after his return to his New York studio was a still life of his army uniform draped over a chair and entitled *Change of Life* (129), which was exhibited and immediately purchased by the owner of the plush, popular Twenty One Club in New York. However, he soon found the studio too confining after the excitement and activity of the war years and left New York to spend six months with the Ringling Brothers-

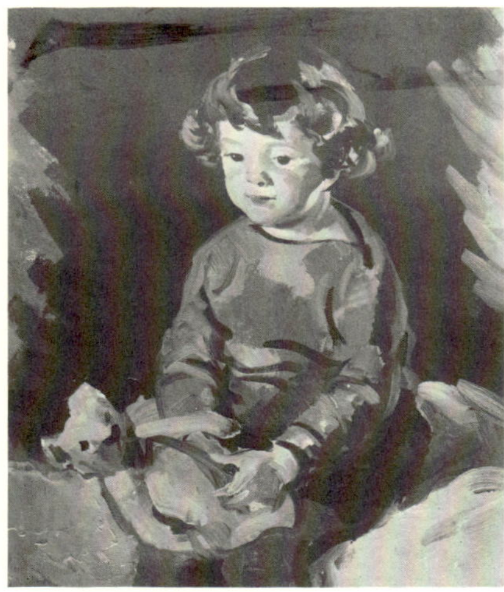

1929
24"x 20"
Oil on canvas

8. Teddy

Barnum and Bailey Circus in Sarasota, Florida.

There, in the tradition of Walt Kuhn, Gifford Beal, John Steuart Curry, and many American artists before him, he became immersed in the glittering excitement, glamour, fantasy, humor, and often pathos of circus life. Many drawings and paintings were produced, including parades, riding acrobats, aerialists, and burlesque dancers, but what evidently attracted him most was the humor, vitality, and poetic sensitivity provided by the clowns. Many of these performers became his friends and served as models for later portrait studies.

Another aspect of this "change of life" during these first years of transition to civilian life was provided by a series of late afternoon and evening classes in philosophy, art history, and criticism which he took under the auspices of the GI Bill at New York's distinguished New School for Social Research. There, his contact with trained minds and with artists active in other media opened new vistas which obliged him to review and reassess his own background, ideas, artistic values, and directions. Part of the excitement of the period, too, was an oil venture in Wyoming, when he became involved with a geologist friend in the exploration of an untapped oil field which promised to develop into a fabulous gusher and then eventually failed.

The art scene in New York had changed during the war years. The presence of many of the leading avant-garde artists as émigrés from Europe; the influence of some of the great teachers of the abstract point of view, such as Josef Albers and Hans Hofmann; the increased recognition of the American Abstract tradition stemming from the Armory Show; the establishment of Abstract Expressionism as the new American modern art, and the enthusiastic endorsement of the new art of this century by the critical press—all provided a fresh atmosphere of excitement and progress.

The result was that many of the traditional figure painters turned toward the more abstract, personal, and deliberately experimental styles. For Nordhausen the excitement provided not a reversal but renewed confidence in the validity of his early efforts, and the experience seemed to justify the conviction—as Delacroix once expressed it—that it is the artist, not the critic, who sets the expressive tone of an age. In this period that tone was not monopolized by a single artist, style, or group but comprised a rich diversity of artistic expression comparable to what was developing in related fields of literature, music, and the theater.

The new enthusiasm and widened horizons of the postwar artist, the prominence given to non-representational art, and the decline in the number of figure painters put Nordhausen in a stronger professional position than he had ever had before. He competed in various shows, won awards, notably in the Pepsi-Cola "Paintings of the Year" exhibition at the Metropolitan Museum in 1948 and that of the Allied Artists of America in 1951 for the best figure painting in the show, and began to attract the attention of private collectors and museums.

New Horizons

RECOGNITION and sales provided him freedom and the means to travel. The idea had already occurred to him in 1940, just before World War II, when he had taken a short trip to Puerto Rico. There he had lived in a primitive cabin on the grounds of a Presbyterian mission high in the hills of the interior where he painted native types. Now he established travel as a more consistent program. He spent four months painting landscapes in northern Italy in 1951 and sold most of them in a one-man show held at the Grand Central Galleries the following year. Another year, 1953, spent in Italy, chiefly in a studio on the Piazza Donatello in Florence and later in Calabria, produced a host of figure studies and landscapes. In the spring of 1962 he went to Greece and the Mediterranean on a U. S. Navy assignment, which was notable for its variety of seascapes and activities on board ship. Later that year he traveled through most of the Scandanavian countries.

The experience of travel, to be sure, was not the packaged regimentation of the modern tourist industry, but a slow and deliberate process of personal study and creative interpretation of people and their environment, especially in the more remote rural areas. The result was a series of warm and sympathetic studies which reflect an attitude developed in his earliest work in Munich—that of a profound respect for nature and the model combined with a mastery of the artistic means of expressing it—but now established as a permanent and consistent form.

Maturity and confidence is revealed in Nordhausen's comments on the work of old and modern masters as he again visited the great museums of Europe during this period. The explosive sensations of the moderns, especially the Americans who were now much more frequently shown in European museums and galleries, were everywhere to be seen; but although the initial impact was impressive, he felt that the effect would soon wear off and that a brand new explosion would then be required to sustain continued creative interest.

Characteristically Nordhausen took a broad, slightly different view from that of many of his fellow artists. Beyond the oversized canvases, the large patches of brilliant color, the bold brushwork, and the heavy application of paint (which so frequently fell off the canvas through lack of technical competence), he looked for something more permanent and meaningful. In Stockholm, for instance, he was impressed by the tremendous stature of Carl Milles, not alone for the size and number of his figures, but more especially for his humor, love of life, and humane enthusiasm. In Oslo it was Edvard Munch whose work he discovered, not only as great in itself, but also as a source of inspiration and justification for the expressive forms of both Oskar Kokoschka and Augustus John.

He looked at Rembrandt again, impressed by his amazing richness of color and solidity of form, as well as Velásquez, with his unbelievable simplicity and subtlety of color. He discovered in Goya a power, sensitivity, and imagination that seemed to go far beyond the achievements of the

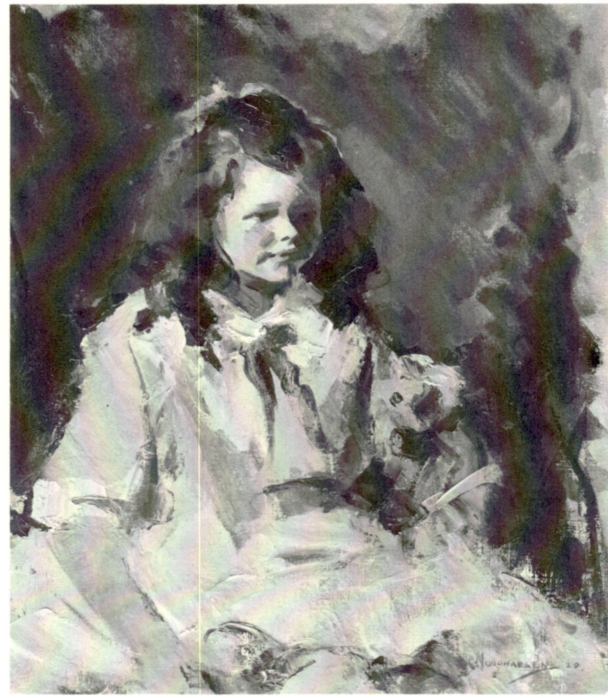

9. Little Girl with Doll

great Velásquez and the old masters of his day: giants eating bodies, a city hovering on a rock, the beautiful draftsmanship and action of figures in the etchings and paintings of Goya that are expressions unique and unexcelled among artists both before and after his time. Goya could thrust figures in an endless variety of positions not taken from a visual reality but from memory and imagination.

Renoir and Degas had always been among his favorite painters, but in this period they seemed to have a new meaning to him. Renoir was a pure painter whose technical mastery, beautiful women, lush flesh, and generally pleasant subject matter provide the spectator with an unconscious and continuous spiritual life. There is something of that character in the work of Degas, whose superb draftsmanship and understanding of people as moving forms re-create the wondrous world of the ballet.

Nordhausen had known and admired Hans Hofmann as a person and teacher since Munich days, but could never understand why Hofmann, with all his artistic ability and creative verve, was never genuinely productive until he came to the

United States. Even then it was difficult for him to comprehend the great master's objectives. During the 1930s Hofmann had a studio on Ninth Street across from Nordhausen's apartment. Nordhausen would often see Hofmann before the window on a hot summer night, bare-chested and in sweaty shorts dueling violently with his canvas in another of his improvisations. ''What a hell of a way to make a living'' was his comment then. He was obliged to admit later, rather ruefully, that in view of Hofmann's international reputation, his many exhibitions, and critical acclaim, and the fantastic prices his pictures brought, he did very well indeed.

Nordhausen's respect for Carl Milles, as well as his longtime devotion to Peter Paul Rubens as an extraordinary painter and personality, is a reflection of his own character and influenced much of his career. An article on Henry Nordhausen by Boylan Fitzgerald in *The Artist* of New York praised the now nearly sixty-year-old artist as ''a highly gifted, multifaceted personality, with a poetic sensitivity enhanced by youthful vitality and genuine love of life and people.'' He was described as a ''master of many media, more than a little scientific . . . an artist with both theoretical knowledge and practical know-how.'' Many are talented, he goes on, ''but few are willing to pay the price in thoughtful, thorough and downright hard work.'' With reference to Renoir and Franz Hals he paid tribute to the artist's respect for the old masters and ''the inter-century fellowship of delineators of a gentle, kindly and human gladness.''*

* *The Artist*, Vol 59, no. 1 (April 1960), p. 15.

The Salmagundi Club

NORDHAUSEN had always been a loyal and enthusiastic participant in the activities of the prestigious Salmagundi Club. This organization, the oldest art club in America and still functioning in a historic brownstone on lower Fifth Avenue, was founded in 1871 as an outgrowth of a small group of artists working in the studio of Jonathan Scott Hartley, then known as the Sketch Club. Its name, referring to any potpourri of ingredients, originally derived from Washington Irving's *Salmagundi* essays, which were much in vogue among intellectuals in the 1860s and 1870s. Over the years it developed what its members liked to call the "Salmagundi Spirit—a contagion of pleasure in the creative mind and its social interchange" and included on its roster such distinguished names as John La Farge, Albert P. Ryder, George Inness, William M. Chase, Louis C. Tiffany, Stanford White, and Thomas Moran.

Under Nordhausen's influence as president (1959-63), the club expanded its activities from the traditional social and exhibition programs to a variety of scholarship, special exhibition, and public educational programs aimed at a wider circle of community art interests. It also inaugurated a scholarship-member program to attract students and young talent into its social and exhibition activities in a congenial form of professional-apprentice collaboration. It was thus established as a tax-exempt educational and charitable organization and continued on a financially sound basis.

At the same time Nordhausen and a group of fellow members with similar experience in the Armed Forces developed a continuation of the nationally known Navy Combat Art Program of World War II into a Navy Art Cooperation and Liaison Committee (NACAL), which used many Salmagundi artists of all types to document navy combat missions as well as its many worldwide activities during peacetime. It was on one of these assignments that Nordhausen accompanied the Sixth Fleet on a tour of the Mediterranean and Greece in 1962.

Professional Portraiture

THE COMBINATION of a resourceful personality, curiosity about and enjoyment of people, and a penetrating respect he had for the model accounts for Nordhausen's later and widespread success in portraiture. To be sure, he had always painted portraits, but more concentrated work in the medium of the commissioned portrait began in 1949 in Selma, Alabama, with that of the ninety-six-year-old Gen. John W. Moore, national commander of the United Confederate Veterans. A host of commissions followed, involving distinguished personalities in business, education, government, and the armed services as well as various social groups. Many of these were concentrated in the Georgia area, so that he found it desirable to establish his own studio in Columbus, Georgia, in 1960.

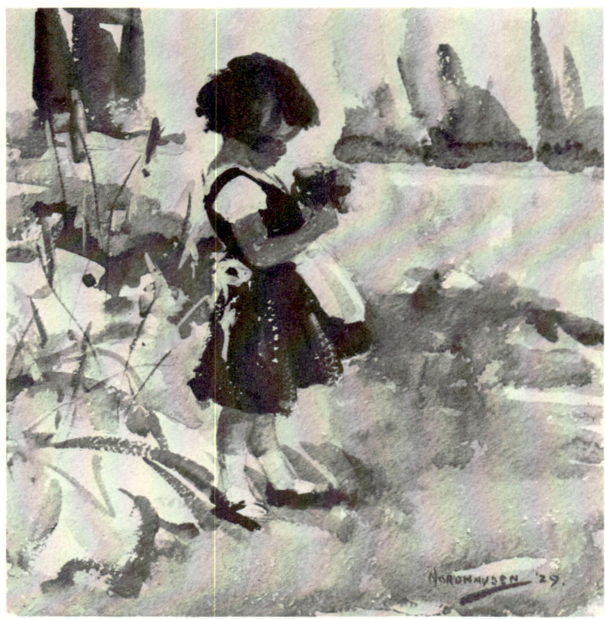

1929
19"x 18"
Watercolor
Private collection

10. Child in Garden

Although the act of portraiture has its limitations—a likeness is mandatory, and the painting, whether it is a good likeness or not, has to be acceptable to the commissioner—it has maintained a firmly established position throughout the history of art. Nordhausen's approach to the problem is that of the realist but, when compared with his other work—the figure studies, ballet dancers, and costumed studio models—there is a consistency of mood which is almost romantic in character. For him the mood is essential, and indeed the execution of a commissioned portrait is doomed to failure if the subject is not sympathetic. It is obviously not the exterior and recognizable features that are important but rather the inner and often hidden character which must be interpreted through the form, color, drawing, and light.

Whereas the earlier portraits have a free and more lucid composition with a greater bravura to the brushstroke, the later ones are more sustained, evidenced by solid form and a greater subtlety of color and texture. Indeed, it is this quality of sober restraint, modest solidity, and sensitive understanding of human values which gives Nordhausen a unique and distinctive position in the art of our time.

In recent years the major portion of Nordhausen's creative effort has therefore been devoted to portrait painting. This has given him a high degree of financial security, but it has also been the fulfillment of the professional ideal toward which he had struggled since his early Munich days. Yet he is constantly intrigued by the human figure and its endless possibilities in terms of color, composition, and spiritual expression. He has continued to paint directly from the model, both nude and in costume, and has enjoyed success in terms of both sales and recognition.

An Artist in Manhattan

THE SIXTY-YEAR RECORD of this artist in Manhattan is thus one of solid performance. It is not a provincial one, for though his roots have always been in New York, as has been noted he has traveled and worked in many areas of the world—in Georgia, Vermont, and the American West as well as in Germany, Italy, Mexico, and many other foreign countries. Nevertheless, he remained a devoted and integral part of New York City, that vast and unique cultural metropolis.

From his early youth Nordhausen was thoroughly addicted to the Manhattan scene, with its colorful burlesque shows, its baseball games, the elevated streetcars, Fourteenth Street, and the studio life of Greenwich Village. He loved Coney Island and the characters seen on the subway late at night. He used to describe some of the pictur-esque scenes—a gaudy drygoods storefront with a big sign, "Levi never loses a customer!" while a bum sleeps across the doorway in a mass of crumpled newspapers—which would be a typical subject for a Reginald Marsh painting but one which Nordhausen would never do. Similarly he had no artistic interest in the sad-faced shopgirls of Fourteenth Street made famous by the Soyers, even though he deeply respected the drawing and composition of their paintings.

It is true that the majority of the artists and certainly the best critics and art historians since the mid-twentieth century have been concerned with the various abstract modes of expression. But the role they have played has not been an exclusive one. The realists and the studio concern for the figure, both within and outside academic circles, have remained very much alive. They have maintained a steady though less prominent tradition with a persistent following that has varied in style from the exuberant freedom of Henri, Luks, and The Eight to the hard-light, precise, detached immobility of Pearlstein and Chuck Close.

Each group, whether modern or traditional, nonobjective or representational, has its own historical analogies and sources, though the historical span of the modern groups seems to be confined more to the art of this century, and the analytical system much more detailed and sophisticated.

Without fanfare Nordhausen's work has remained an essential part of that tradition. The fact that it has not conformed to one or another of the specialized groups that have captured the attention of the critical press serves only to emphasize the pluralistic and many-faceted character of American art during this period of the twentieth century.

The issue of Manhattan as the artistic capital of the nation as opposed to the "provinces" has long been the subject of debate among art critics and historians. The threat of decentralization through the patronage system of the federal government recently brought forth a spirited defense by Hilton Kramer in the *New York Times* for Manhattan's leadership in the arts as "a place where abundant choice, variety and conflict—the conflict of contending traditions and ideas—are the rule rather than the exception in the life of the arts. All artistic experience is comparative experience, and talent prospers where comparisons are vivid, compelling and unremitting, where standards are harshly judged and vigorously defended . . . it is in the nature of a cosmopolitan culture such as New York's that it offers both the best and the most variegated models of what is established and the most exacting terms for moving beyond them and creating new ones."*

To the succession of these variegated models, often criticized as fashion trends, Nordhausen's work represents a quiet stability based on his own deep and integral respect for nature and the figure, a mastery of technical procedure and all the human limitations and possibilities associated with them. His equally deep-seated respect for tradition reaffirms the persistence of both the genuine and the creative.

Conversations on Art

IN THEORY Nordhausen has always felt that art should not be considered a competitive sport, and as we have noted in the swift succession of styles and trends in the New York scene he has maintained his own course. Nordhausen has seldom been blessed with the publicity necessary in our time for stylistic success. His has never been the kind of flamboyant personality that would naturally attract public attention, nor is his subject matter controversial enough to provoke attacks by articulate artists or critics.

Not that he objects: "There is not one type of art to which all men should conform," he said in an interview, "there are as many types of art as there are types of men. Look around and discover the many styles in other times and countries. . . . What is true of the historical styles in the museums is also true of the variety in contemporary art.

"But remember," he went on, "there is good painting and bad painting; non-creative painting and vital, sensitive and imaginative painting. So too there is some fine non-objective painting and a good deal of weak, inept non-objective painting. It is not the classification that insures the quality of art. It is the character of mind and spirit."

The artist is a special type of person. "His true purpose," he said, quoting George Inness, "is simply to reproduce in other minds the impression which a scene or sitter has made on him. A work of art is not to instruct, not to edify, but to awaken an emotion. Its real greatness consists in the quality and force of this emotion."

At another time he made the remark that "talent is an individual capacity. It is not acquired, nor can it be learned; he who has it is simply born that way." With it must go the will and ability to persist, for many an artist, faced by seemingly insurmountable difficulties, will give up the struggle because of "lack of talent" when in reality the difficulties are those involving his own personal growth.

Concerning teaching and the encouragement of the artist, he said, "One tries in the best tradition of each style and form, to develop the individual personality to the maximum of his own possibilities. But the artist needs technical training, a knowledge and understanding of the world and its people, a trained mind and eye as well as a skilled hand. He cannot do it all himself, but needs the guidance of competent instructors to shorten the road toward individual freedom and maturity of expression. Constable said it well with the comment: 'The self-taught artist has studied with a very ignorant master.' "

In an attempt to organize his thoughts on the aesthetic process, he explained what he considered the four basic modes of expression in works of art:

(1) Realism, by which he meant not only the imitation of objective facts present in the act of perception but also the thinking process by which those facts become visually organized as, for example, in Naturalism and Impressionism (Raphael, Rembrandt, Manet).

(2) Surrealism (feeling), the use of visual images and symbols to construct an independent reality, reflecting the unlimited world of the subconscious as suggested in Romanticism and the fantastic (Dali, Andrew Wyeth).

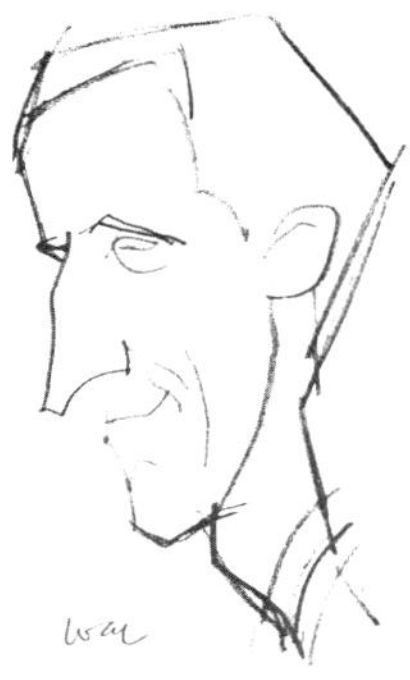

Caricature of Nordhausen
by William Auerbach Levy.

(3) Expressionism (spirit), the plastic reaction to the object or experience in nature to arouse in the beholder a corresponding sensation (Van Gogh, Kokoschka).

(4) Abstraction (intuition), avoiding all imitative elements and inviting an aesthetic response to the purely formal relationship of line, space, color, and mass without conscious use of reason (Picasso, Braque, Hofmann, Pollock).

These concepts, he insisted, are not always separate and independent entities but are often interrelated or fused in a single work. The critic or art historian concerned with analytical clarity may well disagree with these ideas, but they do provide a statement of his own point of view with regard to the succession of artistic styles that has dominated the New York scene through most of his career.

Important here is the primary emphasis on Realism, by which is meant not only respect for the objective facts of nature but the thinking process by which those facts are used and absorbed in the artistic product. All the other concepts are concerned in one way or another with spiritual content—not the recognizable subject matter but the emotional buoyancy which gives the work of art its aesthetic significance.

Nordhausen's approach, therefore, has its parallel in the realism of Henri, Sloan, Luks, and The Eight. His stylistic roots, however, are not to be found in their work but rather in the same sources they used—the great achievements of Hals, Velásquez, and Goya—which he had discovered through the academic discipline he experienced in Munich.

The persistence of the style and its acceptance as part of the Manhattan scene can be followed in the work of the next generation of artists whom he liked and with whom he felt a certain affinity: Eugene Speicher, Bernard Karfiol, George Bellows, and Leon Kroll. Those of his own age and generation such as Reginald Marsh, Moses Soyer, and Raphael Soyer present many parallel elements of style but also significant differences in social content and orientation.

As observed many times before, Nordhausen had always maintained a deliberate detachment from the obvious problems of social or political content. Throughout his life he has had his share of frustration, tragedy, and disappointment as well as the thrill of personal achievement. But it is extremely difficult to discover those personal experiences as such in his work, where they are transformed into the mood and artistic structure of the created product. At the challenge of the war after Pearl Harbor, for example, he did not turn to the obvious use of his art to produce patriotic cartoons, condemn the enemy, or glorify the heroes, but enlisted in the army as a private. Through a long and arduous process his technical skill, creative imagination, and artistic experience combined to make a major contribution to the collective war effort.

In reviewing this remarkably productive career of over sixty years, the usual historical problems of stylistic evolution, iconographical implications, and social or political significance seem less important than the elementary yet inexhaustible problems of the painter and his work. In conversation one is always aware of the artist's enthusiastic, almost exuberant response to people, events, and the world about him; but the discussions on art, whether they are about his own work or that of his contemporaries or the old masters, invariably revolve about the artistic problem, its challenge and final solution, which results in that which we call aesthetic quality.

This is usually the experience one has when visiting the artist's studio in New York. An unfinished painting on the easel recalls another of the same model painted some weeks before. This in turn forms an intriguing contrast as a nude study to that model in an elaborate Victorian costume with its much more complicated problems of design in space and variations in flesh tones and material textures.

As the discussion develops, the artist brings out other paintings from the racks in the back of the room: a series of landscapes or still lifes, or again circus and clown paintings—each with its own set of design problems, technical procedures, or personal anecdotes.

The following selection of work and the accompanying comments are the result of such discussions. The work includes not only the best—that is, those the artist feels are the most successful and completely realized from his own point of view—but also those selected by impartial juries in various open competitions over the years and those which are historically important in understanding the artist's character and development.

II

NORDHAUSEN

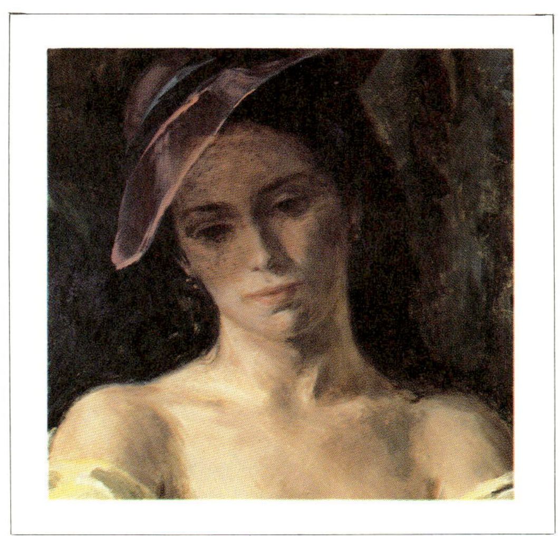

A COLOR PORTFOLIO

1923
15″x 11″
Oil on canvas

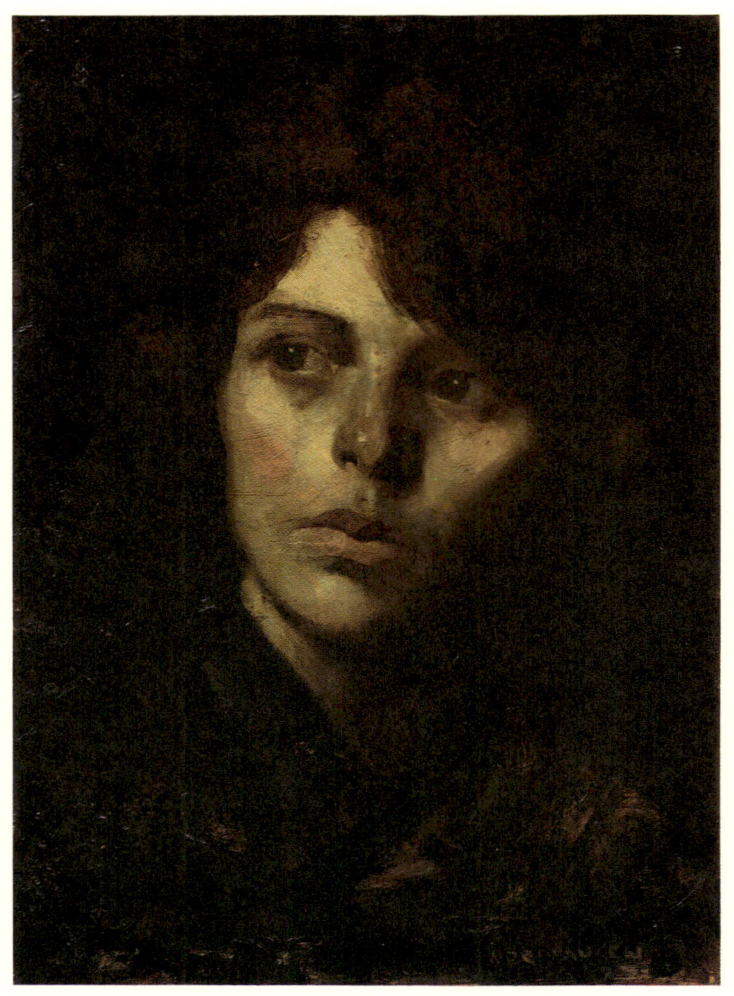

11. *Head of Woman*

1930
20″x 16″
Oil on canvas

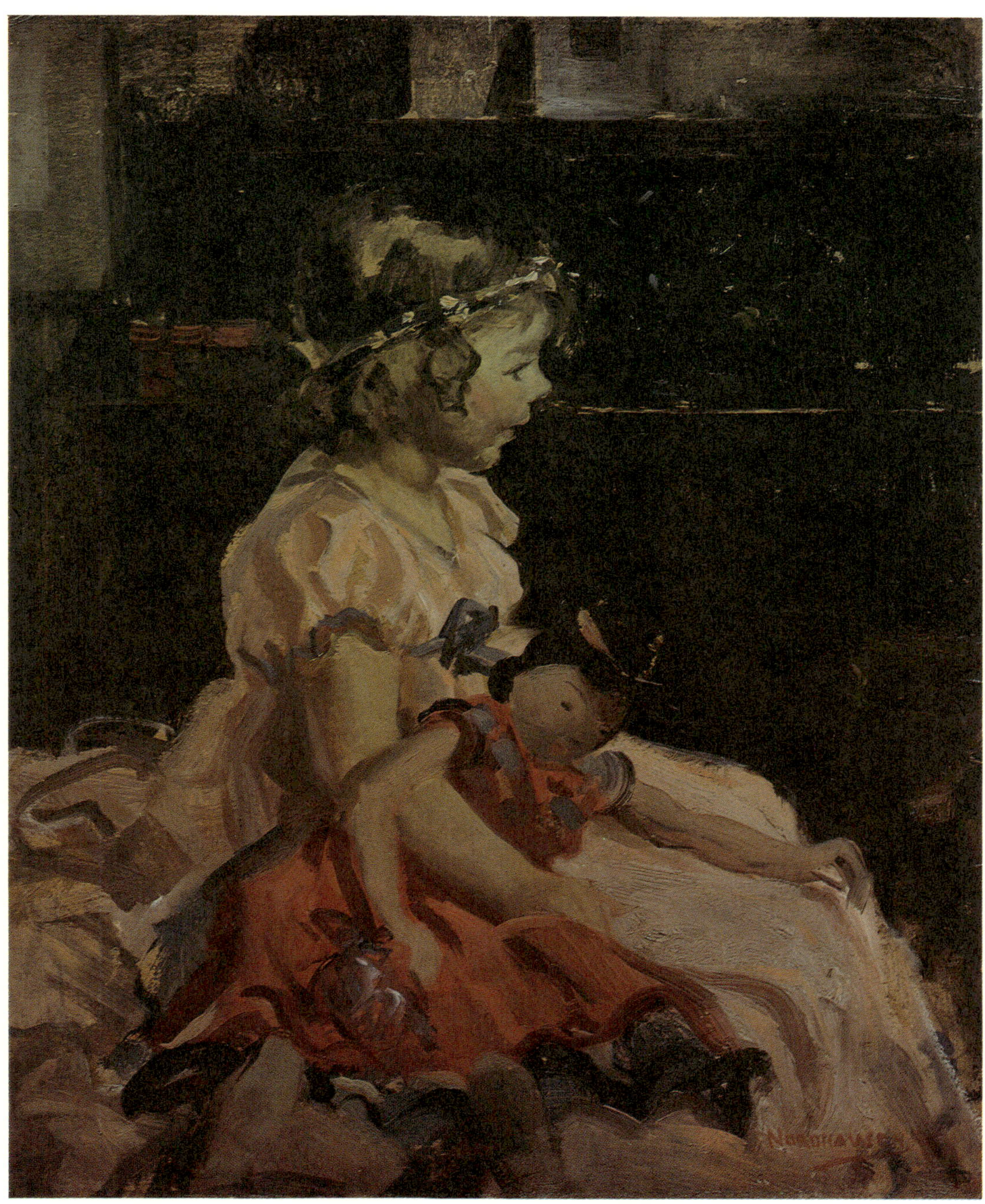

12. *Baby Gwenn*

1938
30″x 24″
Oil on canvas

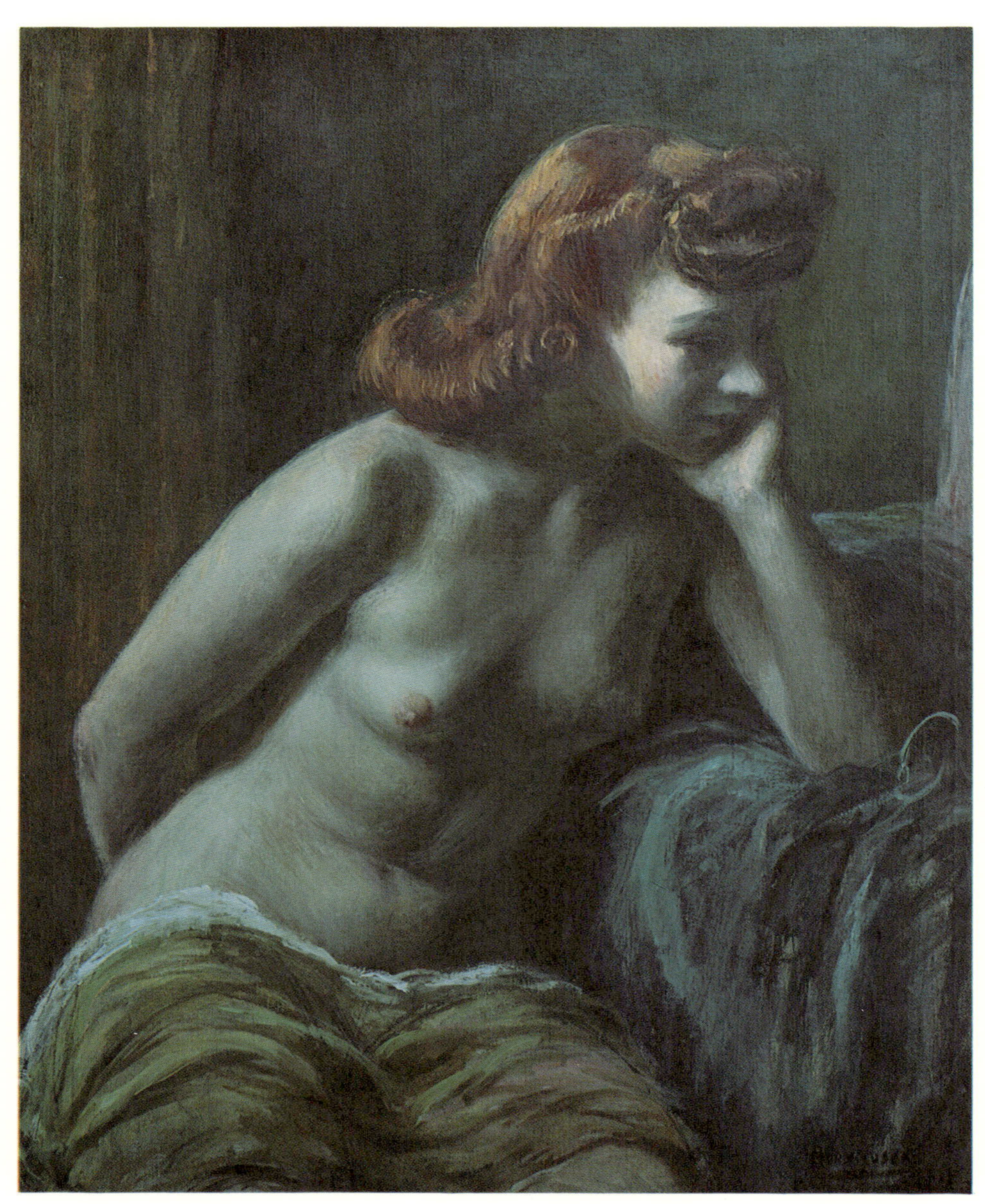

13. *Red Headed Nude*

1938
24″x 20″
Oil on canvas

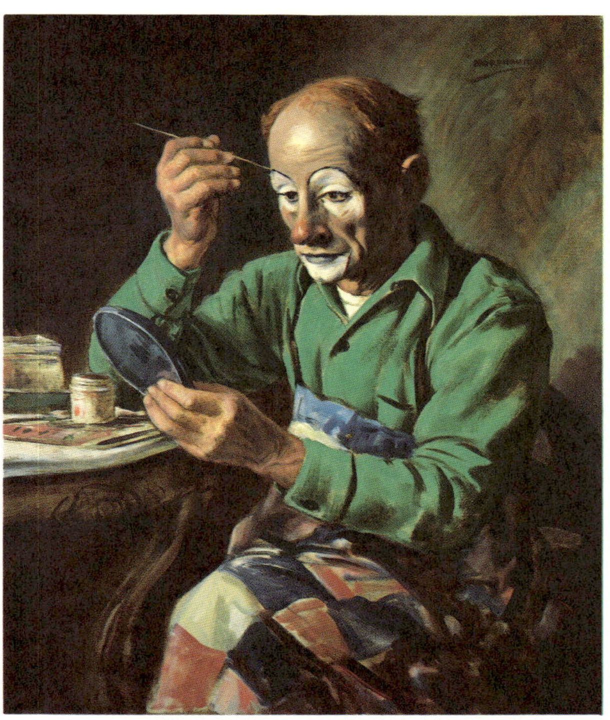

14. Clown Making Up

1938
20″x 16″
Oil on canvas
Private collection

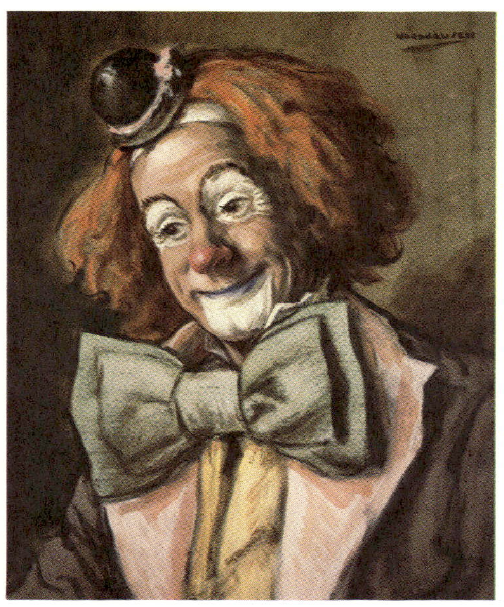

15. Clown with Green Bow

1940
24″x 20″
Oil on canvas

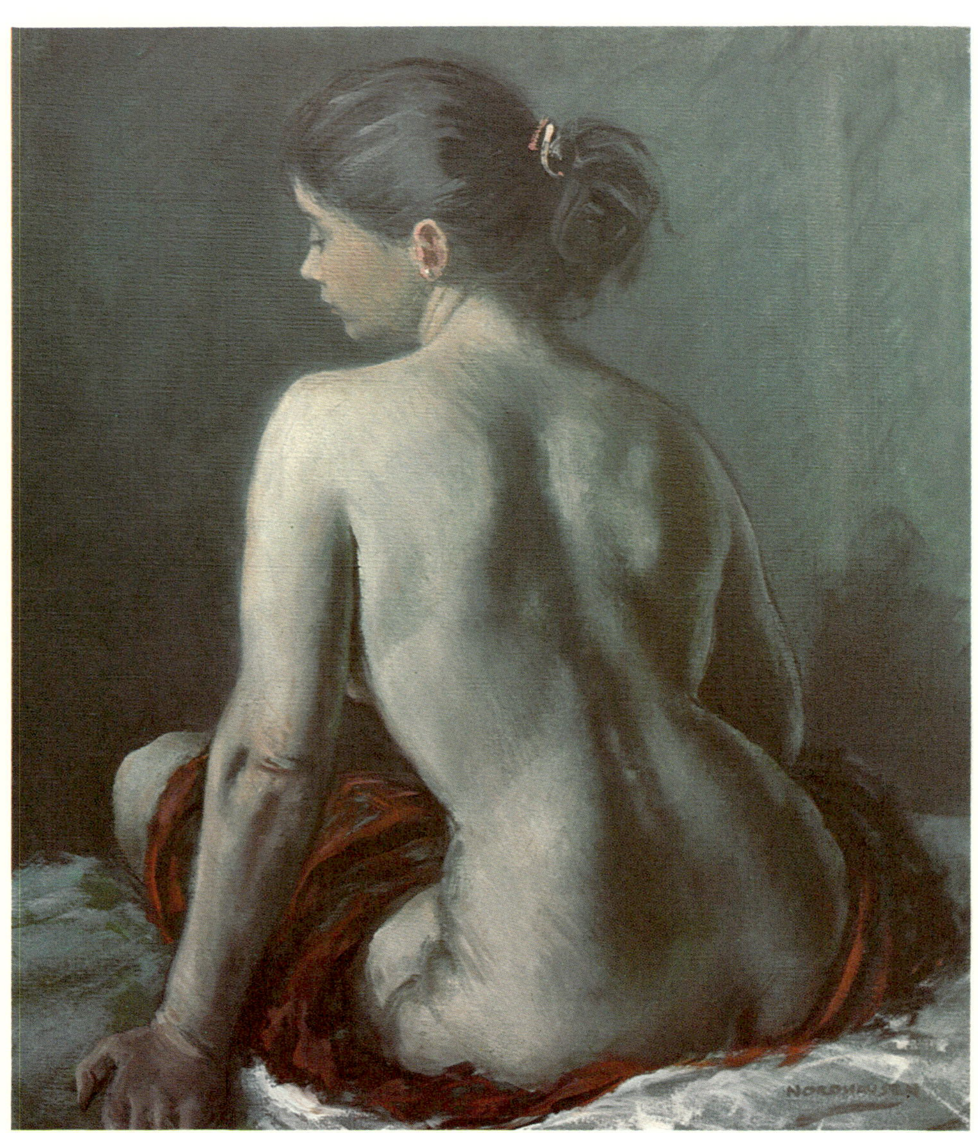

16. *Nude Back, Seated*

1947
30''x 25''
Oil on canvas
Audubon Artists Award, 1947
Collection: Syracuse University

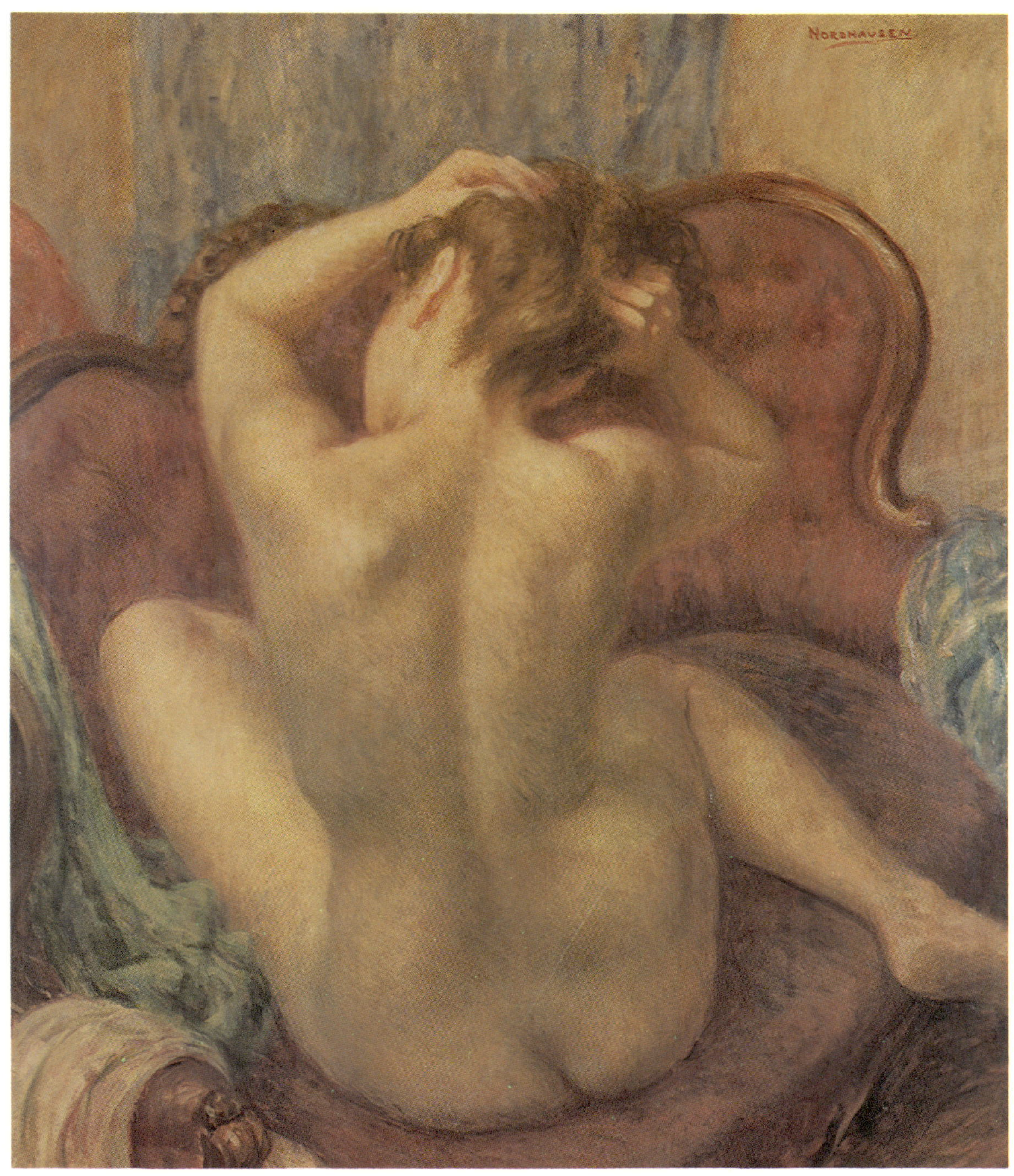

17. Nude on Mulberry Couch

1948
16″ x 12″
Oil on canvas
Digby W. Chandler Prize, 1958

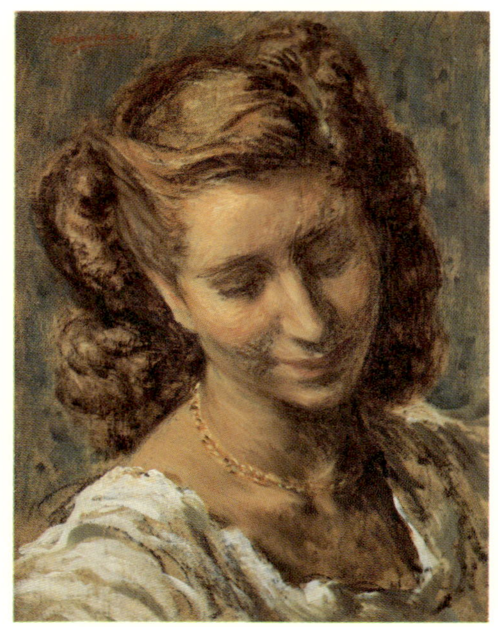

18. Clarisse

1950
38″x 30″
Oil on canvas

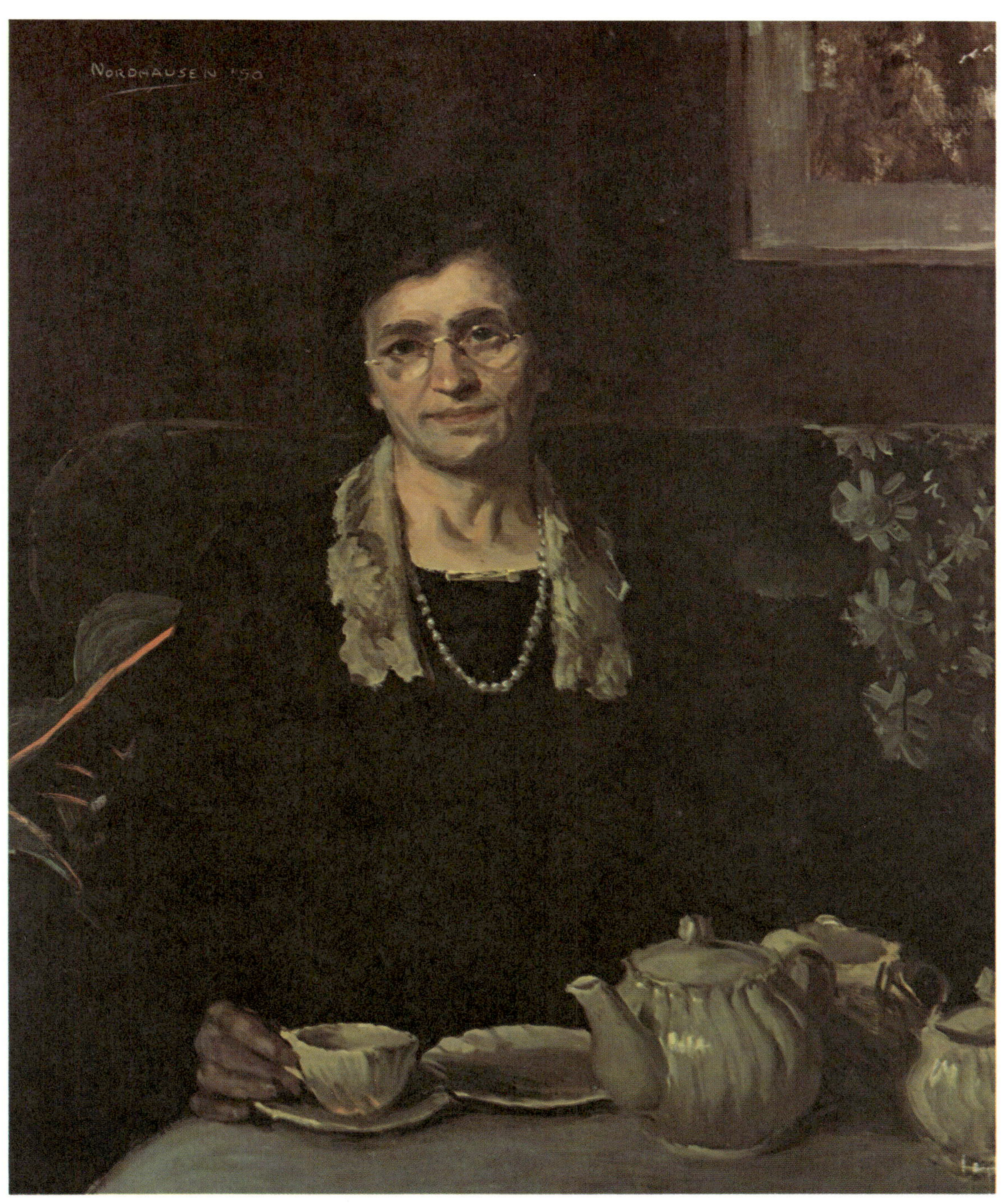

19. *Portrait of the Artist's Mother*

1950
20''x 16''
Oil on canvas
Allied Artists of America Gold Medal Award, 1951

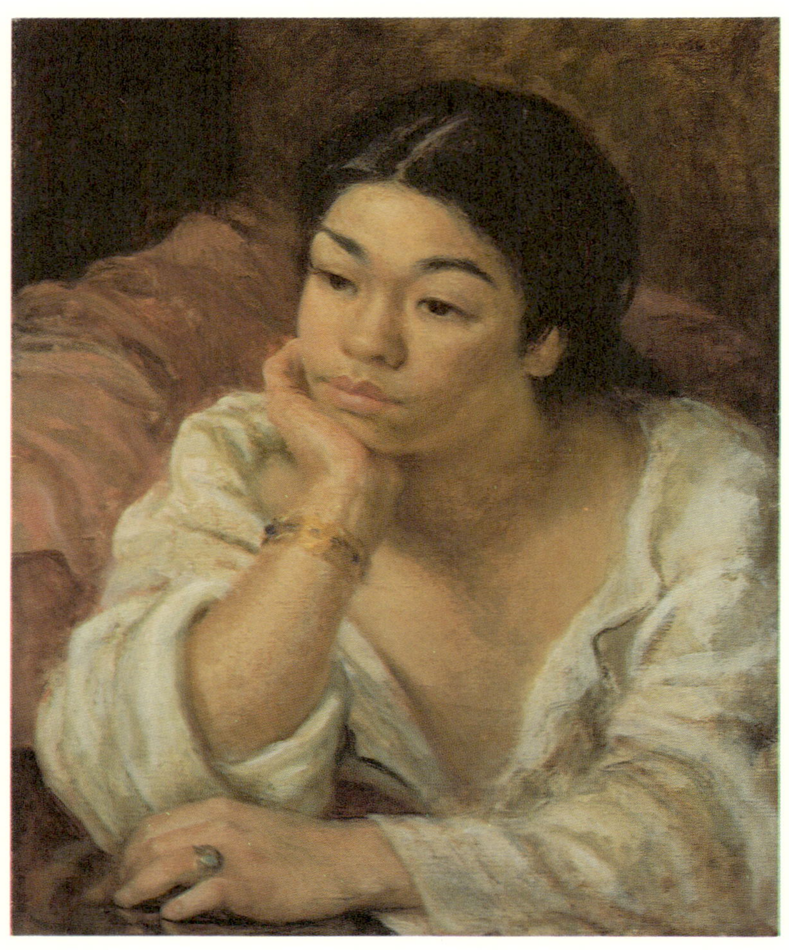

20. Natalia

1950
20″x 16″
Oil on canvas

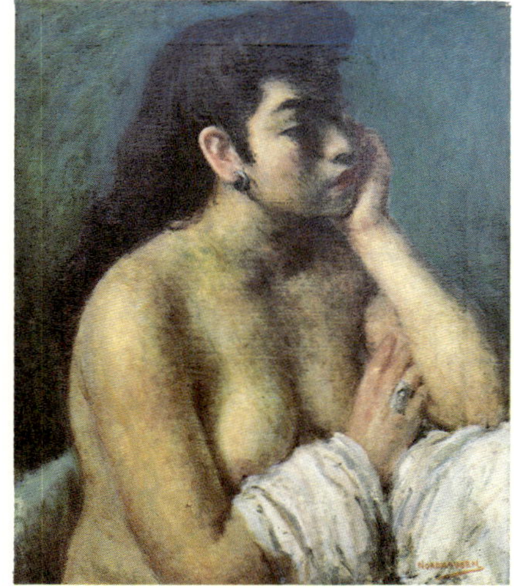

21. Natalia Half Nude

1950
30″x 25″
Oil on canvas

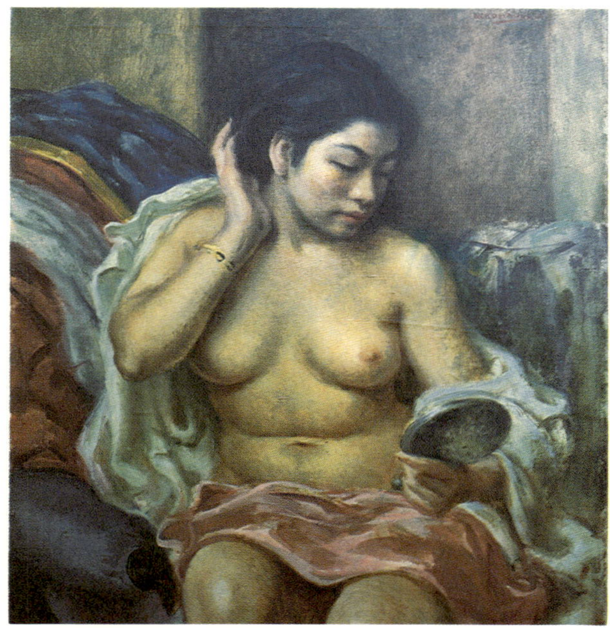

22. Natalia Nude

1952
60″x 40″
Oil on canvas
Collection: Virginia Military Institute

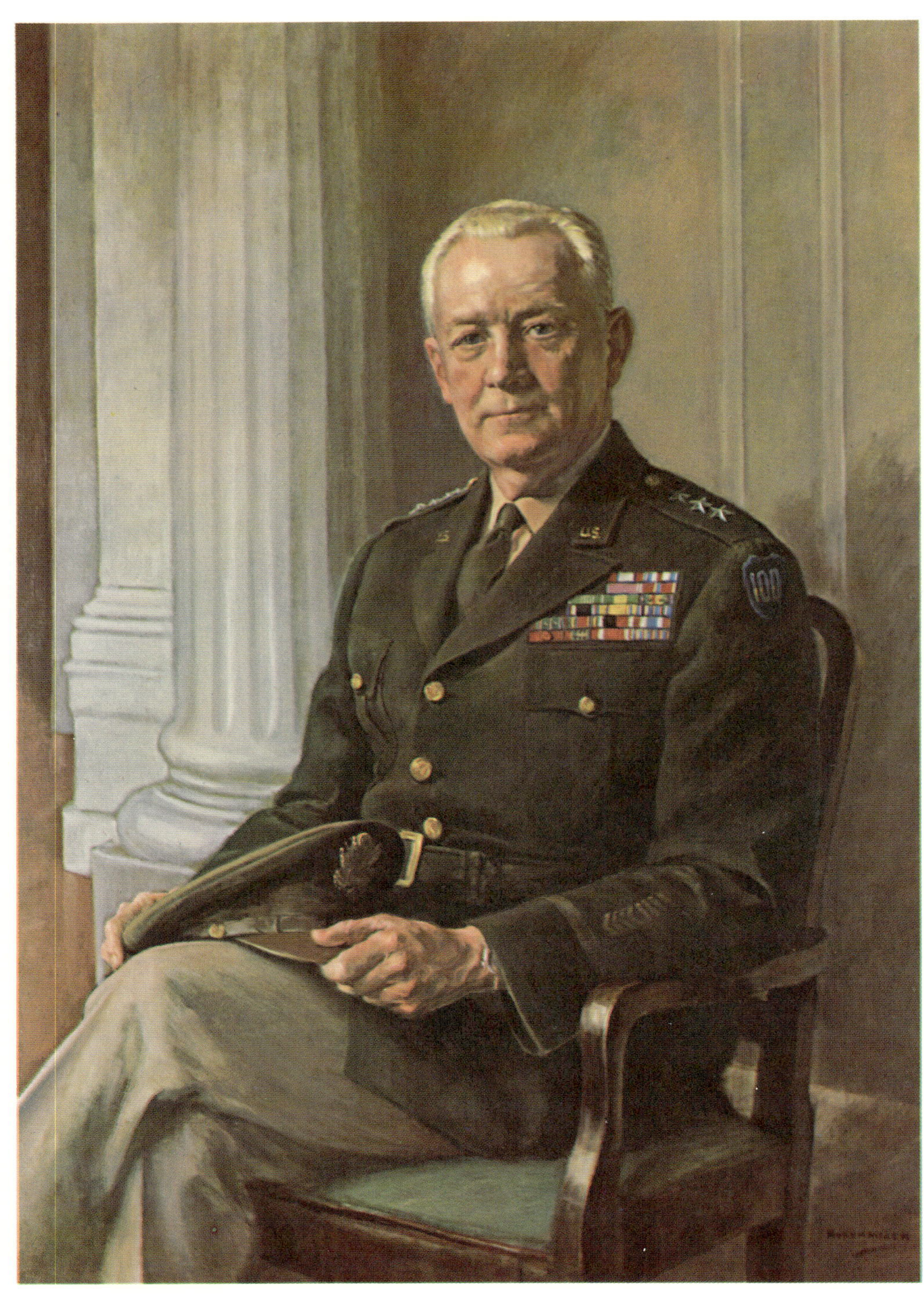

23. *General Withers A. Burress*

1954
36''x 30''
Oil on canvas
Yashitoni Collection, Dobbs Ferry, N.Y.

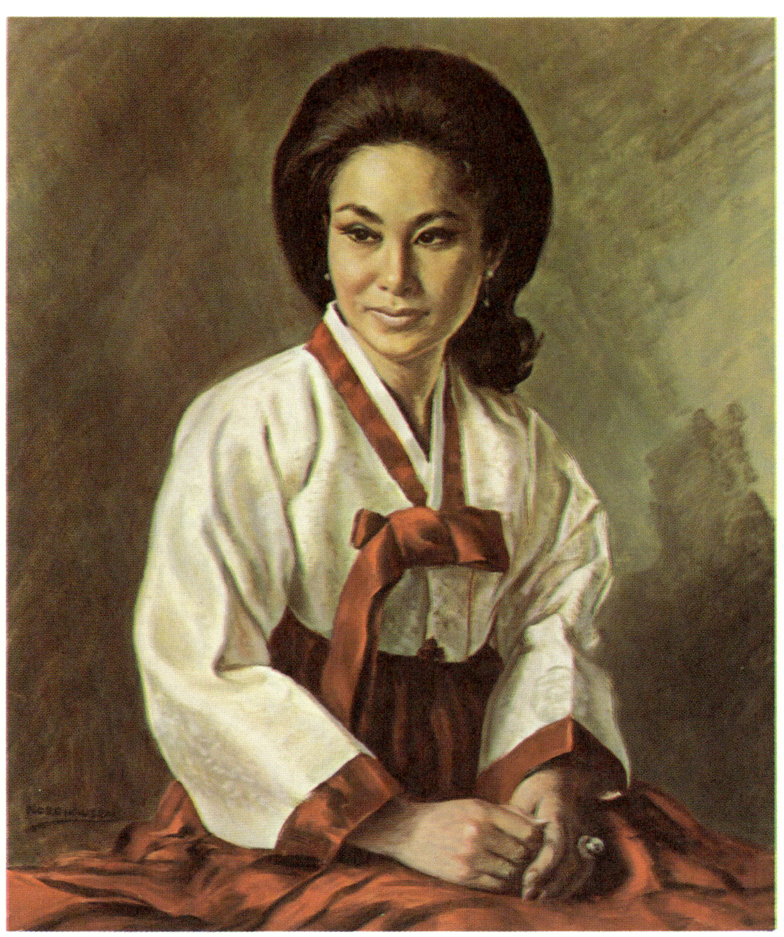

24. Okhee Chae

1955
18″x 15″
Monotype

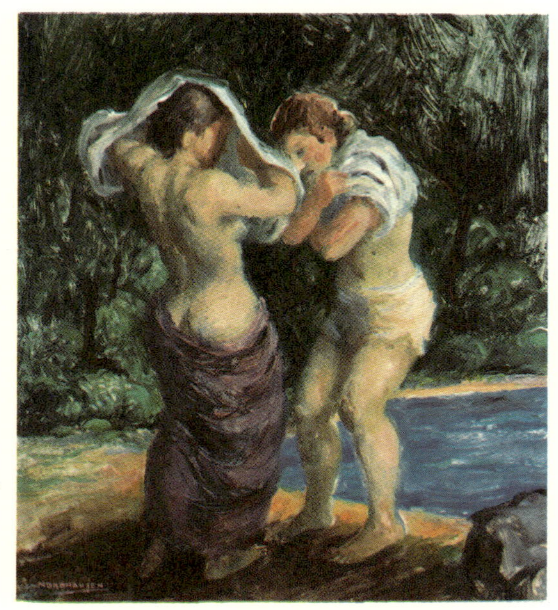

25. The Bathers

1956
35''x 27''
Oil on canvas

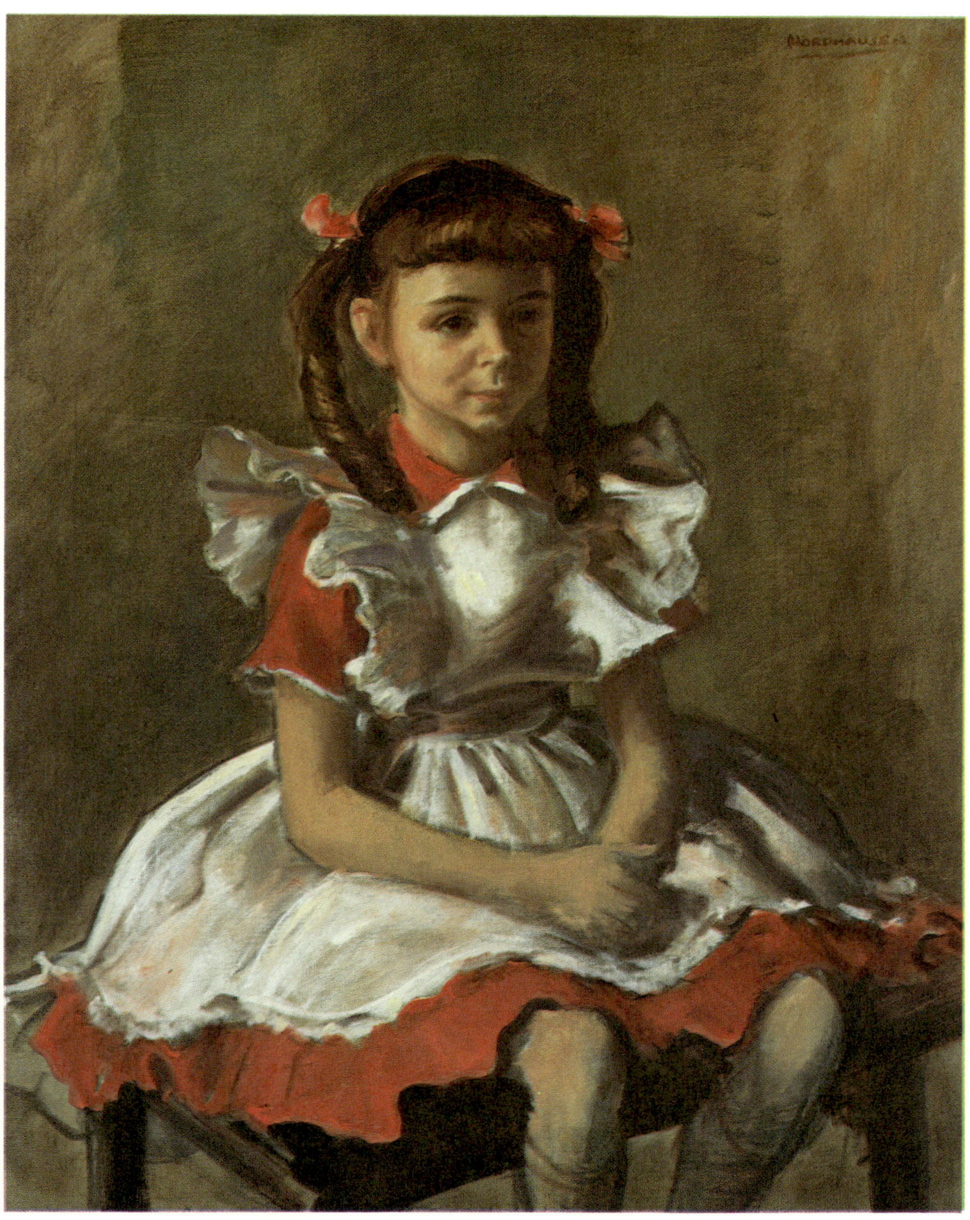

26. *Girl in Pinafore*

1957
36''x 30''
Oil on canvas
Louis E. Seley Award, 1961
Collection: College of the City of New York

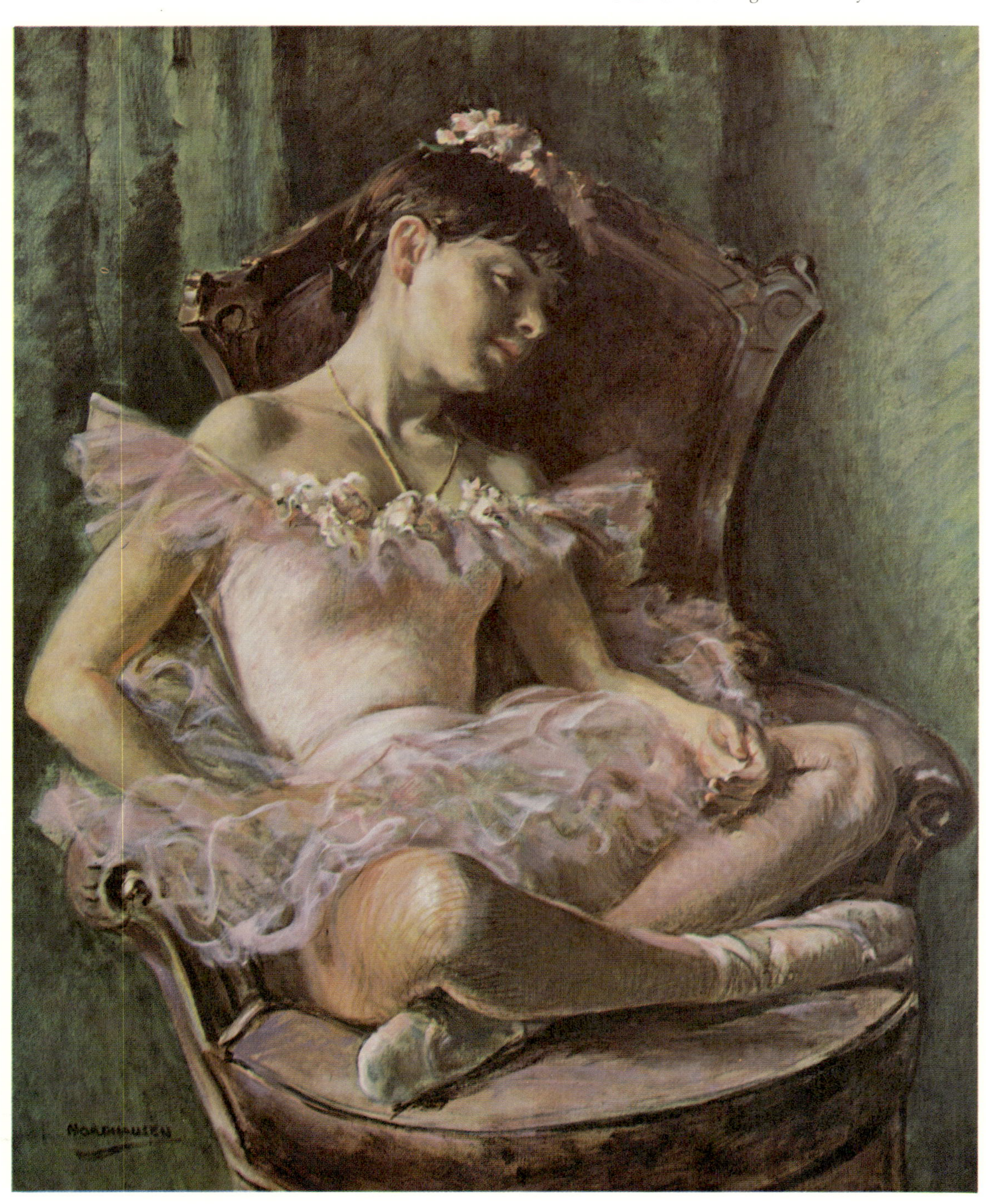

27. *Seated Ballerina*

1958
25″x 20″
Oil on canvas
Woodruff Collection, Columbus, Ga.

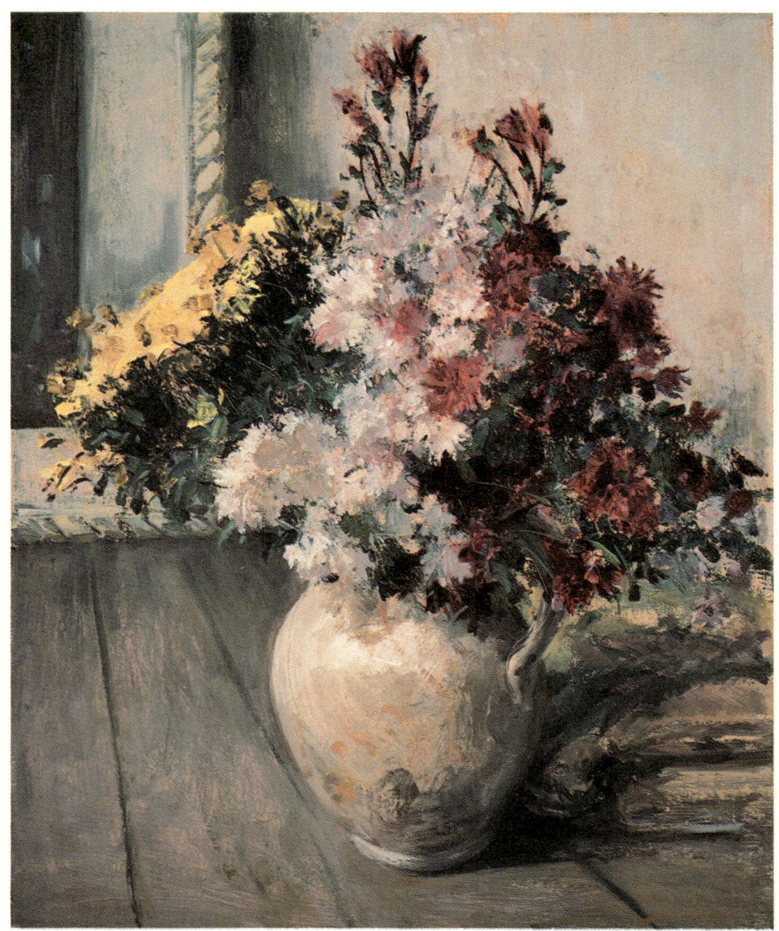

28. Autumn Flowers

1958
36″x 30″
Oil on canvas
Collection: Columbus Museum of Arts and Sciences

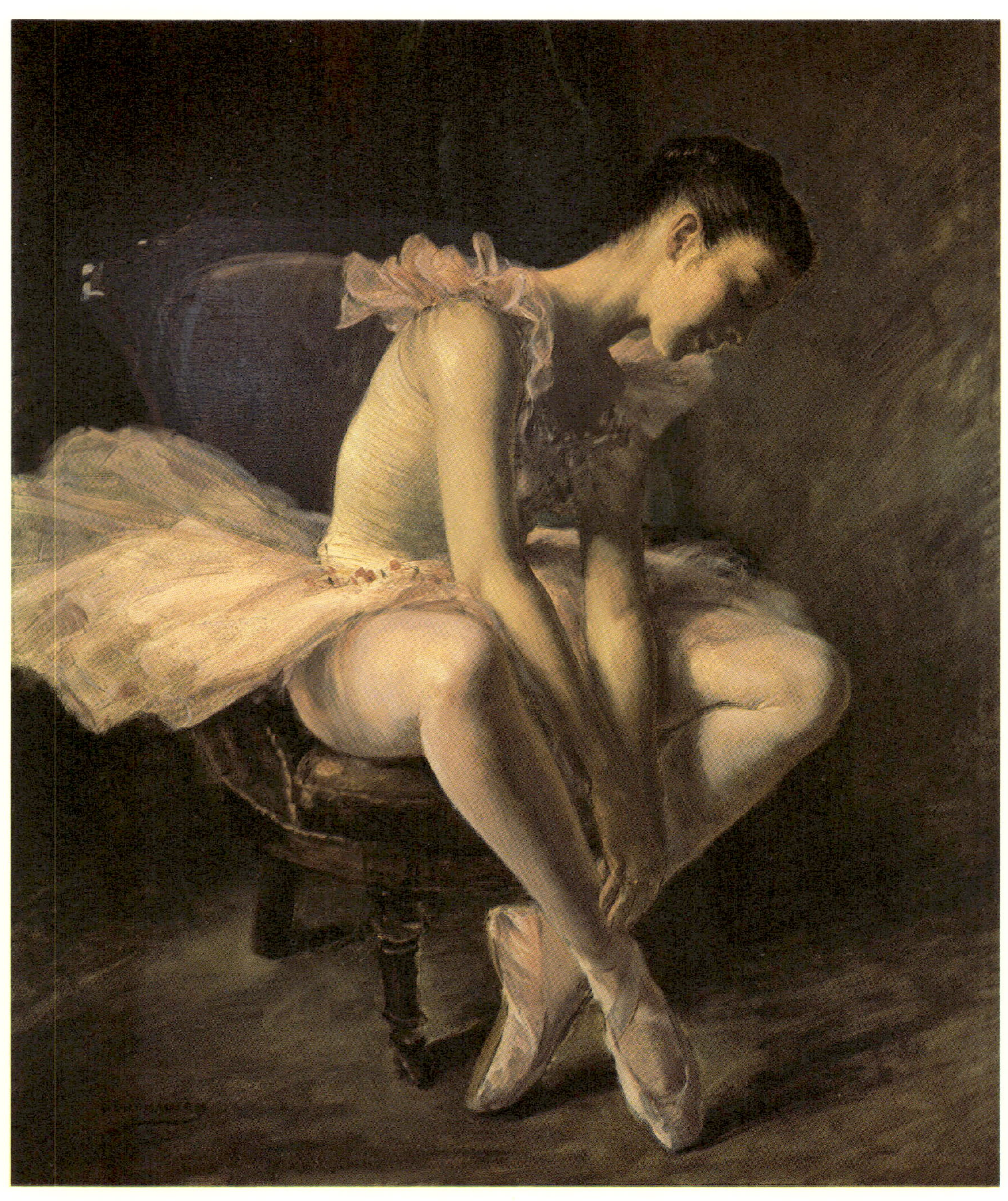

29. *Tying Her Ballet Slipper*

1958
25''x 20''
Oil on canvas
Huff Collection, Columbus, Ga.

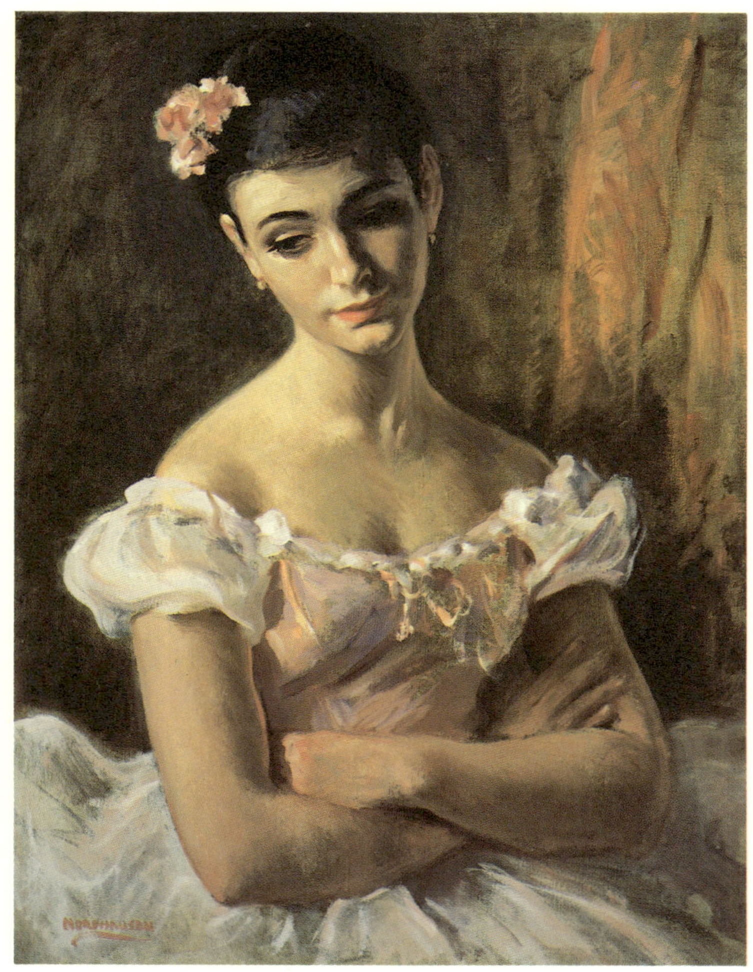

30. Ballerina

1958
35''x 27''
Oil on canvas
Glenn Collection: Columbus, Ga.

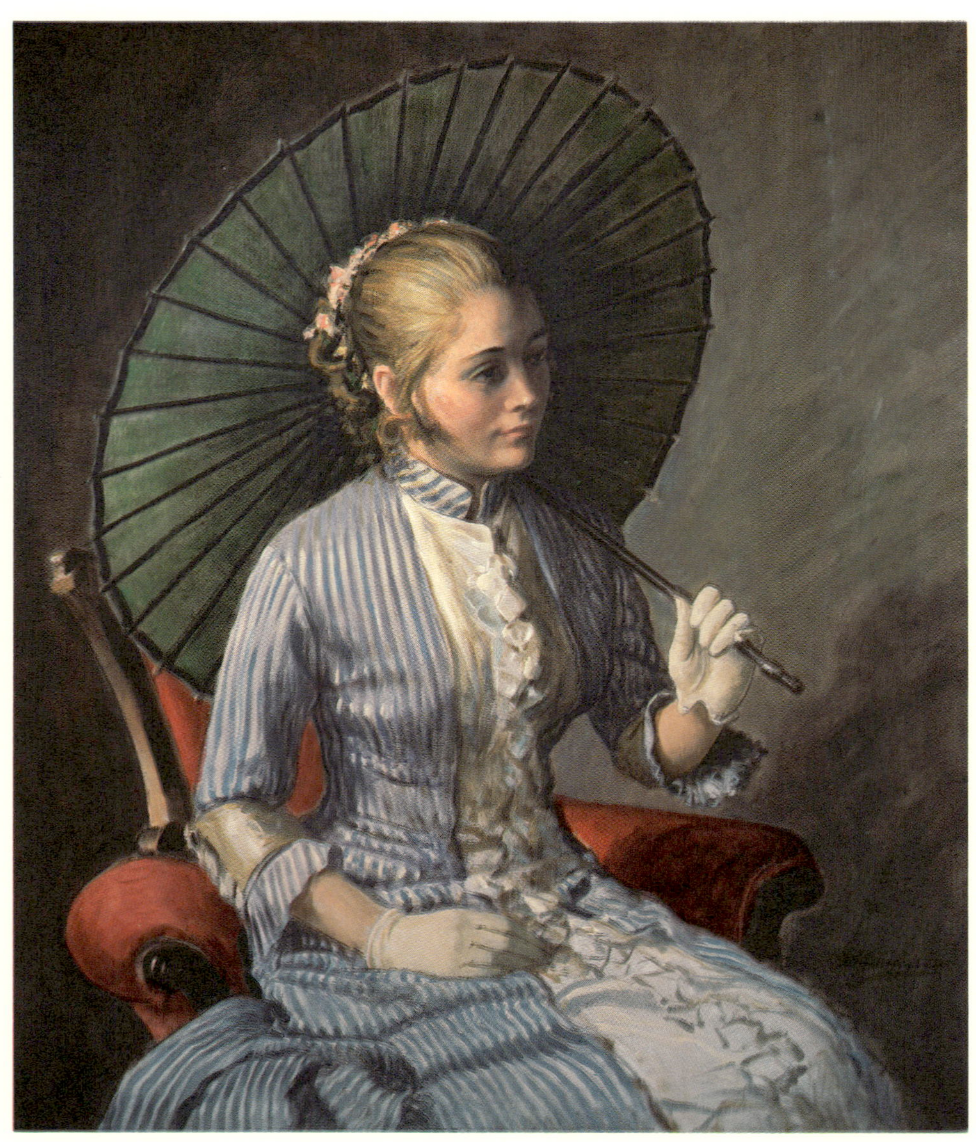

31. 1870 Costume with Parasol

1958
40″x 30″
Oil on canvas
Collection: Syracuse University

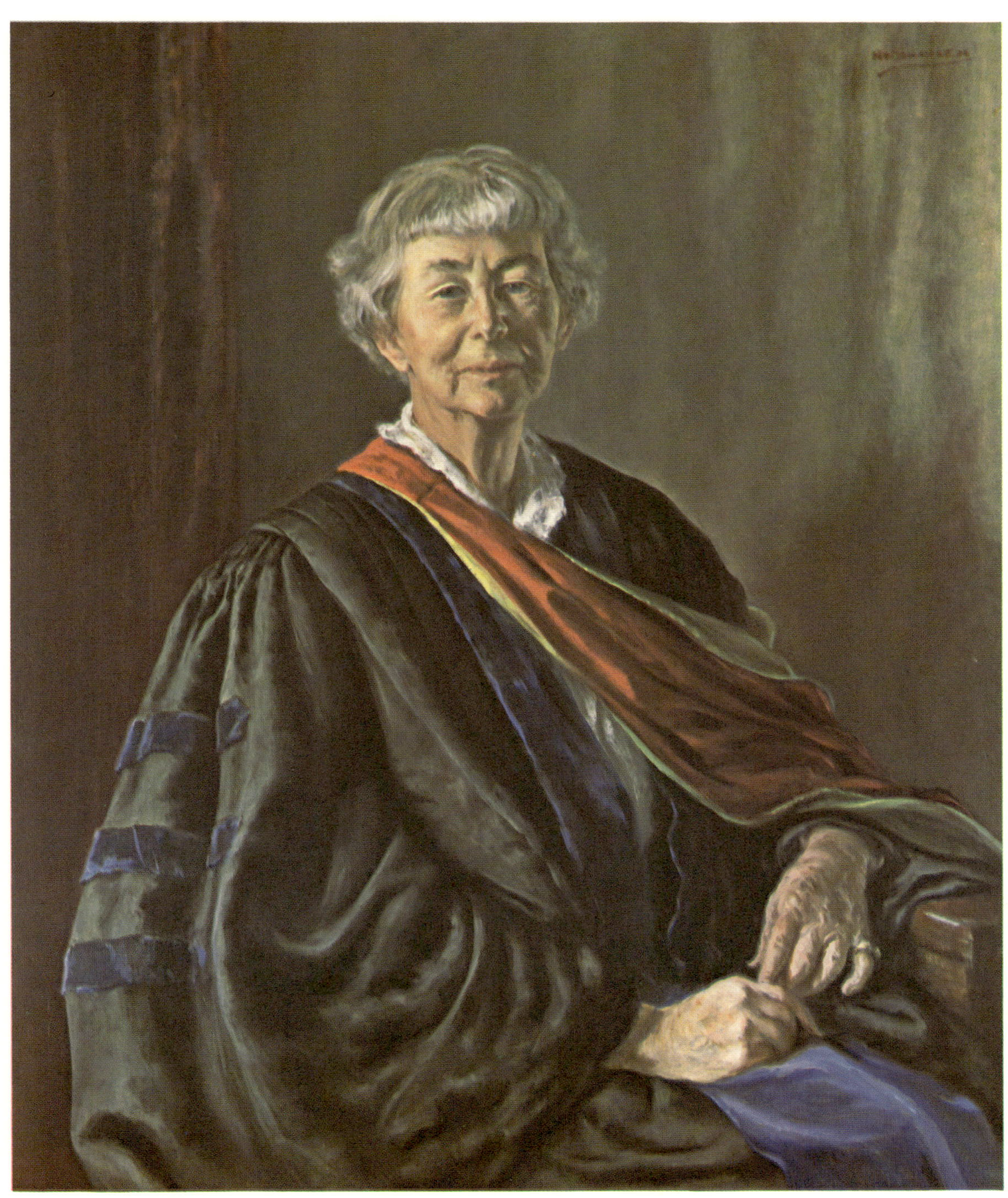

32. Dean Annie Louise MacLeod

1961
45''x 35''
Oil on canvas
Collection: The Pentagon, Washington, D.C.

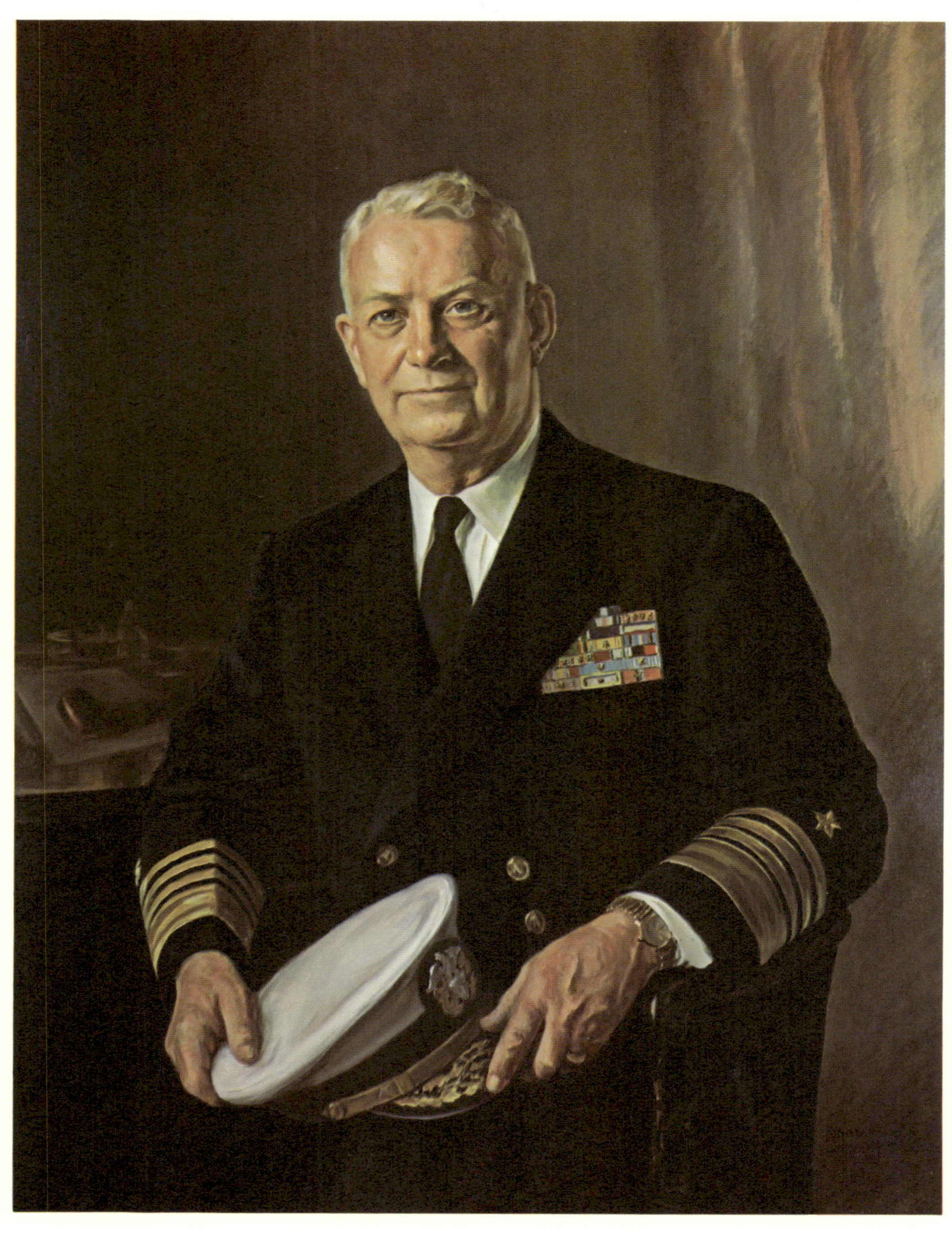

33. Admiral Arleigh Burke

1962
30''x 20''
Watercolor
Chrissoveloni Collection, New York City

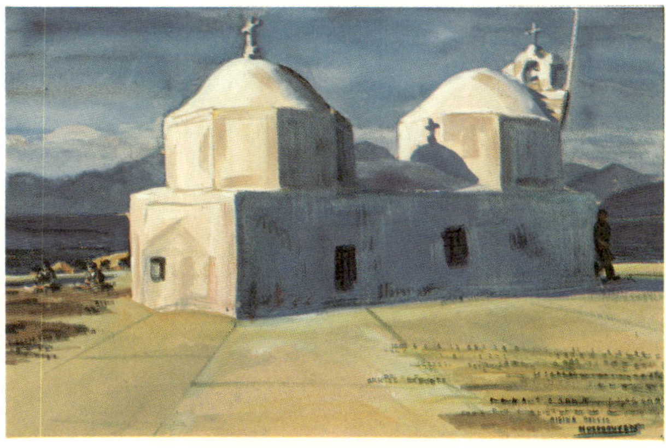

34. *Byzantine Church, Aegina, Greece*

1965
20''x 25''
Oil on canvas

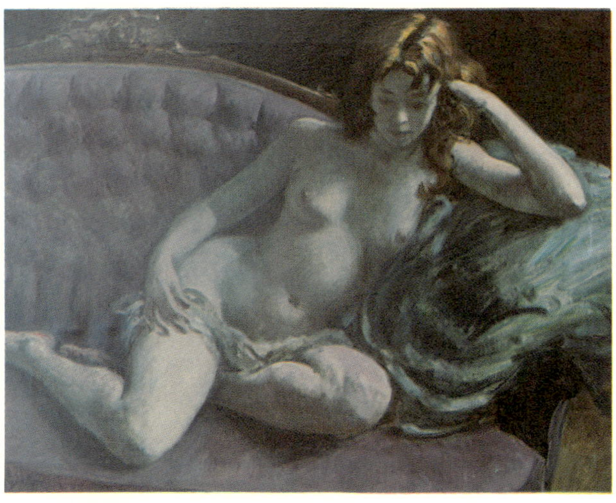

35. *Nude on Purple Couch*

1967
40″x 32″
Oil on canvas
Hardaway Collection, Midland, Ga.

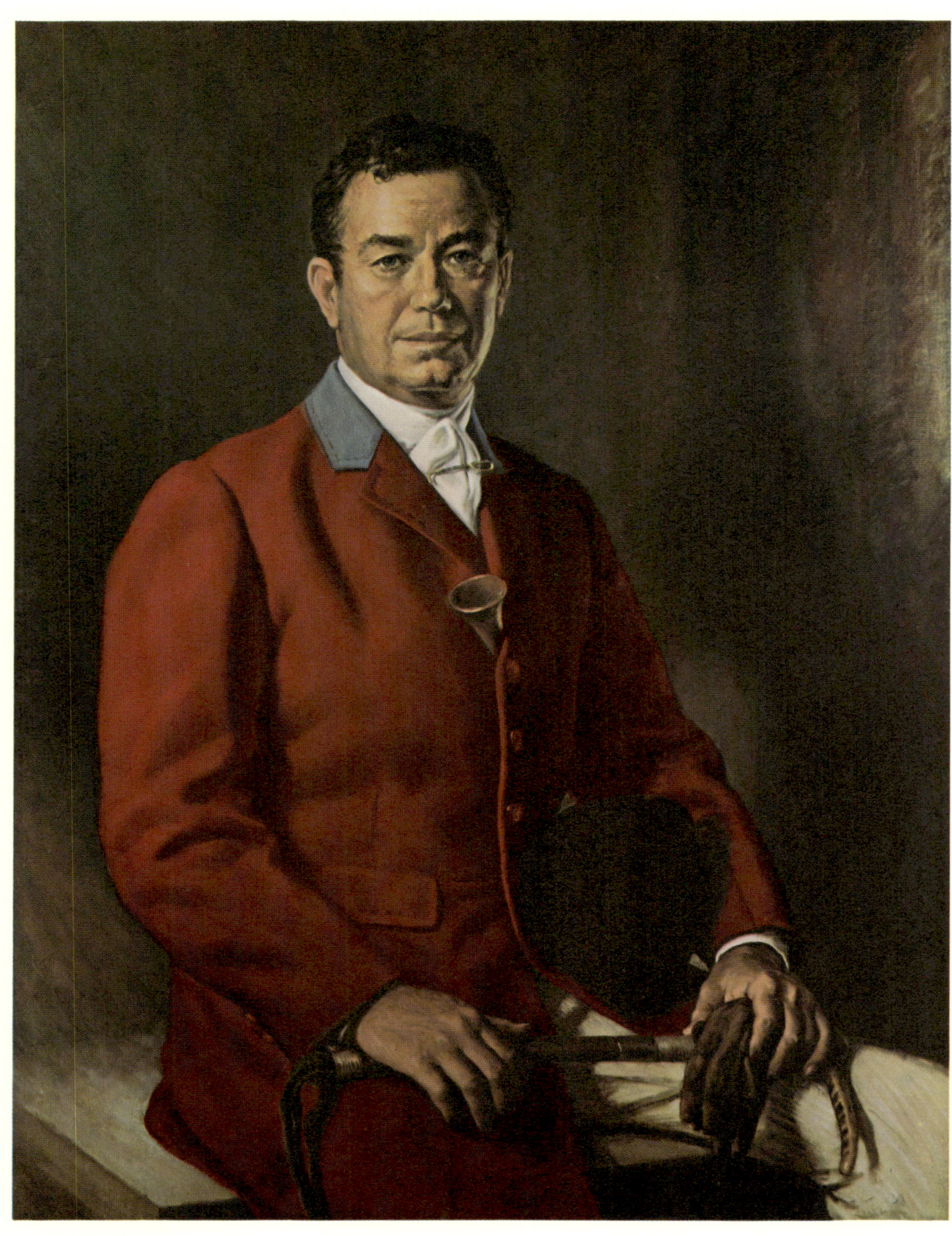

36. Ben Hurt Hardaway III

1967
25''x 20''
Oil on canvas
Foley Collection, Columbus, Ga.

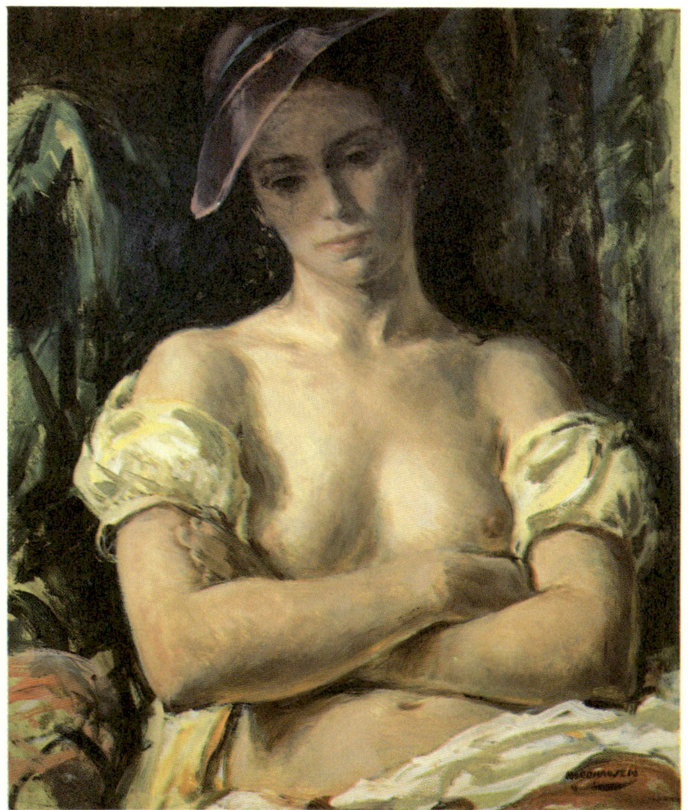

37. *Nude with Hat*

1968
36''x 30''
Oil on canvas
Gynne Lennon Award, 1974
Williams Collection, Columbus, Ga.

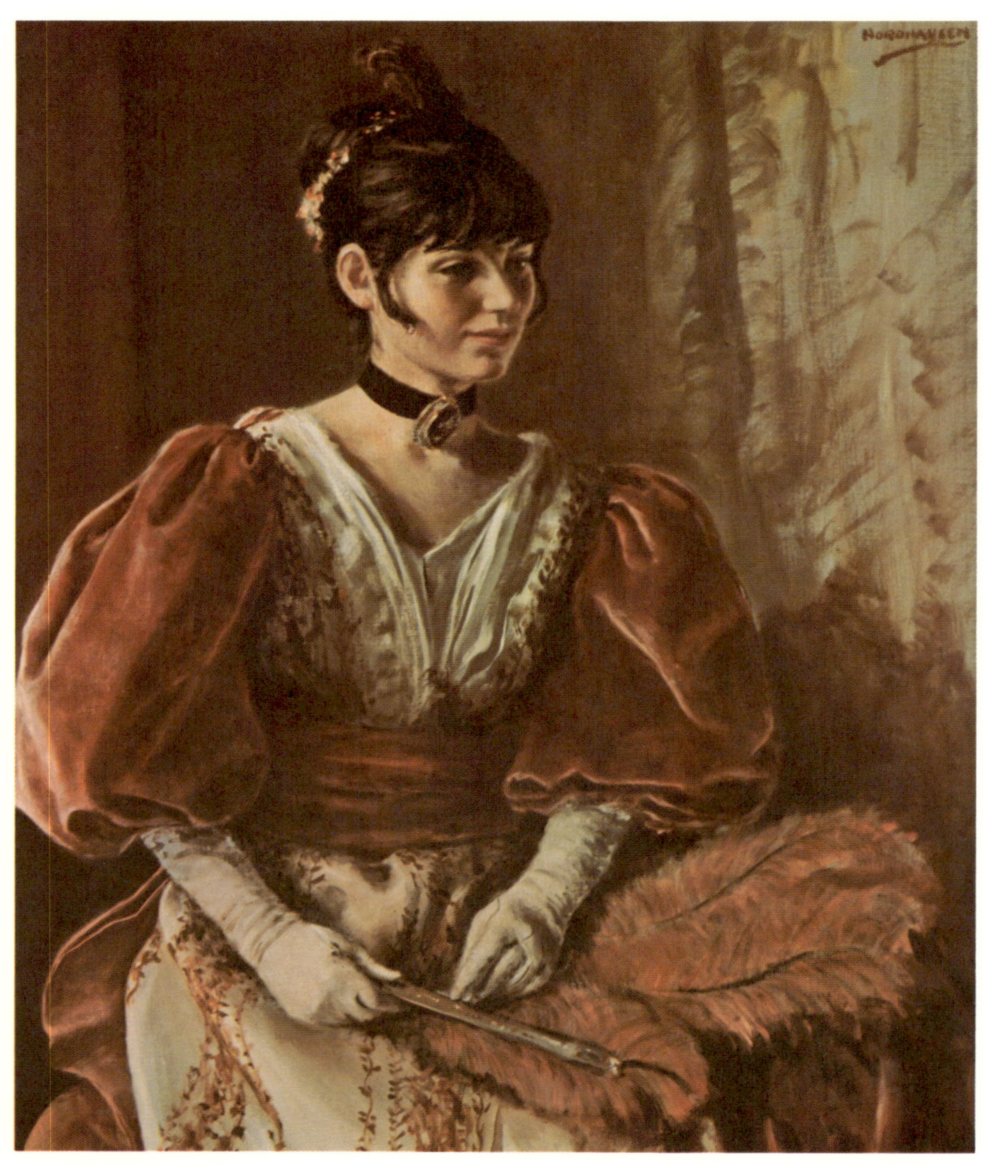

38. The 1890 Costume

1967
42"x 32"
Oil on canvas

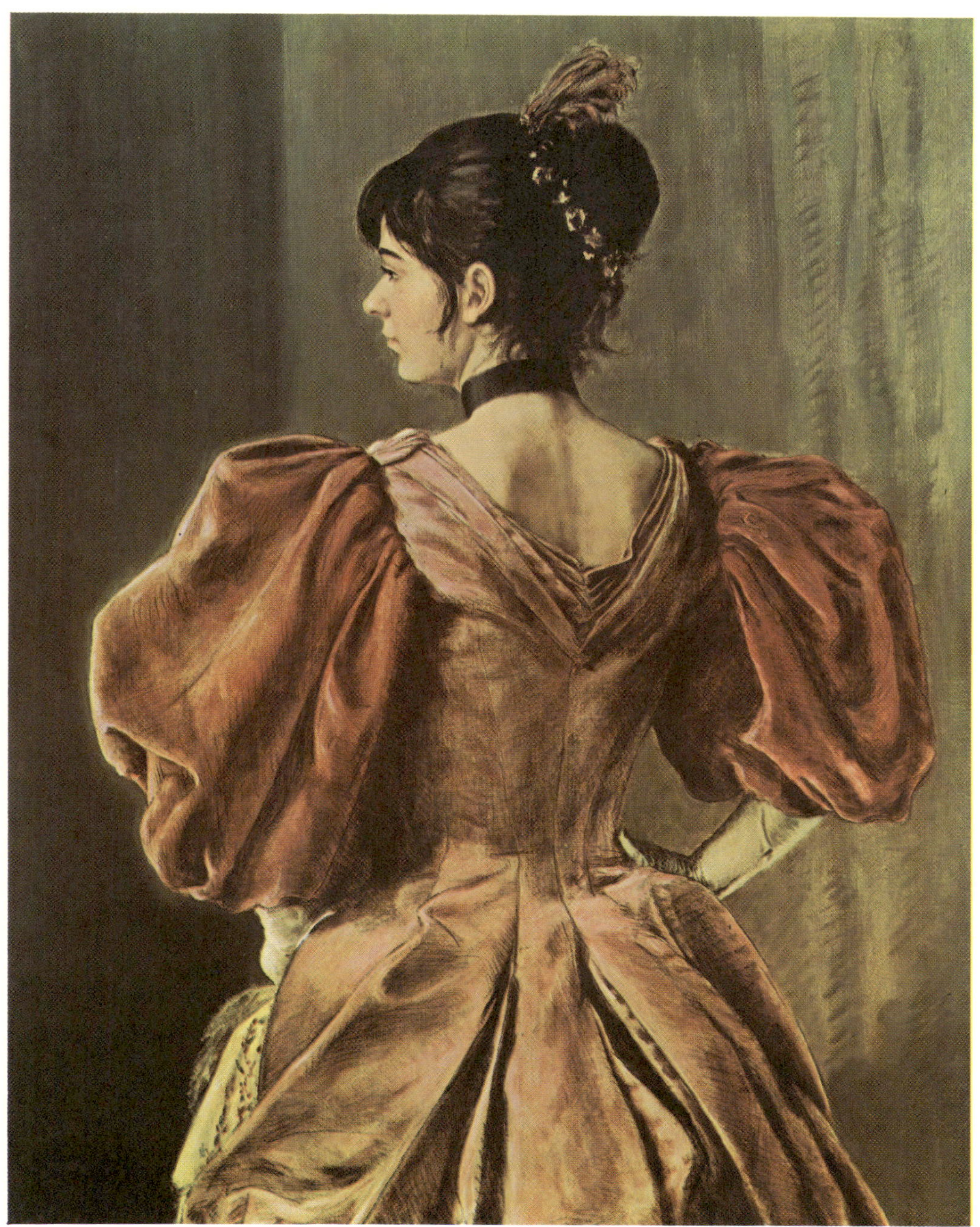

39. 1890 Costume Standing, Back

1968
38''x 30''
Oil on canvas
Passailaigue Collection, Columbus, Ga.

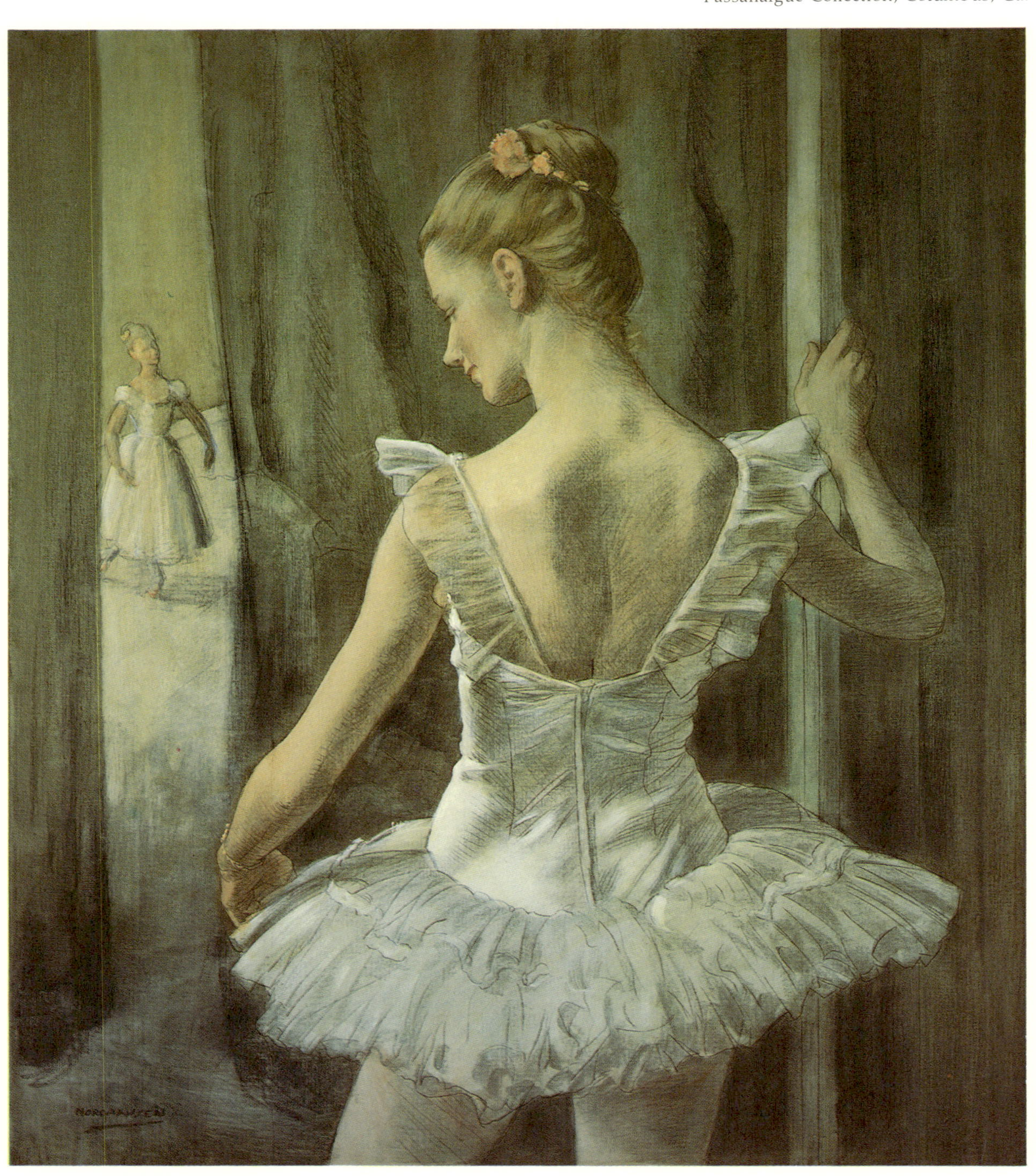

40. *Ready to Go On*

1970
25″ x 20″
Oil on canvas

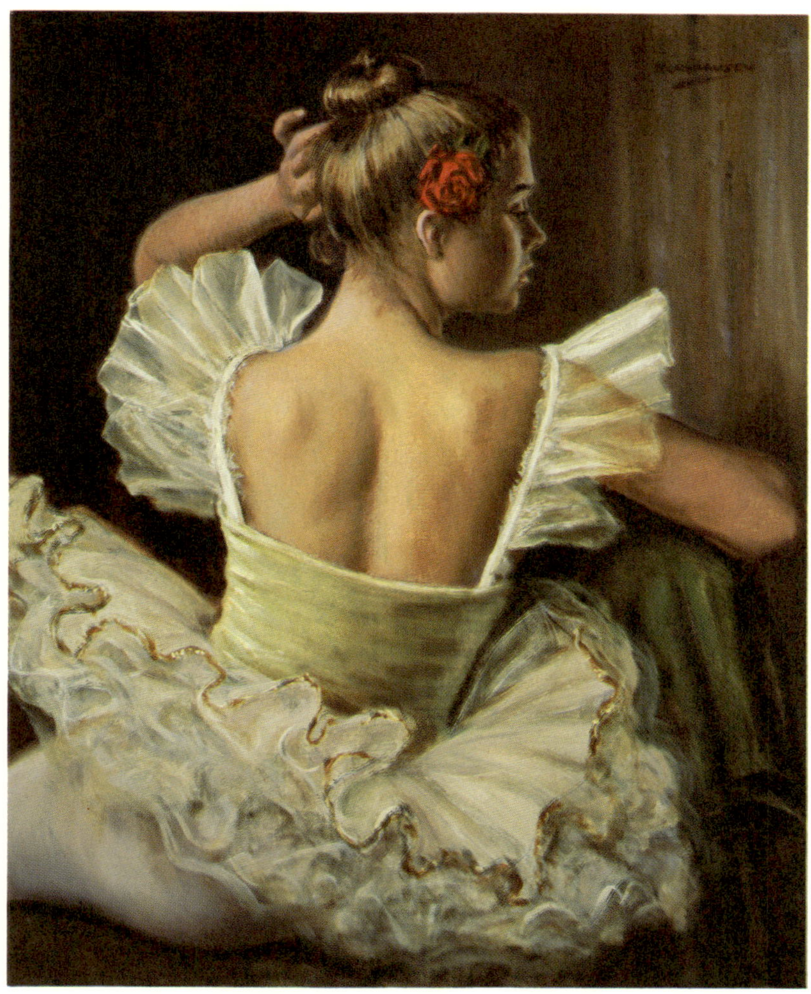

41. *Seated Ballet Figure (The Red Rose)*

1970
30''x 25''
Oil on canvas
Desind Collection, Bethesda, Md.

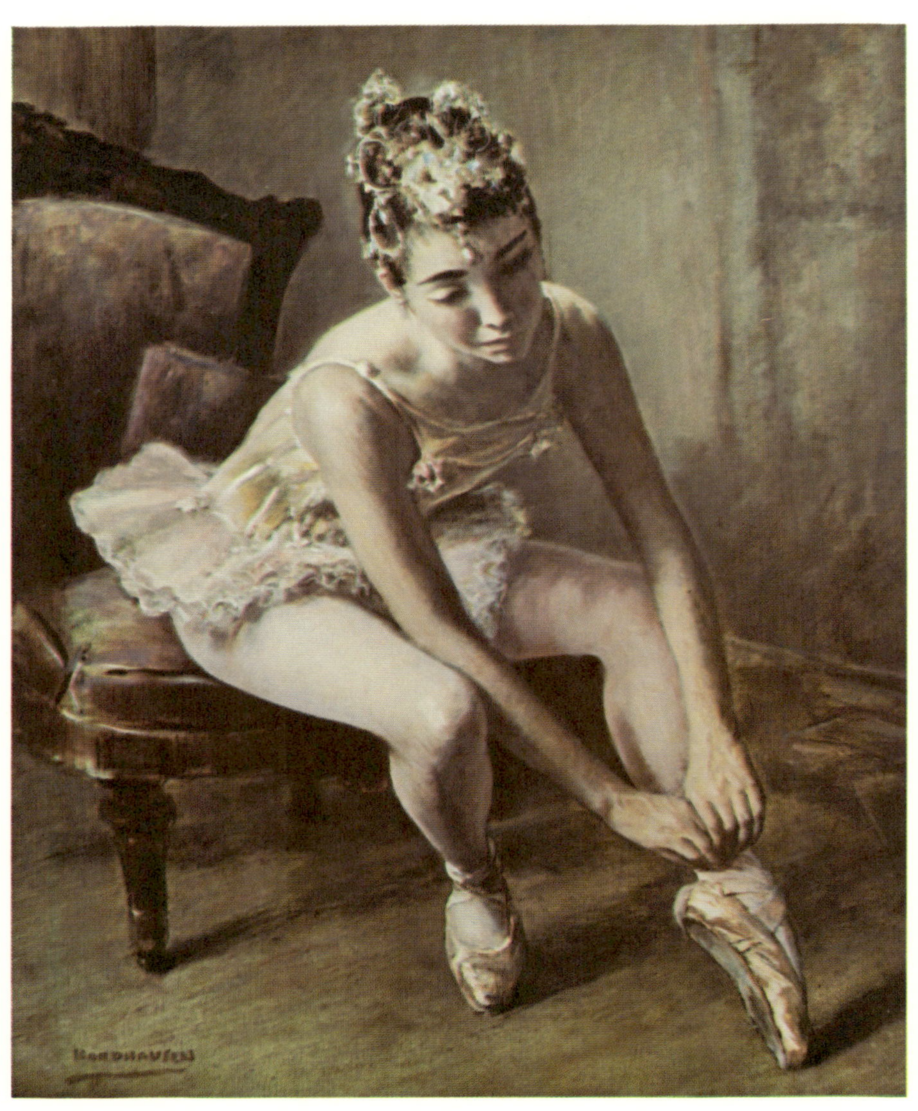

42. *Tying Her Slipper*

1971
38''x 30''
Oil on canvas
Collection: Salmagundi Club, New York City

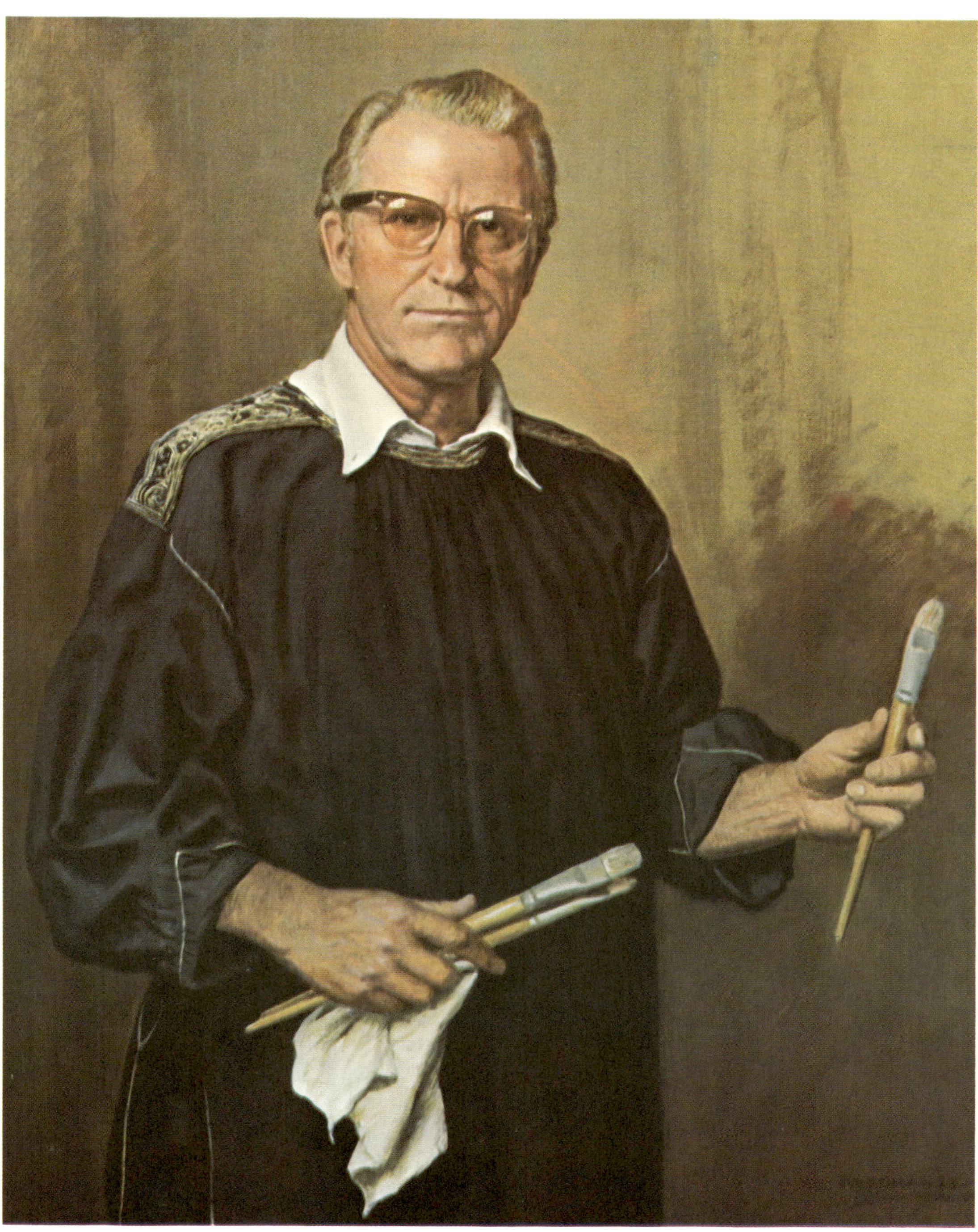

43. Self Portrait

1974
40''x 32''
Oil on canvas
Collection: University of Georgia

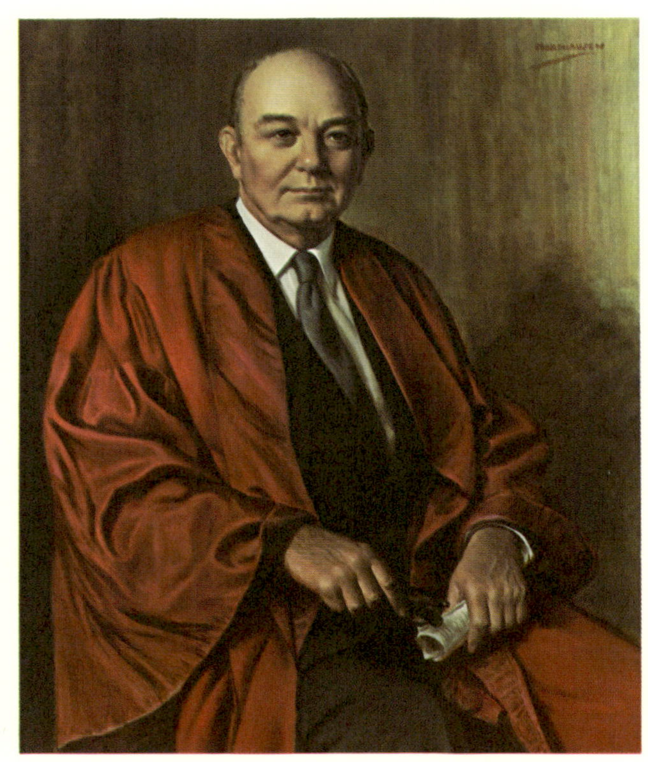

44. Professor Dean Rusk

III

NORDHAUSEN

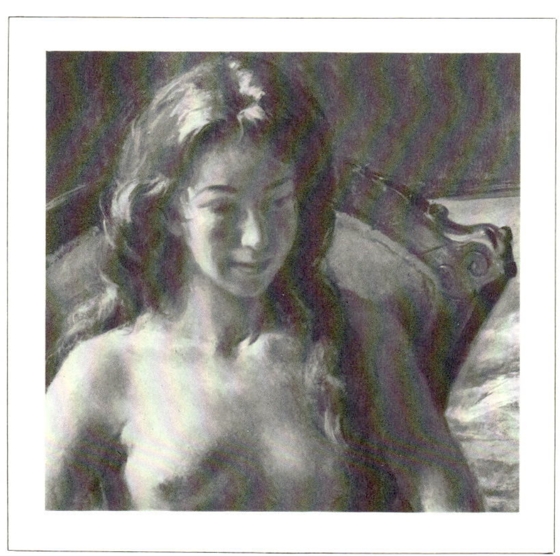

PLATES AND COMMENTARY

NORDHAUSEN'S REPUTATION among artists—indeed, his major creative effort throughout his career—has been based on the human figure. In its purest form it is the nude, and he has often said that "if you can paint the nude, you can paint anything."

The themes may involve the full female figure, standing, reclining, or seated, but often they are concentrated studies of the torso, the back, the head, or the half-length head and torso. The emphasis is on the form and its structural framework, which motivates the soft and subtle movement of related forms within the total complex. With these movements is associated the play of light over and through them, the flesh tones that shimmer from light into shadow, from one form to another, as seen in the various sections of the back or torso, the breasts and diaphragm, the arms and shoulders, the hips and thighs. The flesh tones glow with a luminous, warm, or silvery light which is evident in the transitions from light into shadow and around the form into the surrounding space.

Drapery, as pointed out earlier, is frequently used as a foil to enhance the effect of flesh and form—over the shoulder, around the waist, over or under the breasts, or under the buttocks. The silken texture and luminous green of tightly fitted underpants combine with the flesh tones of the torso and the gold of the background drapery to create a solid and striking effect. Sometimes instead of drapery the artist uses a newspaper or a Victorian chair or sofa with its more elaborate color and texture as well as often exotic shapes.

Action is not the objective in these figure compositions; the model does not *read* the newspaper, nor does she *see* the images in the mirror or look out at the spectator as though she were about to speak. The essential quality is that of a quiet, self-contained detachment, a subtle and spiritual mood into which the spectator is drawn. The careful placement of arms or hands about the head or face, the act of fixing the hair, or even the suggestion of sleep serve to enhance this contemplative atmosphere. Sleep in these cases is not a state of physical unconsciousness but conveys a mood of emotional expectation.

The design of the figure is seldom built in a parallel to the frame of the picture but rather as a diagonal in contrast to it so as to give the figure space in which to breathe and move. Frequently, a seated or kneeling figure is placed slightly off balance, as though about to move from one position to another, which serves to enhance this quiet tension. Nordhausen does not draw the abstract form, but abstract relationships are built into the recognizable forms. There are various instances in which sensuous appeal is made explicit through a recognizable subject, such as the *Venus and the Devil* (46) from the first Munich period and a later oil sketch of *Susanna and the Elders* (50), painted in the mid-1930s.

Nordhausen has often spoken about the emotional excitement involved in the color and light of good flesh painting, but there are many similar and contrasting qualities to be found in an inanimate thing such as cloth. The light on a piece of silk as it glistens across the shining surface can create an excitement quite different from that caused by the slow, heavier quality of a piece of wool or cotton. Velvet has a rich, caressing effect with an obscure depth and mystery in which the brush-stroke seems to lose itself.

Light sometimes plays a special role of its own, such as in a foreshortened figure where the major illumination is on the torso, and the head and shoulders lie back in a transparent shadow. A head may be tipped slightly forward, or a hat may be placed on the head so that the eyes and form of the face remain subdued in a mystery of shadow.

Different models stimulate different forms of expression, depending on their physical or psychological character. These frequently develop into series of studies, varying from the slender elegance of youth to the more mature sensuousness of middle age. Similarly, there is an attraction to different racial types, as can be seen in the various studies of Latin, Anglo-American, Israeli, and Oriental characters.

It is therefore not accidental that the artist has painted so many elaborately costumed figures which are Victorian in character. The ideas usually come from the discovery of a particular type of personality in a model, which leads to the search for a compatible costume in an antique shop, the church rummage sale, or the family storage closet. A fine old lace collar, velvet mutton sleeves, tight silk bodice and bustle, worn with unselfconscious dignity and elegance reflect a mood that is both historical and strangely prophetic. Some of the extraordinary color combinations of cool grays, blue-greens, purples, and salmon, contrasted with the warm flesh tones of the figure, serve to enhance this effect.

The wonderful world of the ballet had a similar attraction for Nordhausen, who had always ad-mired Degas, not necessarily because of his subject matter, but because he was a great artist—any form of art he worked in, whether it was drawing, pastel, or painting, was superb. Nordhausen's interest, however, was vastly different from that of Degas. Certainly he liked the movement, grace, and beauty of the ballet as an art form, but more important to him was the specific character of the figure and personality that was produced by the rigid training necessary for participation in that artistic activity.

So again, it was the figure that fascinated the artist—a lithe, finely tuned physique that was graceful in every pose or move the ballerina undertook, whether sitting, standing, walking, or bending over to tie her ballet slippers. The dancers he used as models, mostly from the New York City Ballet, were attractive young women, but thoroughly dedicated, hardworking professionals. One was a little Indonesian girl who at the age of seventeen was a star in George Balanchine's company. Another was a newly arrived blonde Israeli who was studying ballet but working part-time as a waitress; another a handsome Italian ballerina from the Naples Opera; and still another a dental hygienist from Georgia who was studying ballet and hoped to make that her full-time profession. They were usually used as costumed figures in which the filmy buoyant skirt (the tutu) and delicate colors of the satin ballet slippers and bodice became an essential part of the figure concept.

The circus is still another world with its own particular type of glamour and pageantry and the unique character of its dedicated performers and athletes. Nordhausen had painted a number of circus clowns and burlesque dancers in the mid-1930s, but the circus became a major focus of his effort immediately after World War II, mentioned earlier, when he was struggling to adjust to civilian life. During this period he produced hundreds of drawings, paintings, and monotypes which reveal a lively, loose, easy freedom in both technique and composition that brought him confidence and a new sense of purpose after the hiatus of the war years.

The subjects involved a wide variety of themes, including aerialists, tumblers, bareback riders, and performing horses; groups of actors backstage, and scenes in the dressing rooms. But Nordhausen's major interest as it developed centered on the clown, which provided him with the opportunity to study a particular type of character, with his humor and pathos, the odd combinations of color and design in his makeup and costume, and his earnest dedication to the job of being funny. A number of these paintings were shown in a special exhibition devoted to the circus at the Ferargil Galleries in New York in 1948, which included, along with Nordhausen's, works by Gifford Beal, Russell Cowles, Alexander Calder, Marc Chagall, Jean Dufy, Bernard Karfiol, Barse Miller, Georges Rouault, and Karl Zerbe.

All of Nordhausen's character studies have a special fascination for the romantic temperament. They are not portraits as such but constitute a more concentrated and tentative probing into that most elusive and mysterious medium of the human psyche, the human face. The depictions of the characters' faces vary from those in which the subject looks directly at the spectator, to those with half-closed eyes, to those that look but somehow do not see, to those that express the pathos of the absolute blind. The subjects are sometimes men or boys but are mostly women. The delicate wistfulness of a full-length ballet figure is often found concentrated in the head. The naïve photos of a native child, as in the Puerto Rican girl which the artist called *Forget Me Not* (184), has its parallel in the soft-eyed, dark beauty of *Gypsy Girl* (178) and *Sardinian Girl* (186). Against these expressive Latin types is the classic solidity and composure of the Chilean girl *Natalia* (20).

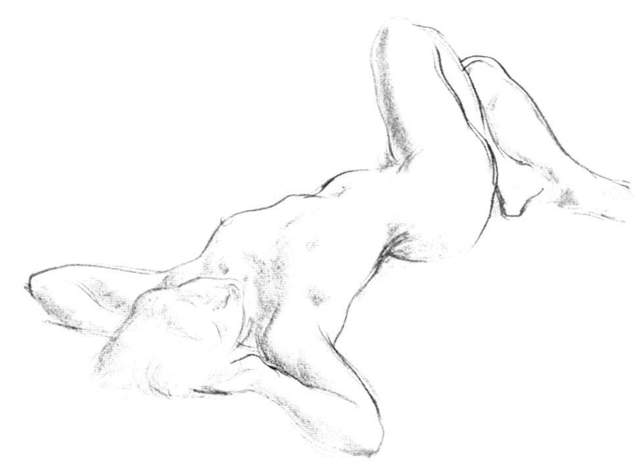

1924
24"x 17"
Oil on canvas
Private collection

1924
18"x 24"
Oil on canvas
Private collection

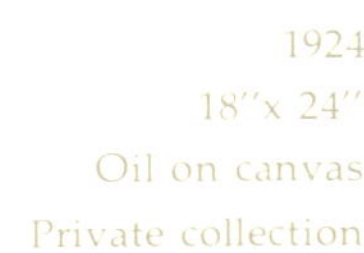

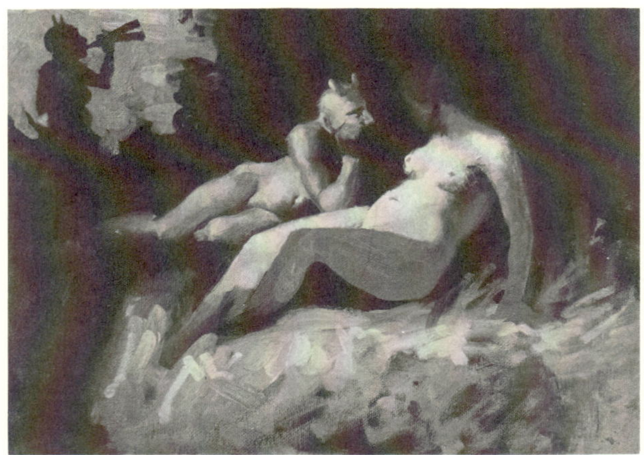

46. *Venus and the Devil*

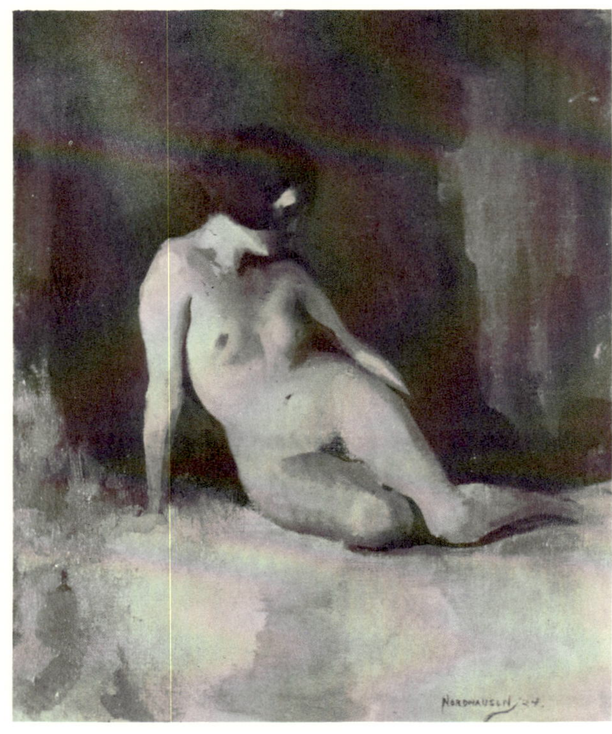

45. *Nude*

1925
10"x 8"
Oil on canvas
Turner Collection. Columbus. Ga.

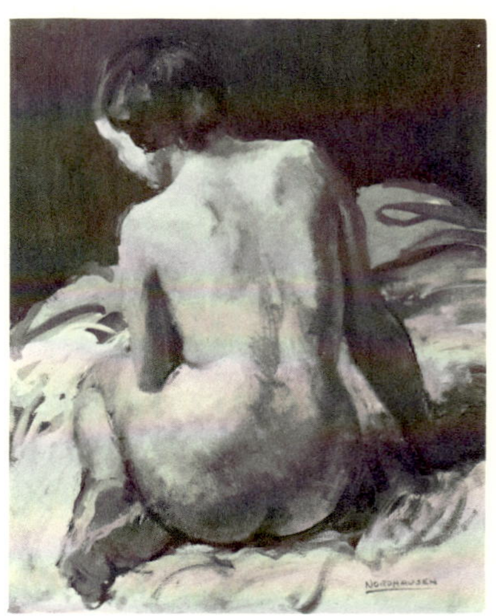

47. *Seated Nude, Back*

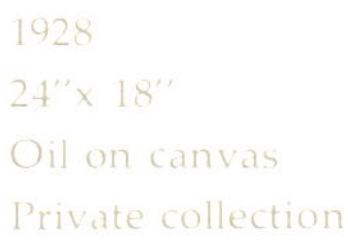

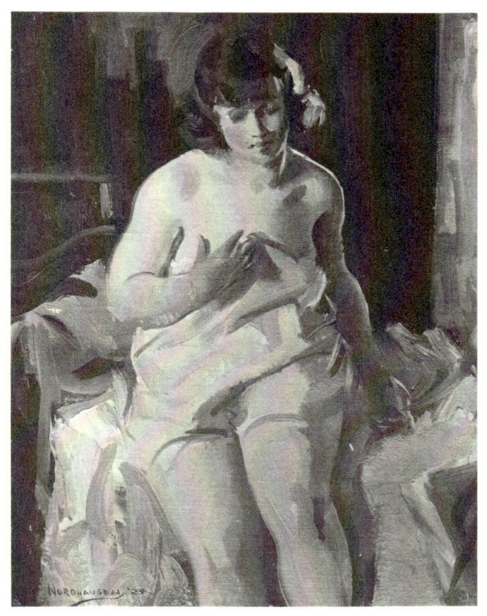

49. *Nude*

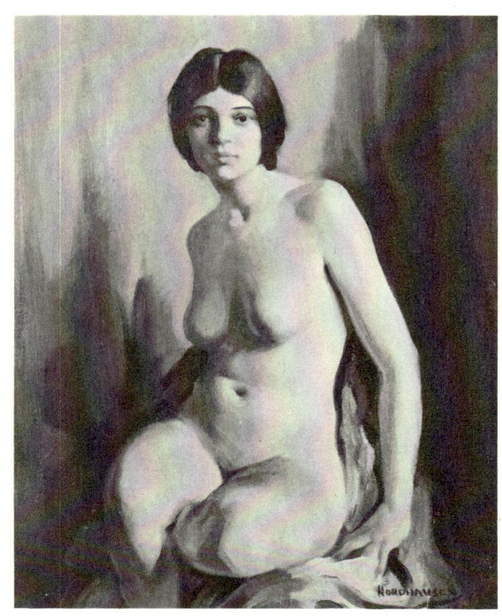

48. *Nude*

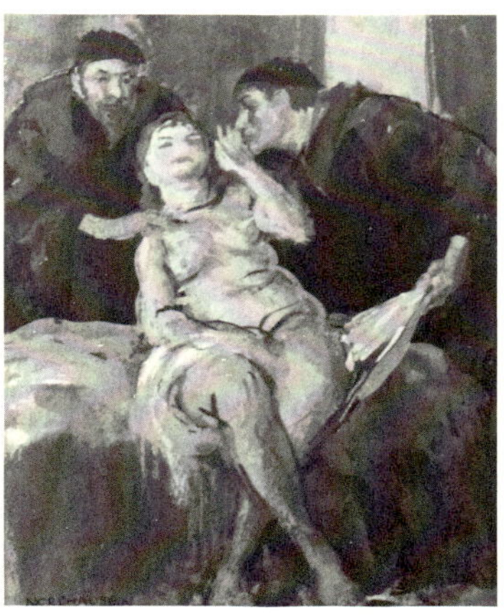

50. *Susanna and the Elders*

1930
19"x 16"
Oil on canvas

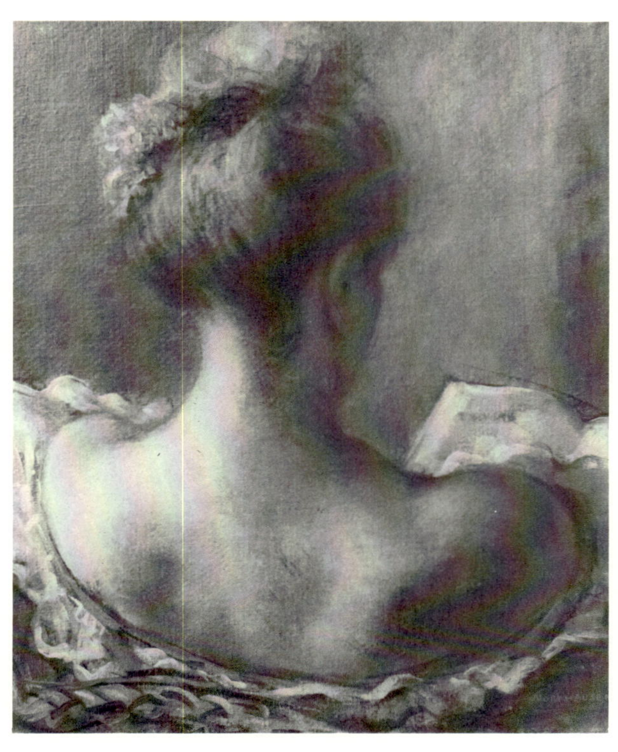

51. *Woman Reading*

1930
20"x 16"
Oil on canvas
Mink Collection, New York City

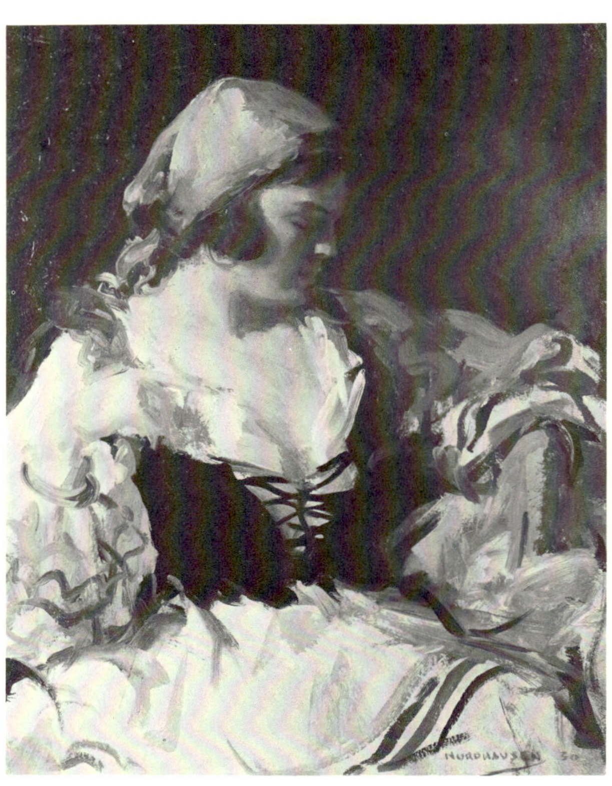

52. *Girl in Peasant Costume*

1930
30" x 25"
Oil on canvas
New Haven Paint and Clay Club Award, 1931
Esther Gold Collection, New York City

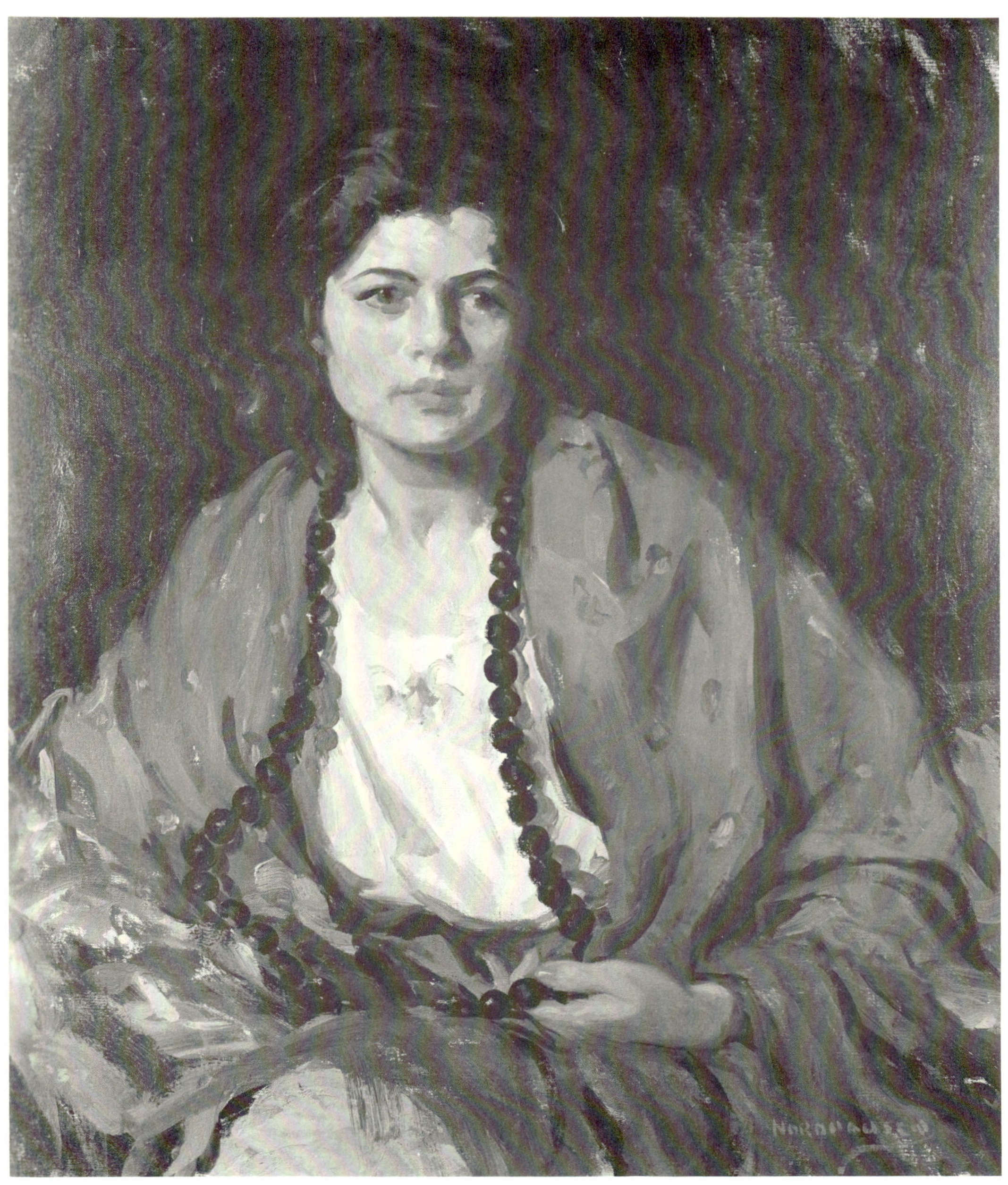

53. *Girl with the Red Shawl*

1934
25''x 30''
Oil on canvas
Millman Collection, Washington, D.C.

1934
20''x 16''
Oil on canvas
Rayvid Collection, Mount Vernon, N.Y.

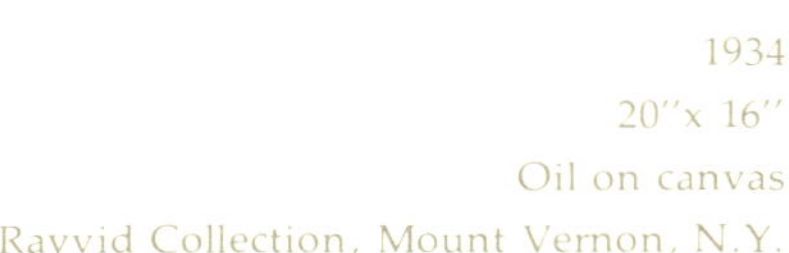

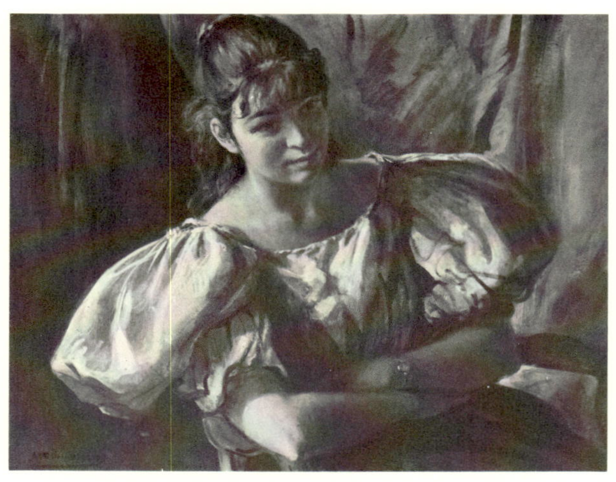

54. *The Old-Fashioned Blouse*

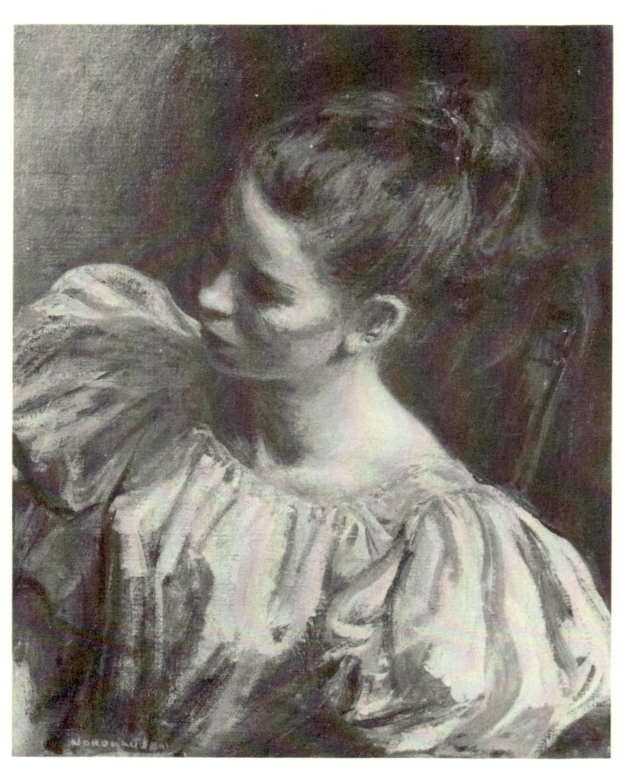

55. *Girl with Puffed Sleeves*

1934
18"x 10"
Oil on canvas
Destroyed in fire

1934
24"x 18"
Oil on paper

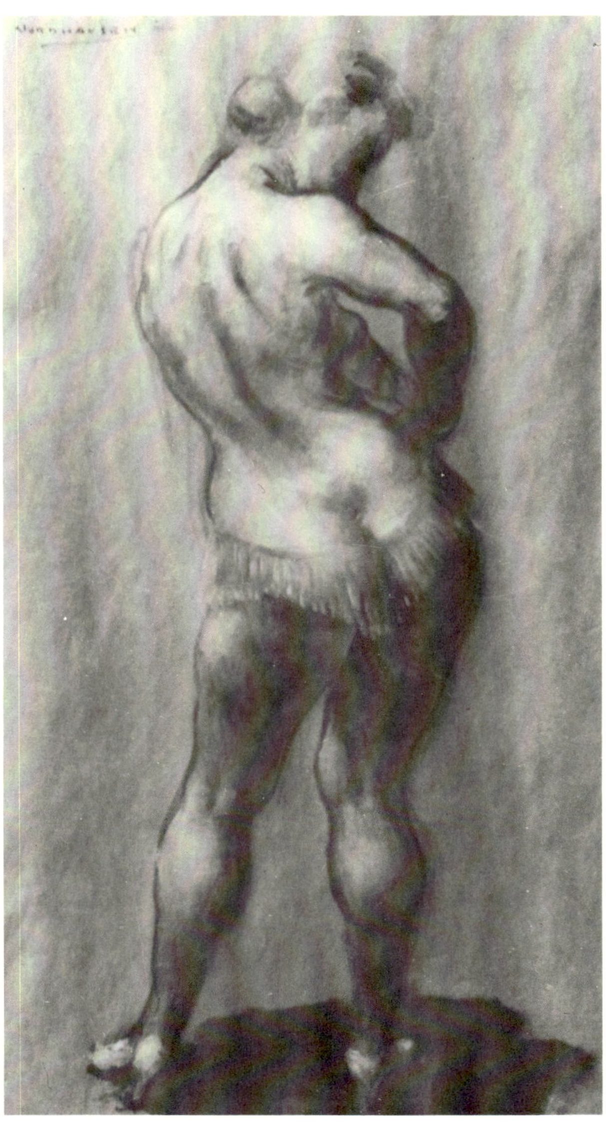

56. *Burlesque Figure*

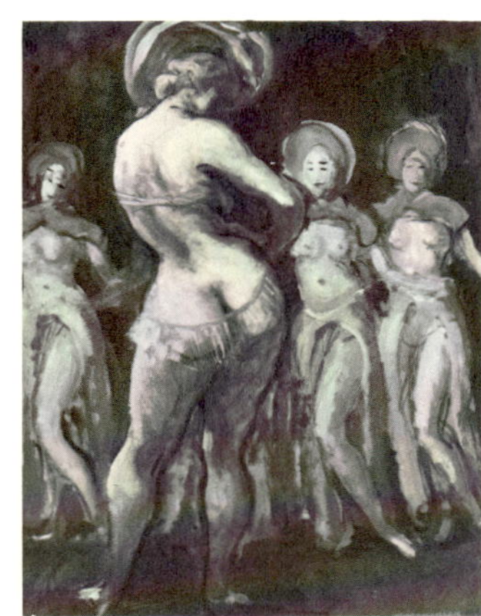

57. *Burlesque Dancers*

1935
26"x 18"
Oil on paper
Private collection

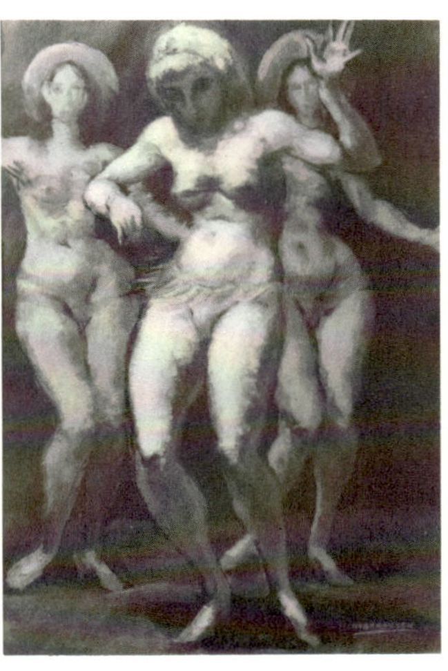

58. *Burlesque Bump*

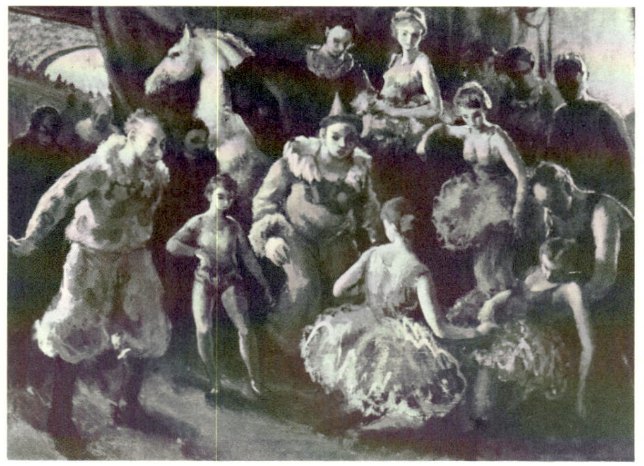

59. *Injured Performer*

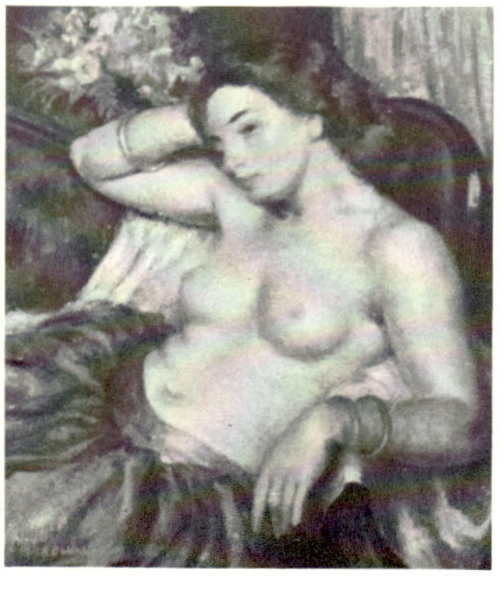

60. *Half Nude*

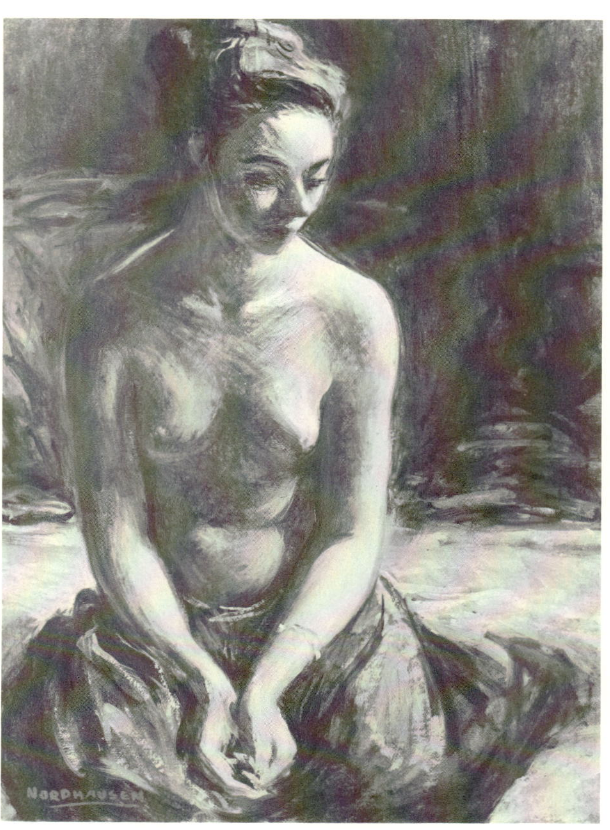

61. *Seated Half Nude*

1935
16" x 12"
Tempera and watercolor on paper
Collection: New Britain Museum of Art

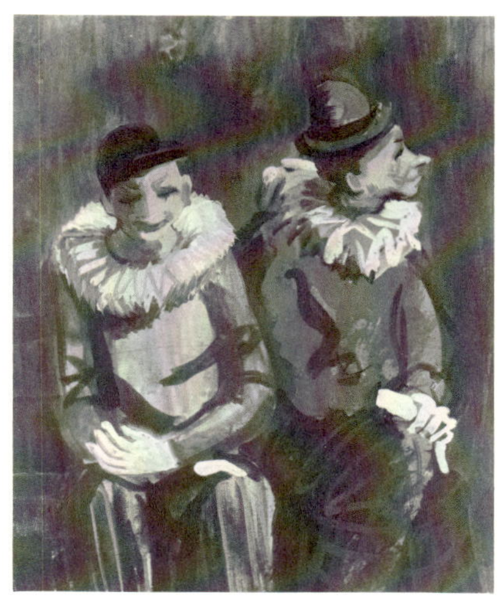

62. *Clowns Resting*

1935
16" x 22"
Tempera and watercolor on paper
Ranger Fund Purchase Award (Exhibition, National Academy), 1949
Collection: University of South Carolina

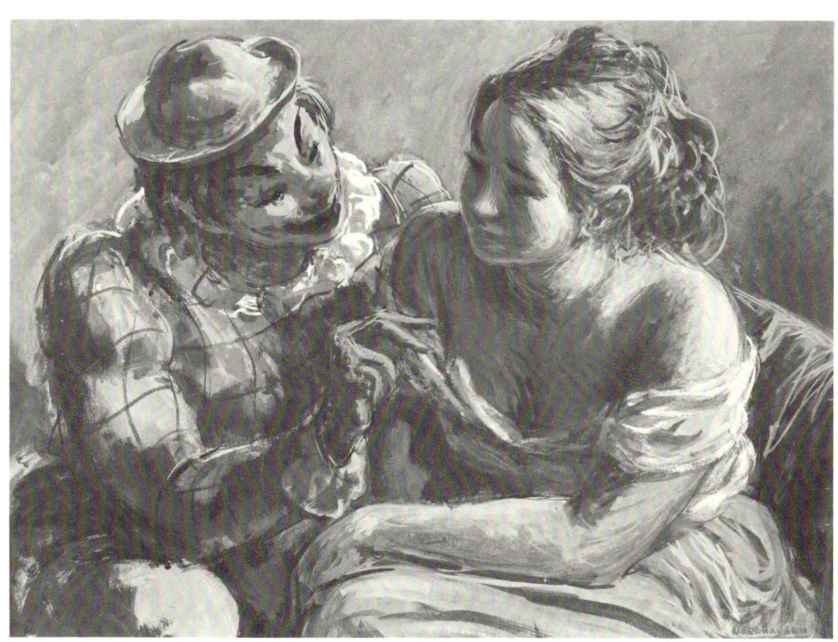

63. *Circus Friends*

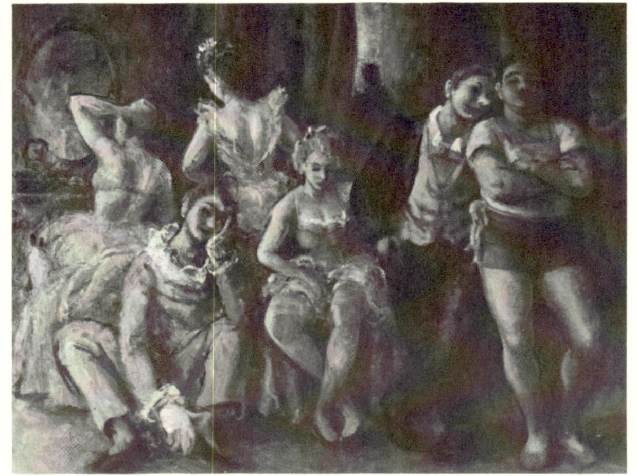

64. *Circus People*

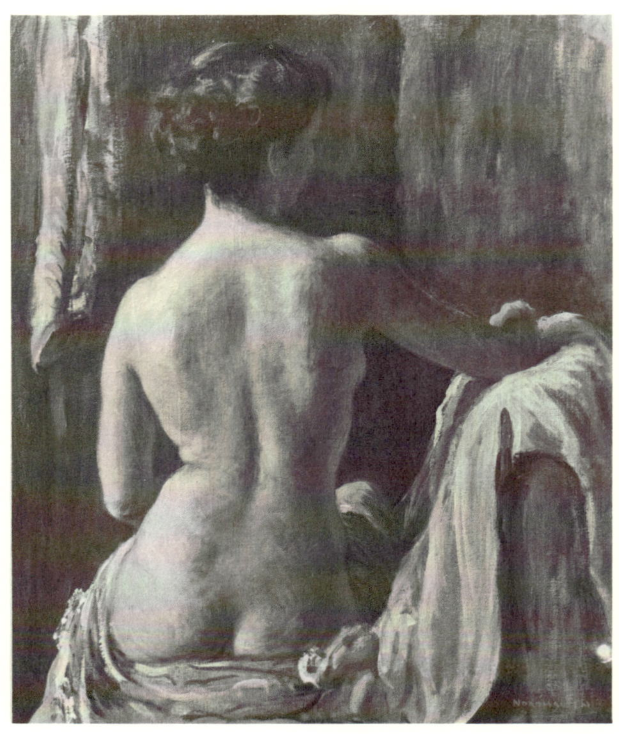

66. *Nude Back, Seated*

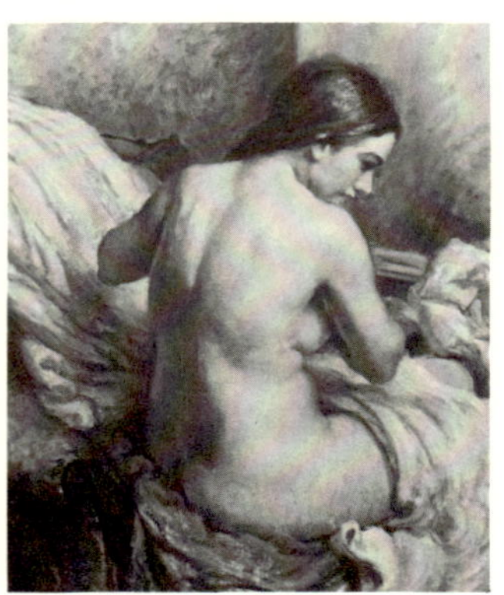

65. *Nude Fixing Hair*

1936
22″x 14″
Tempera and watercolor
Wall Street Art Association Award, 1963

1936
19″x 15″
Monotype
Williams Collection, Columbus, Ga.

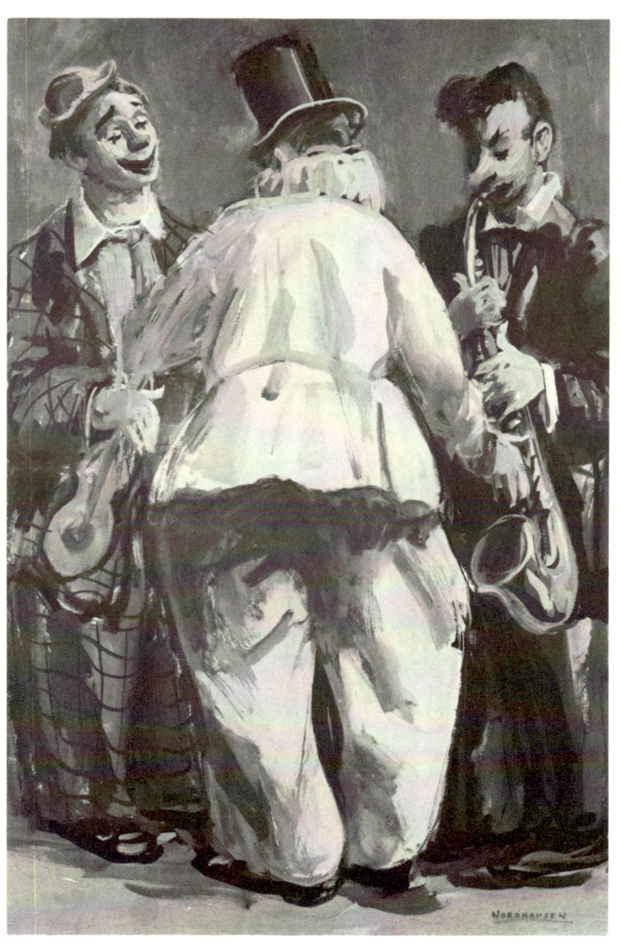

67. *Musical Clowns*

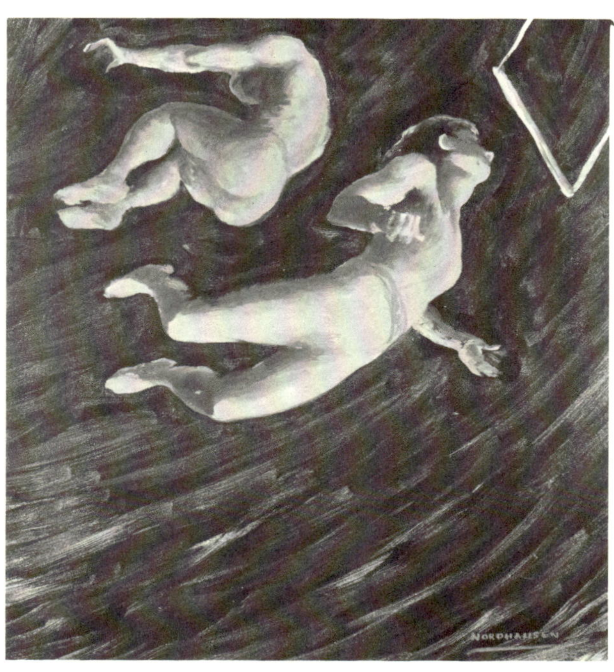

68. *Flying Trapeze*

1936
18″ x 14″
Oil on canvas
Taylor Collection, Atlanta, Ga.

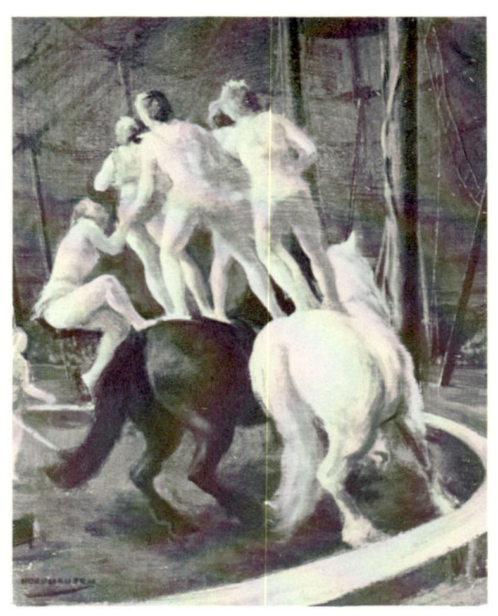

69. *Bareback Riders*

1936
15″ x 20″
Watercolor
Private collection

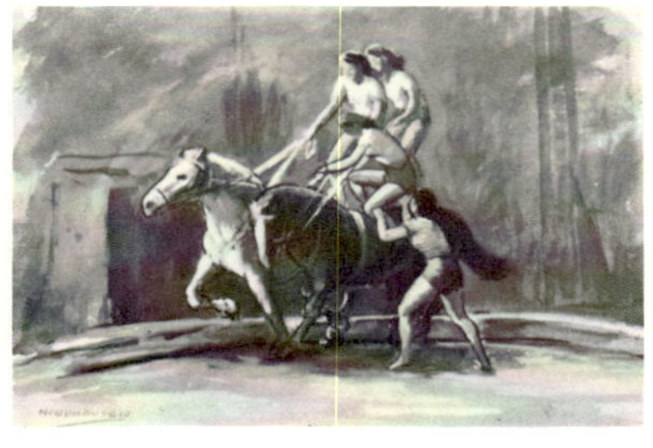

70. *Bareback Riders*

1936
19″ x 17″
Monotype
Riley Collection, Columbus, Ga.

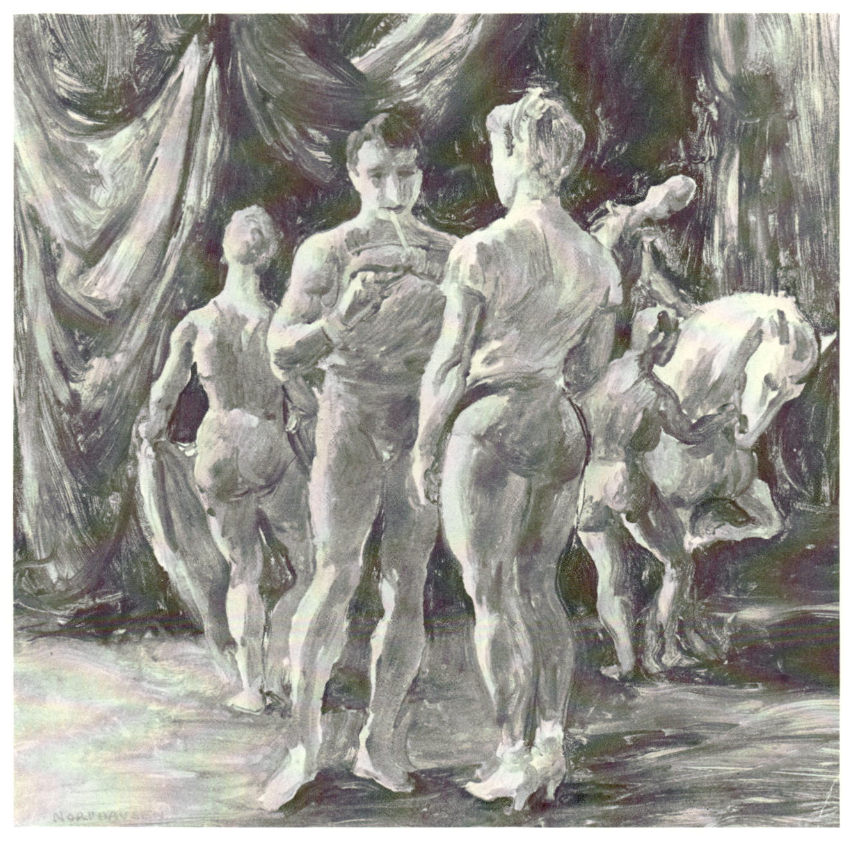

71. *Circus Folks*

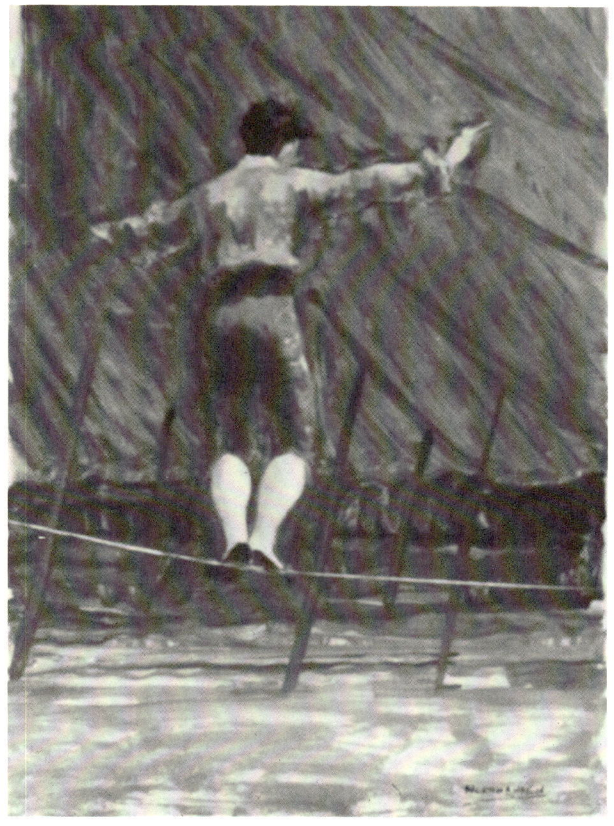

72. Balancing Act

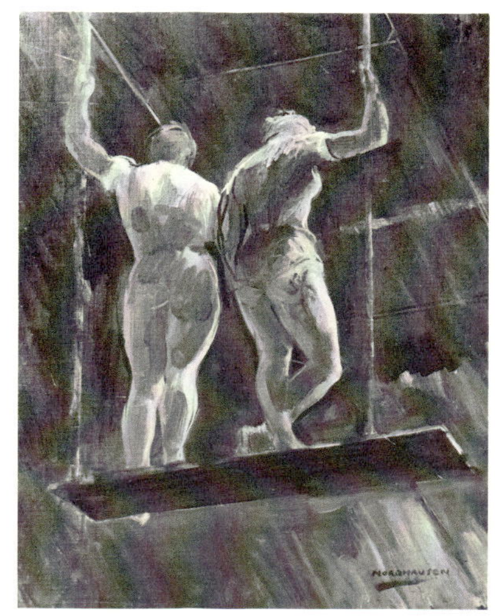

73. Flying Trapeze

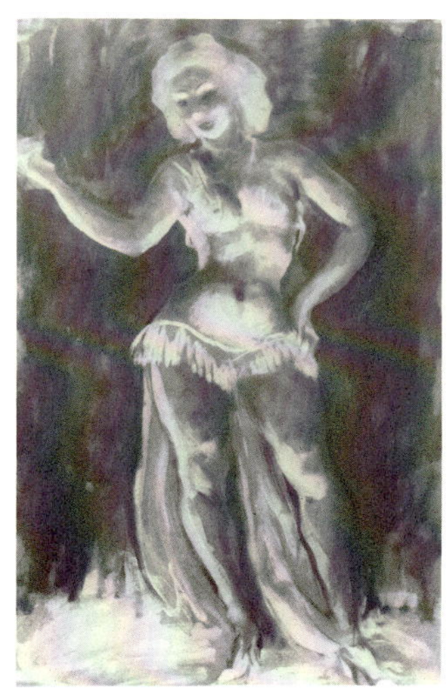

74. Burlesque

1937
18''x 8''
Oil on canvas
Destroyed in fire

1937
18''x 8''
Oil on canvas
Destroyed in fire

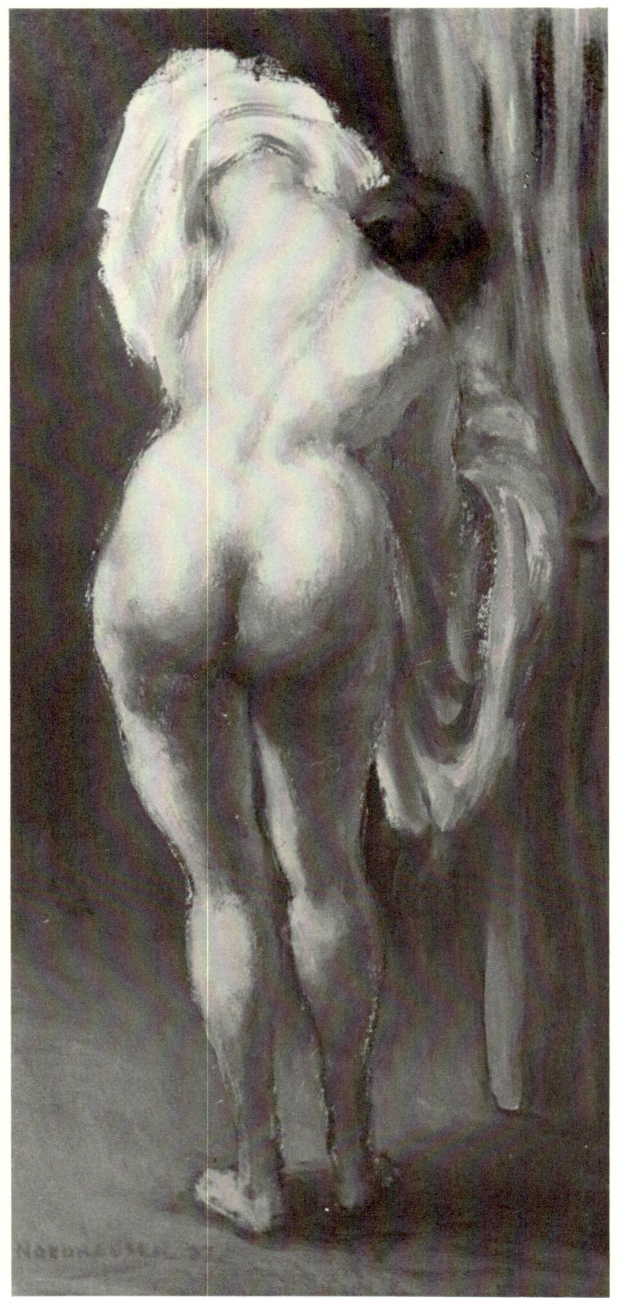

75. *Standing Nude, Back*

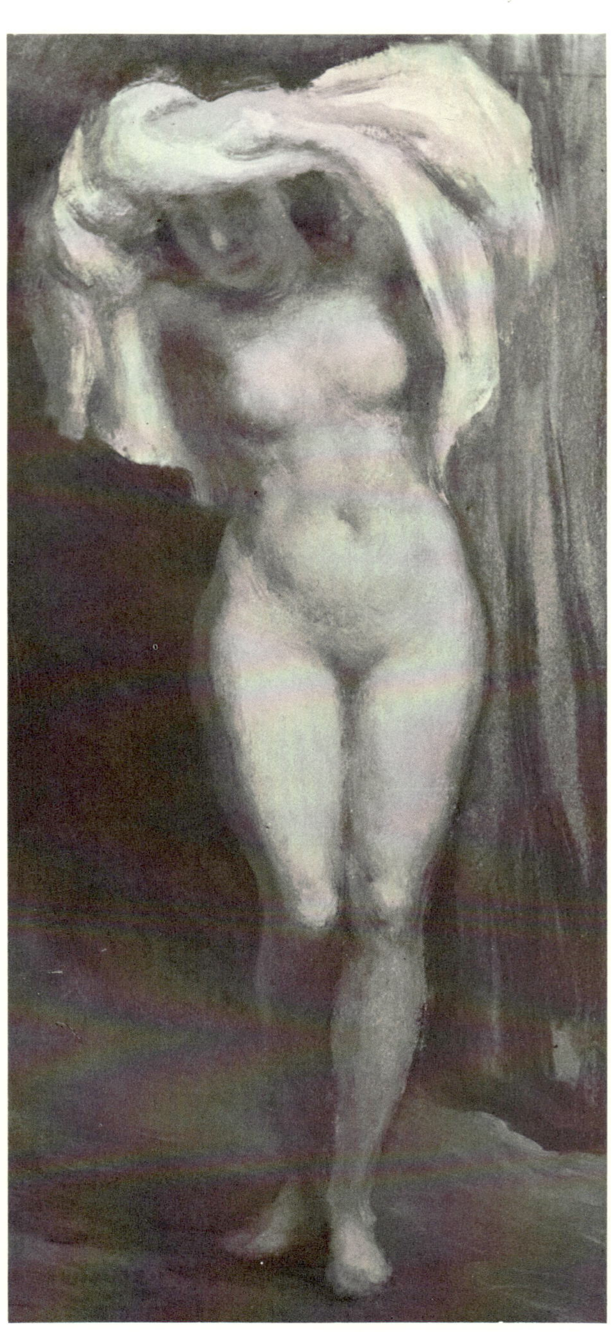

76. *Standing Nude, Front*

1937
28"x 22"
Tempera and watercolor
Ted Kautsky Memorial Award, American Watercolor Society, 1957
Private collection

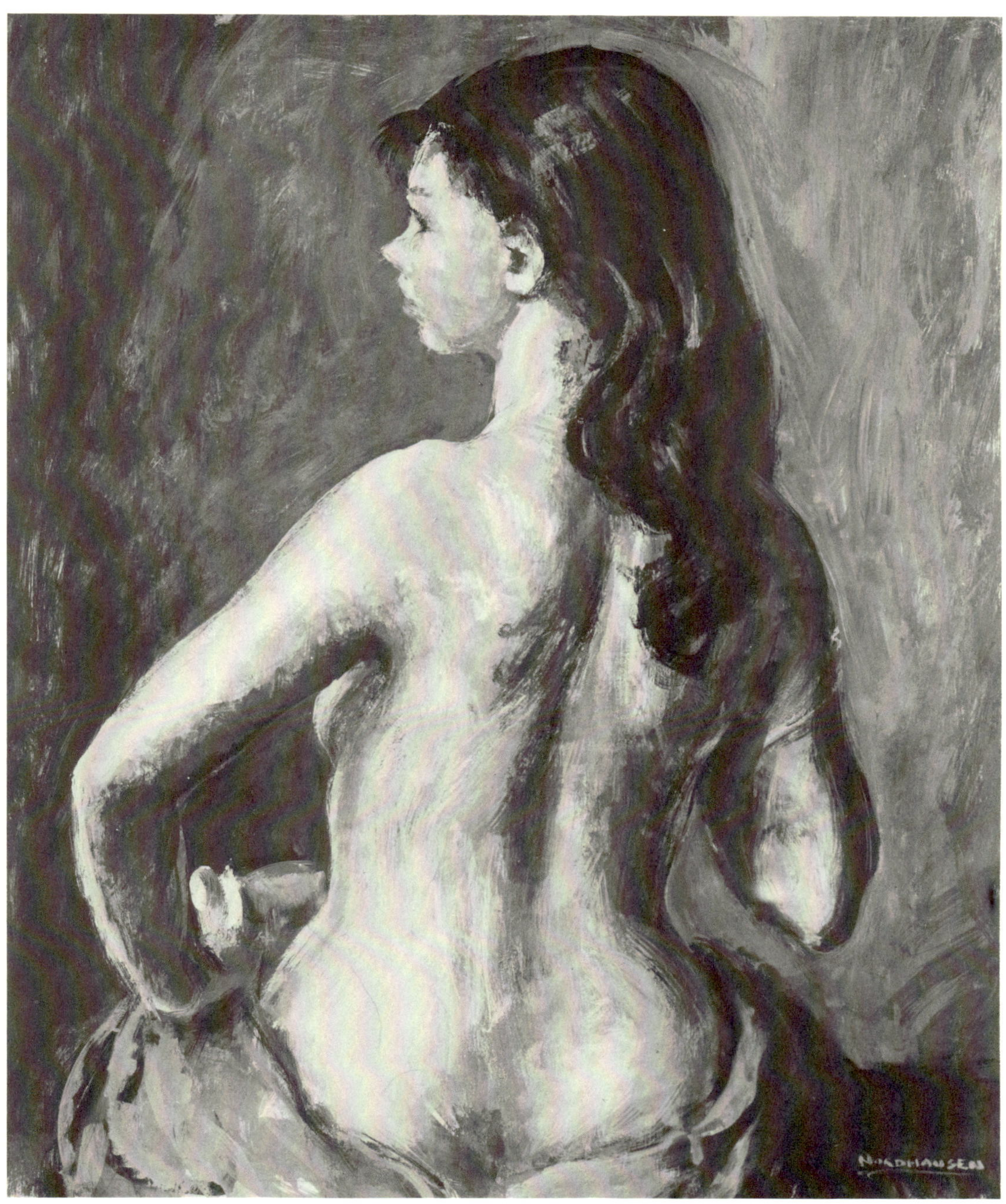

77. Seated Nude

1937
22″x 28″
Oil on canvas
Matt Collection, New York City

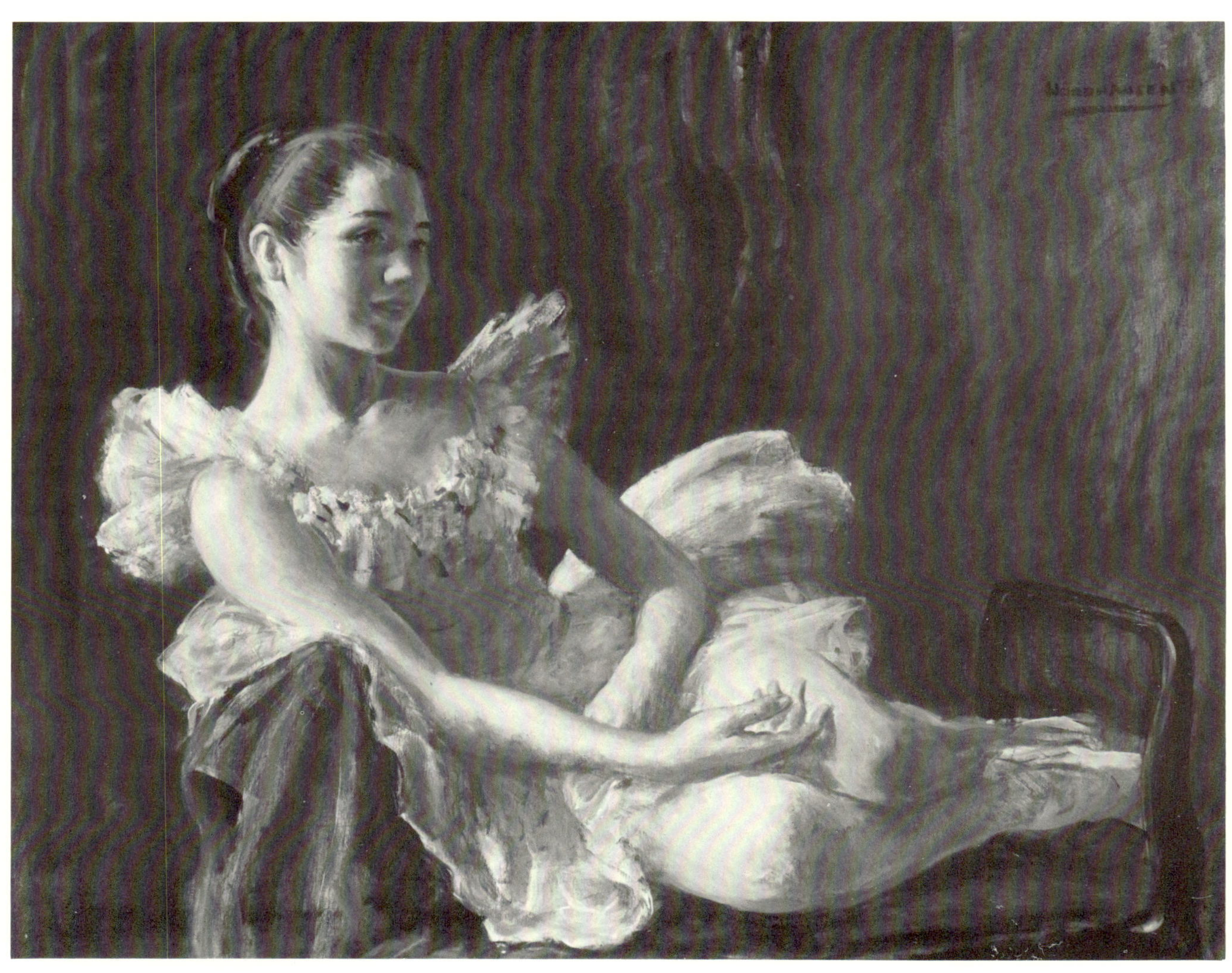

78. Indonesian Ballerina

1938
30''x 24''
Oil on canvas
Joseph S. Isidor Prize, 1939
Collection: William Connor Foundation

1937
20''x 16''
Oil on canvas
Shorter Collection, Columbus, Ga.

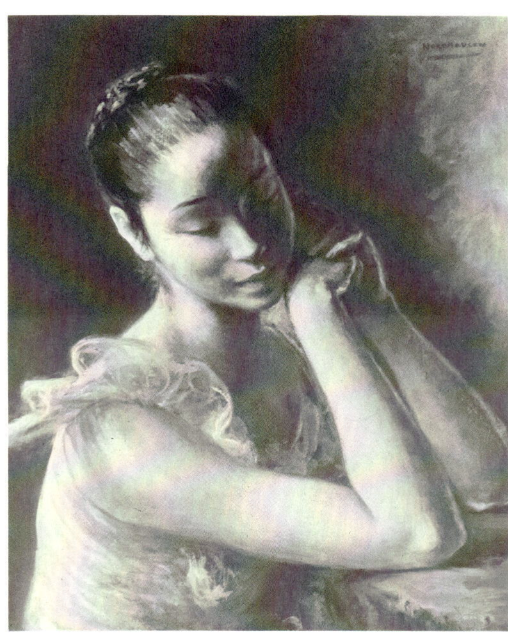

79. *Indonesian Ballerina (Durine Dieters)*

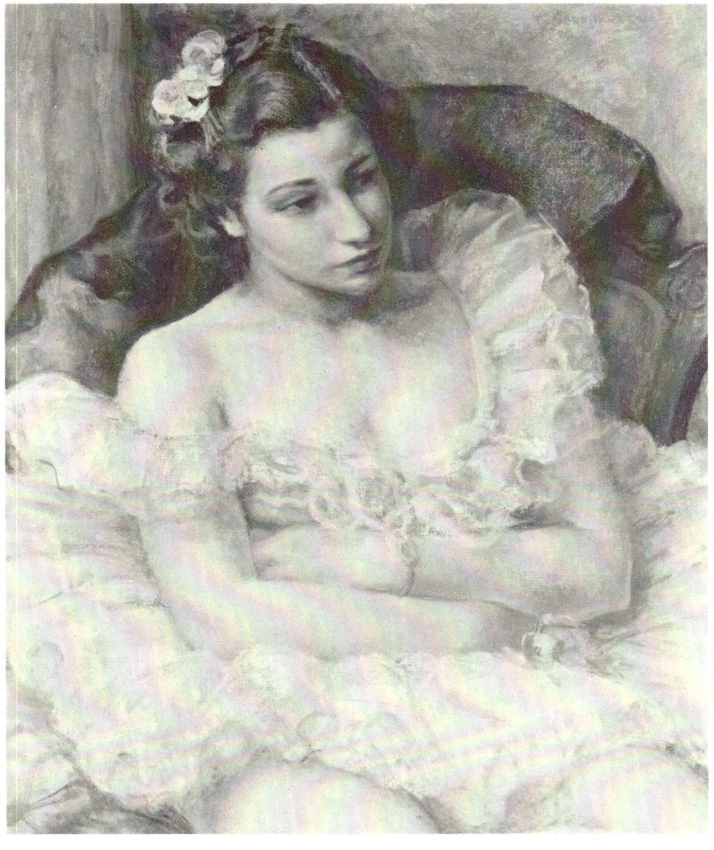

80. *Ballet Dancer (Eda)*

1938
25''x 20''
Oil on canvas
Private collection

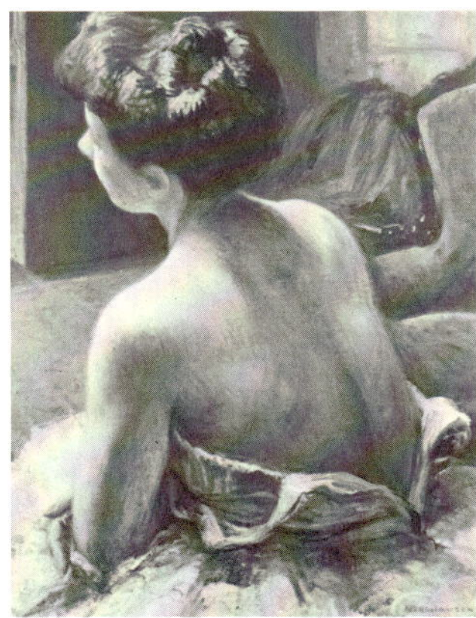

81. *Ballerina Resting (Eda)*

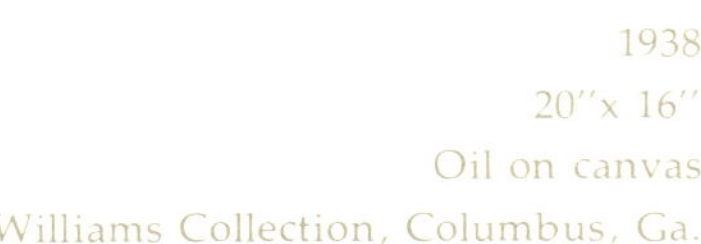

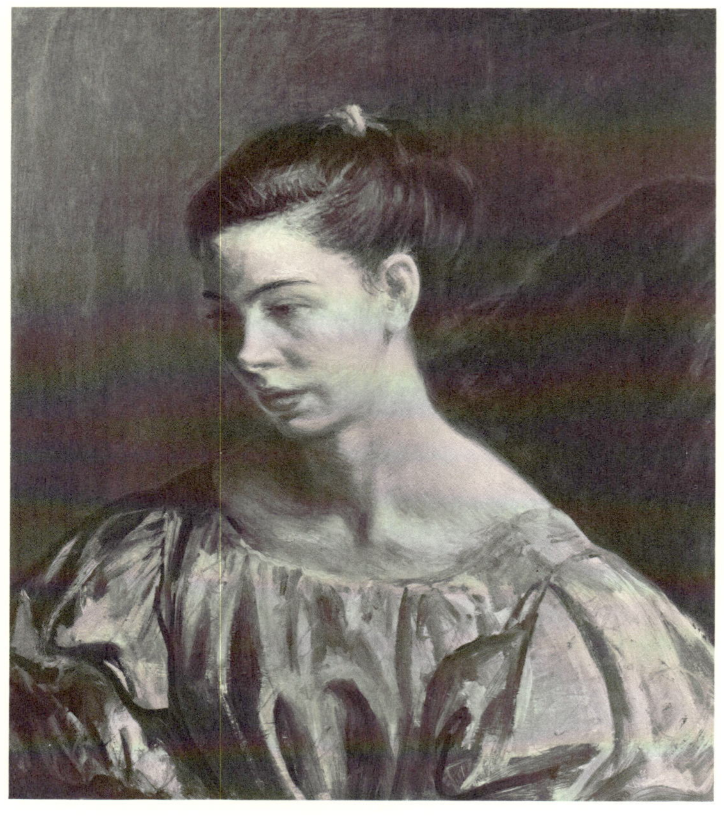

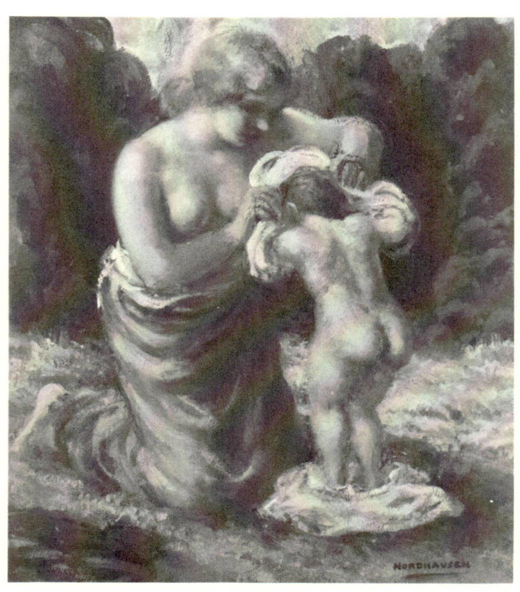

83. *Mother and Child*

82. *Old-Fashioned Blouse (Sera)*

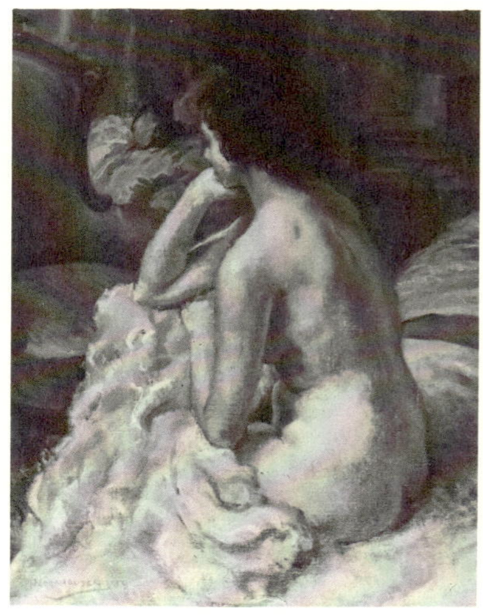

84. *Nude Study*

Nordhausen / 86

1938
16"x 12"
Oil on canvas
Esther Gold Collection, New York City

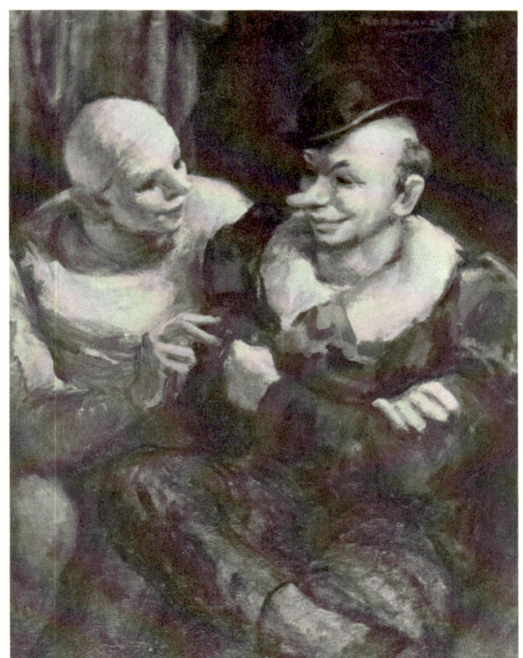

85. *Two Clowns*

1939
18"x 14"
Monotype
Private collection

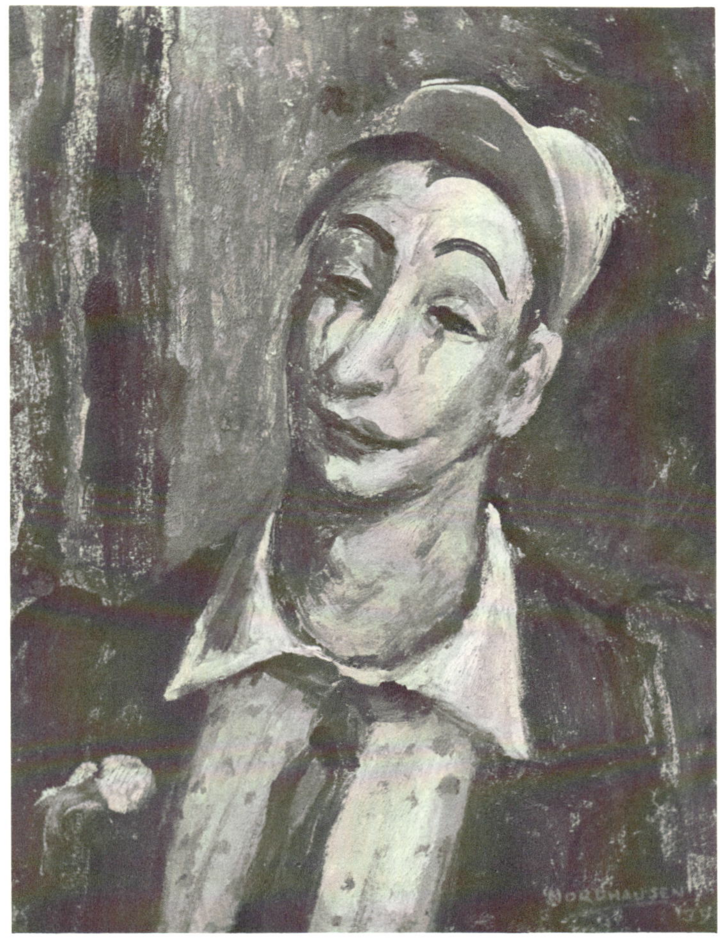

87. *Clown with Hat*

1938
28"x 22"
Oil on canvas
Private collection

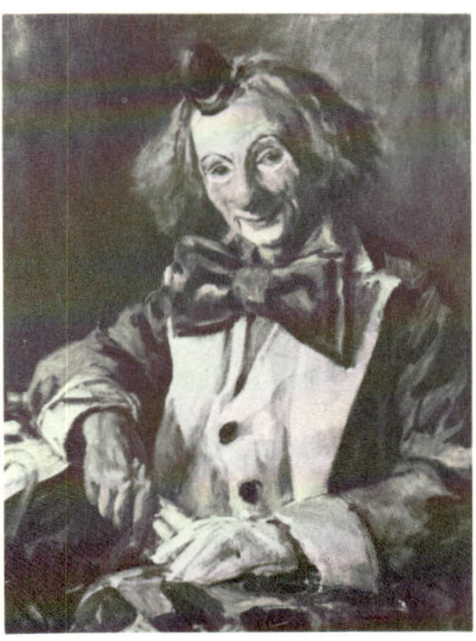

86. *Clown with Red Wig*

87 / *Figure Painting*

1940
24"x 20"
Oil on canvas
Private collection

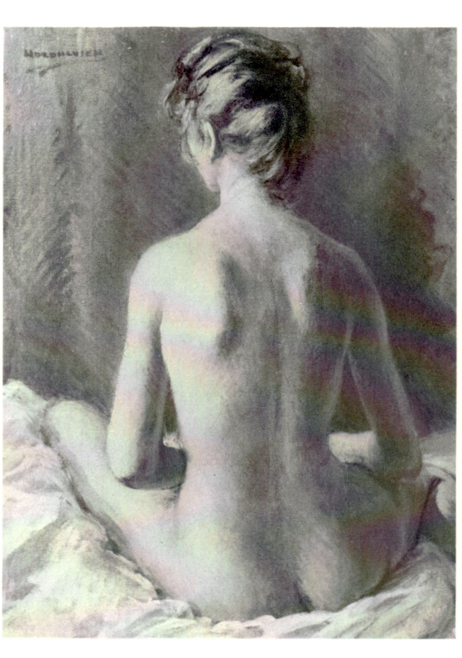

89. *Nude Back, Seated*

1939
30"x 25"
Oil on canvas
Liskin Collection, New York City

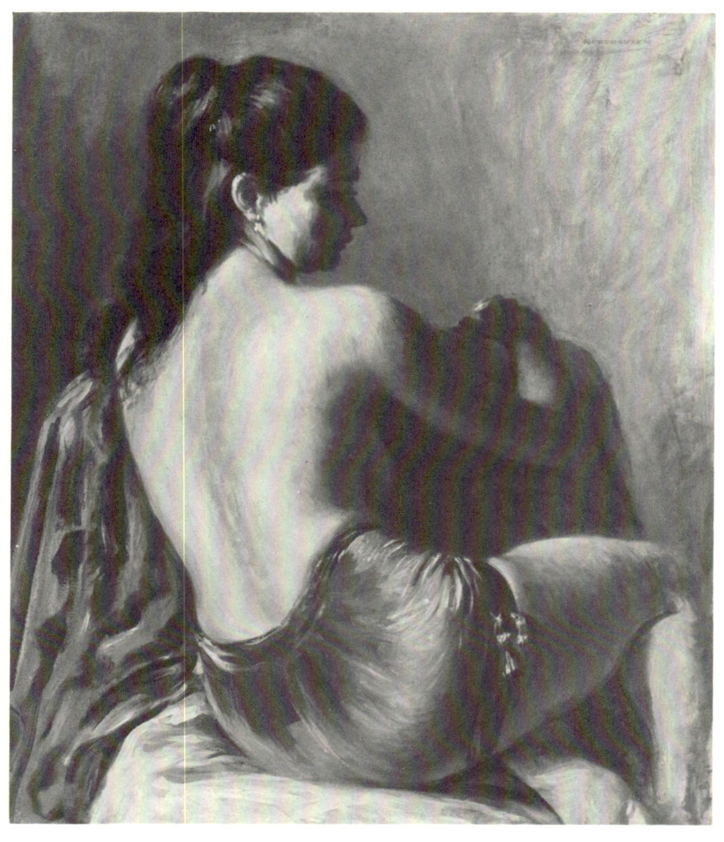

88. *Study in Green and Gold*

1948
20"x 16"
Oil on canvas
Hughston Collection, Columbus, Ga.

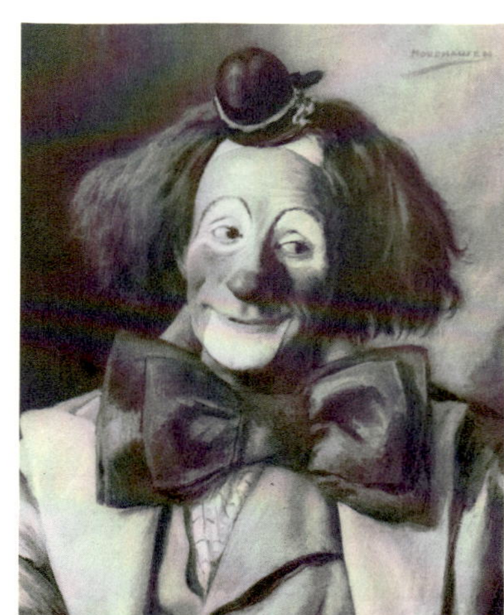

90. *Clown with Green Bow*

1949
30″x 25″
Oil on canvas
Mischa Lempert Prize, 1949
Collection: Cleveland Museum of Art

1949
24″x 20″
Oil on canvas
Collection: New Britain Museum of Art

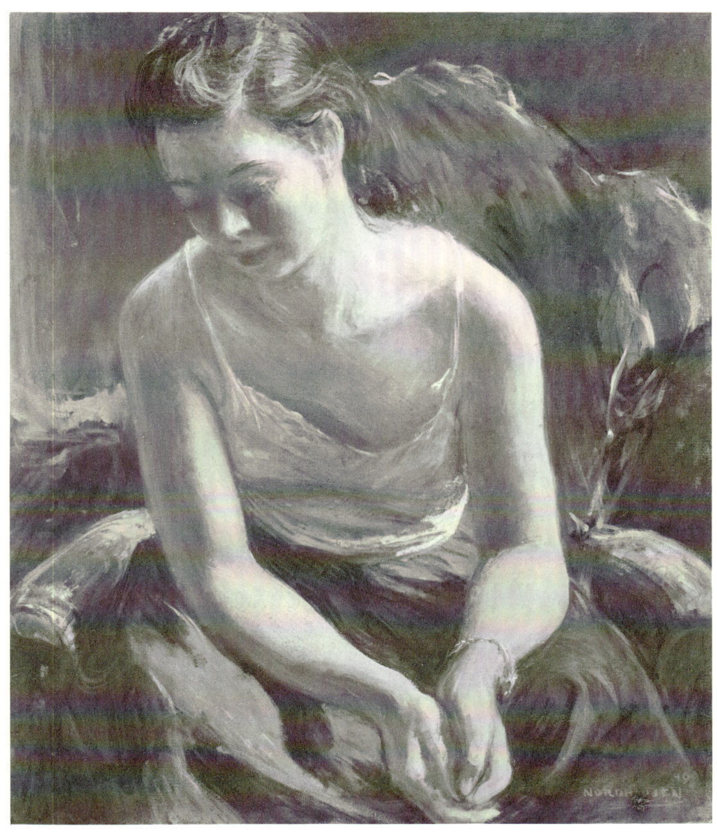

91. *Thoughtful Youth*

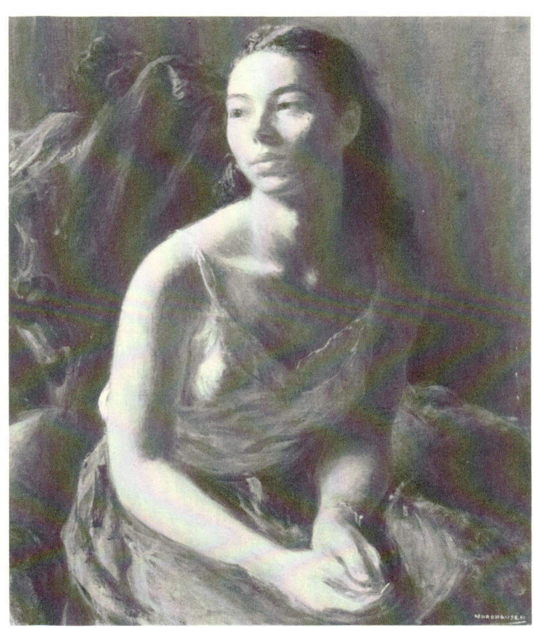

92. *Sara in Slip*

89 / *Figure Painting*

1953
30''x 25''
Oil on canvas
Private collection

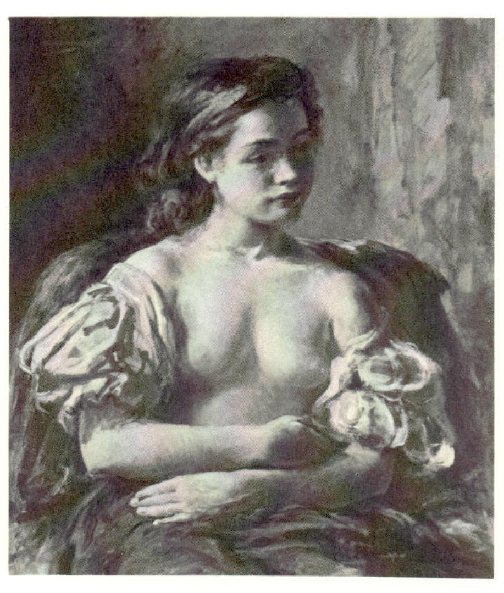

94. *Pensive Youth*

1950
30''x 24''
Oil on canvas
Kriendler Collection, New York City

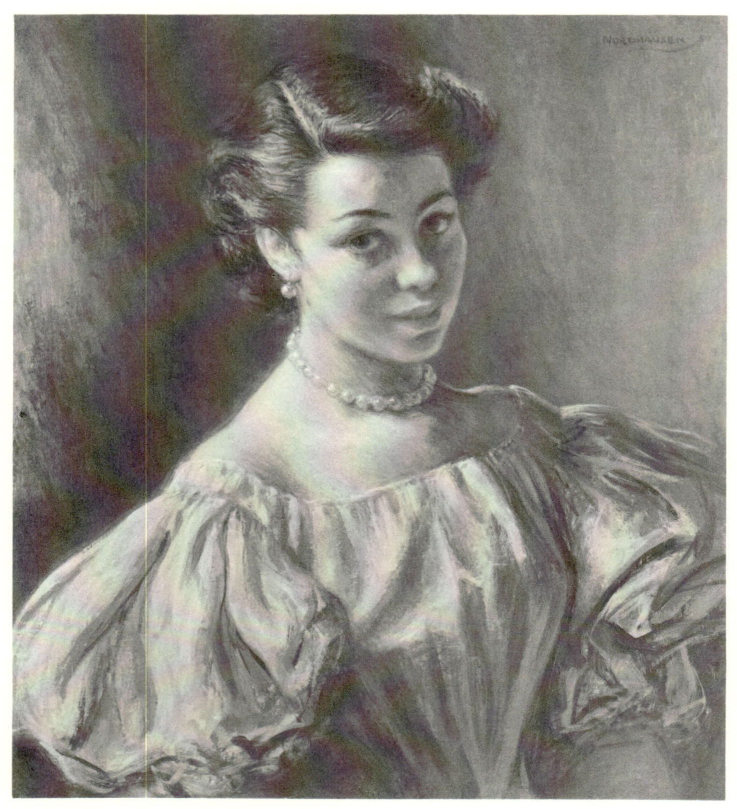

93. *Lala*

1953
30''x 25''
Oil on canvas
Haskins Collection, Kendall Park, N.J.

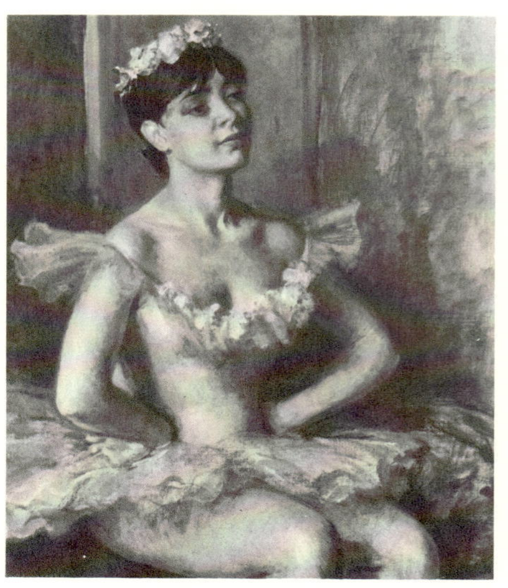

95. *Susie in Tutu*

1955
25″x 20″
Oil on canvas
Stolen

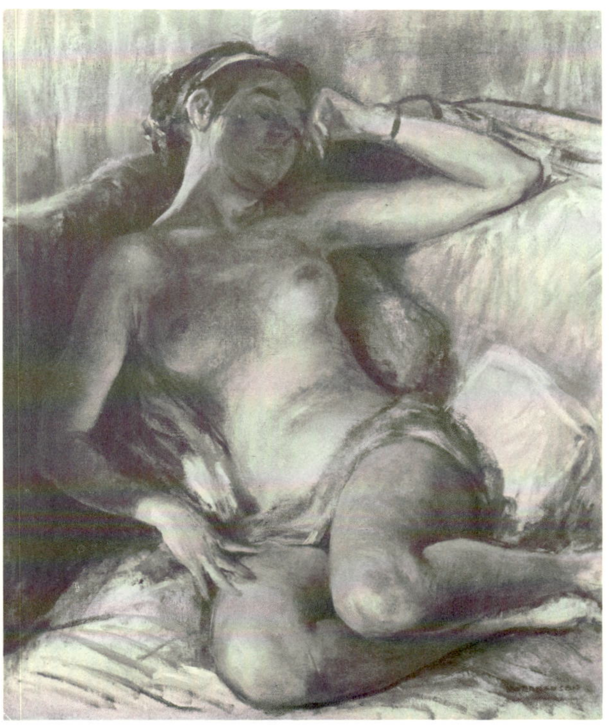

96. *Nude in Half Shadow*

1955
22″x 28″
Oil on board
Collection: Syracuse University

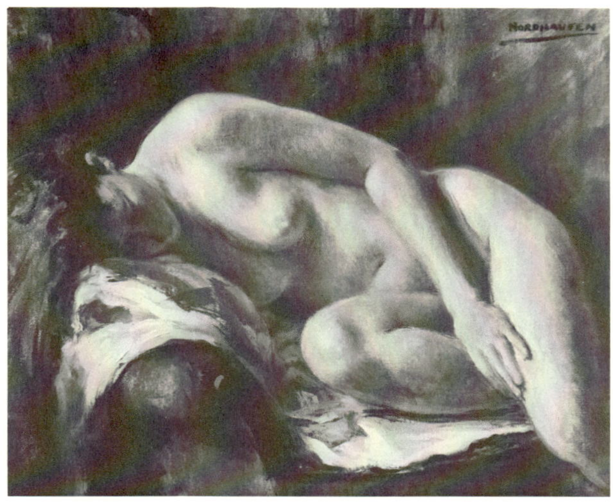

97. *Nude Resting*

91 / *Figure Painting*

1957
22″x 18″
Oil on canvas

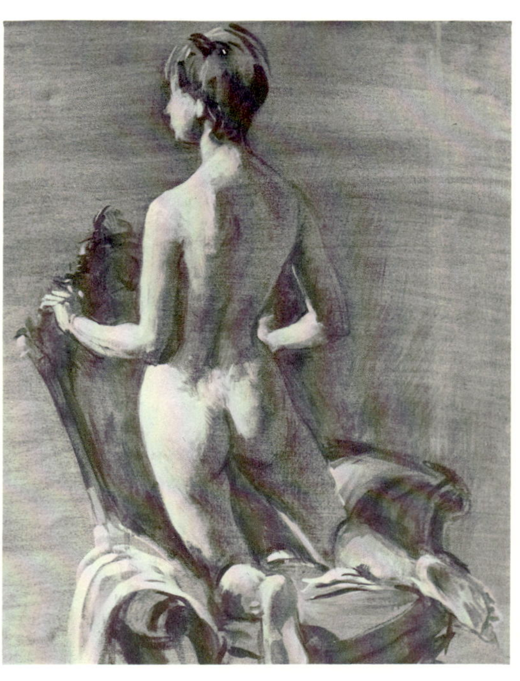

99. *Nude Kneeling on Chair (unfinished)*

1956
21″x 17″
Tempera on board
Collection: Syracuse University

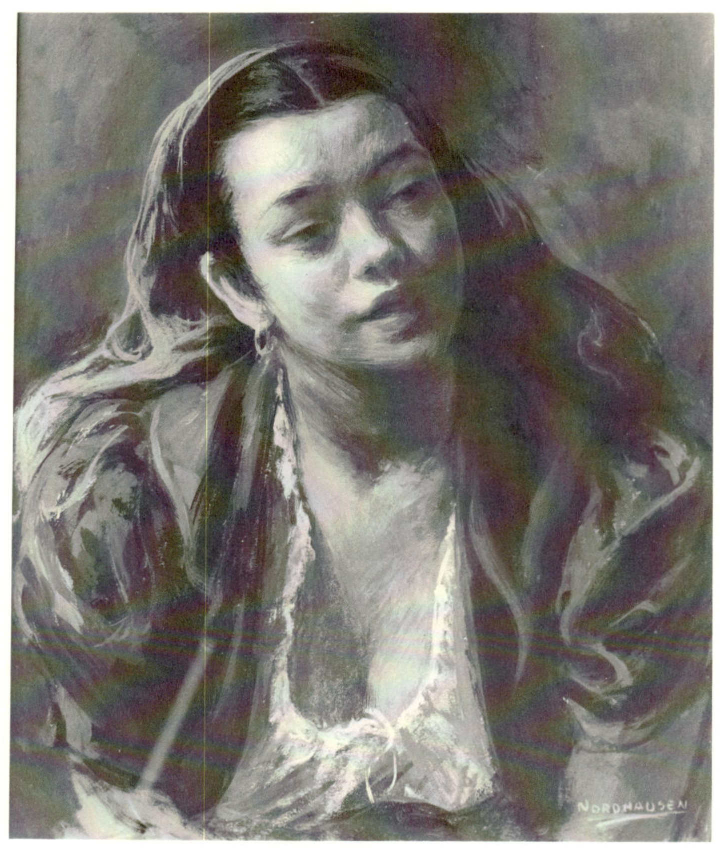

98. *Italian Girl*

1957
30″x 25″
Oil on canvas

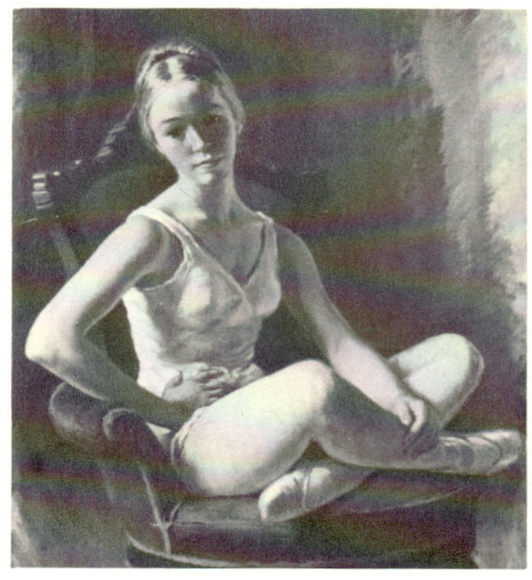

100. *Ballerina Seated*

1958
40"x 30"
Oil on canvas
Collection: St. Lawrence University

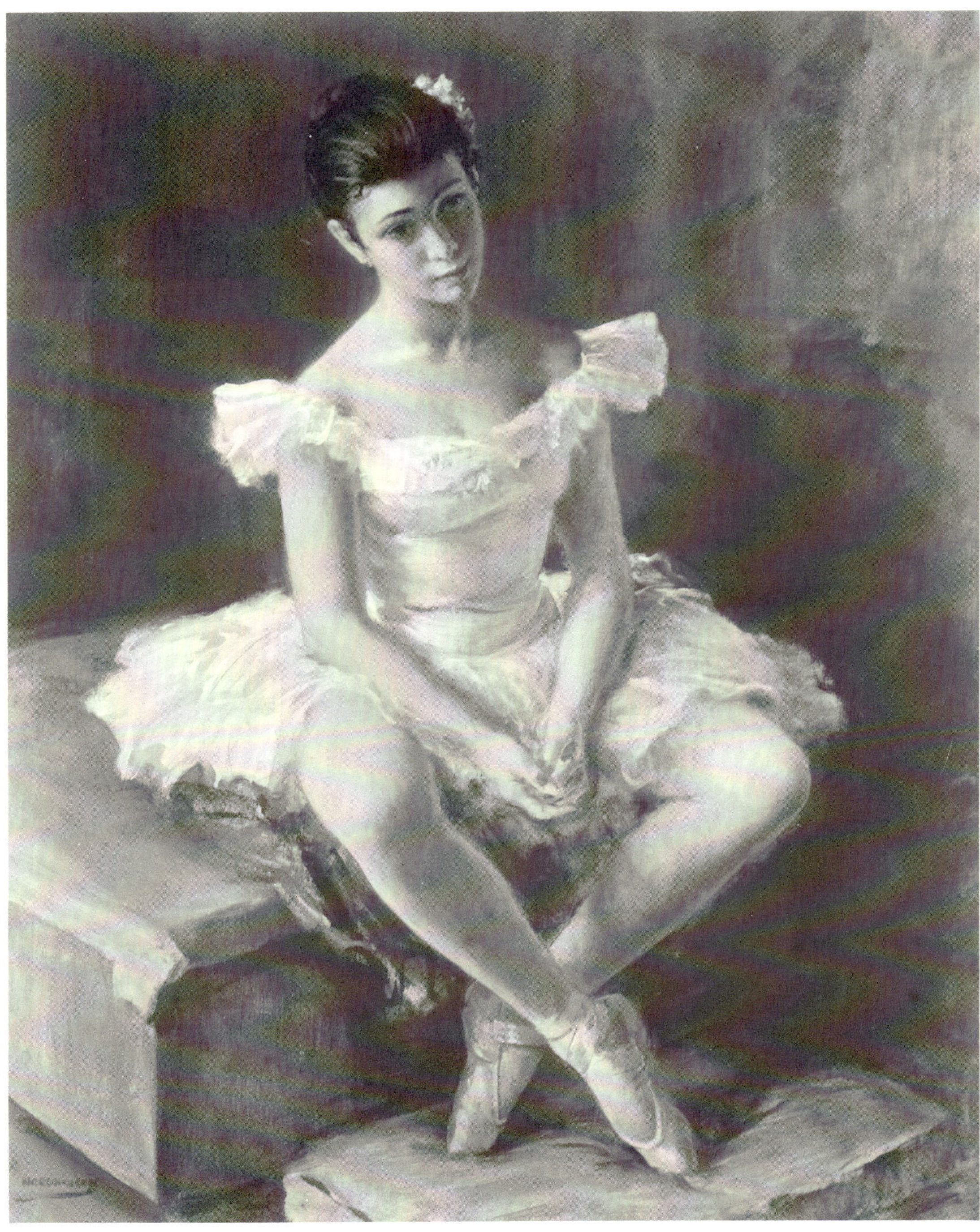

101. *Seated Ballerina*

1958
35''x 27''
Oil on canvas

1958
30''x 25''
Oil on canvas

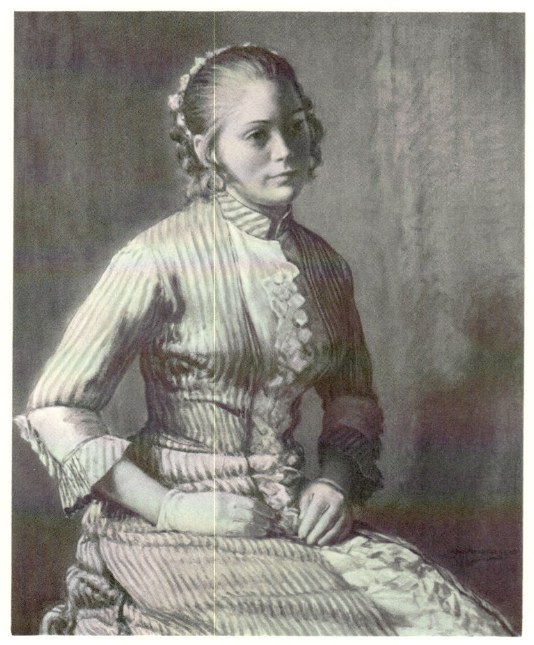

102. *1870 Costume with White Gloves*

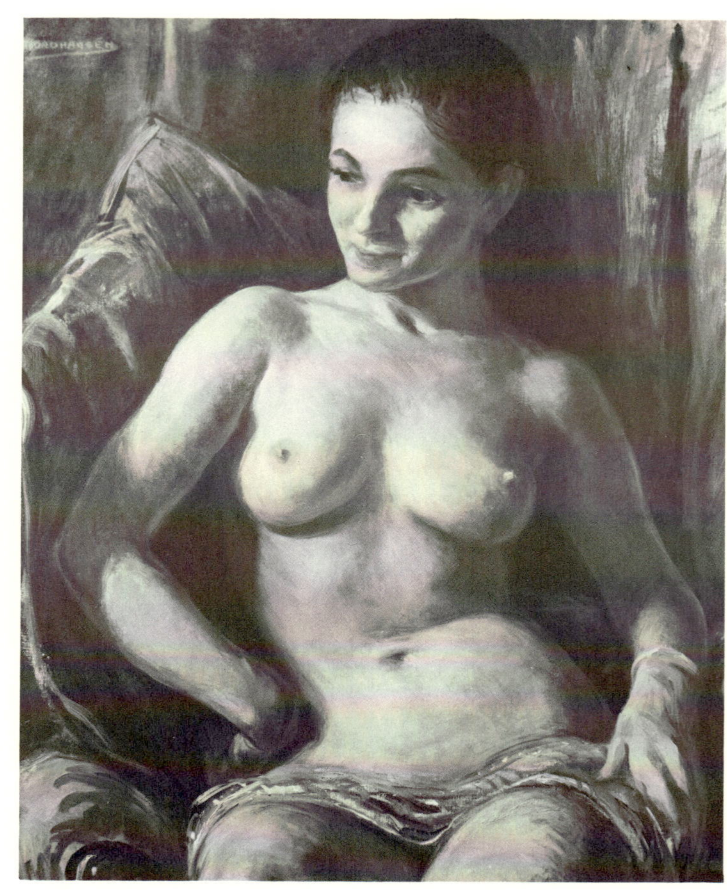

103. *Half Nude*

1959
20″ x 16″
Oil on Canvas
Glick Collection, Bethesda, Md.

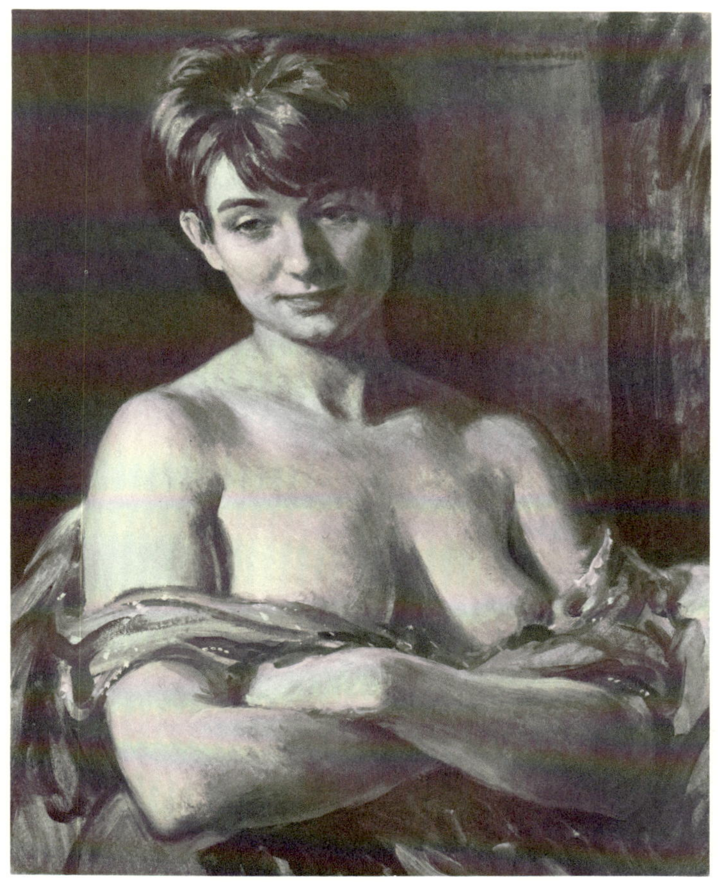

104. *Half Nude with Arms Folded*

1961
16″ x 12″
Oil on canvas

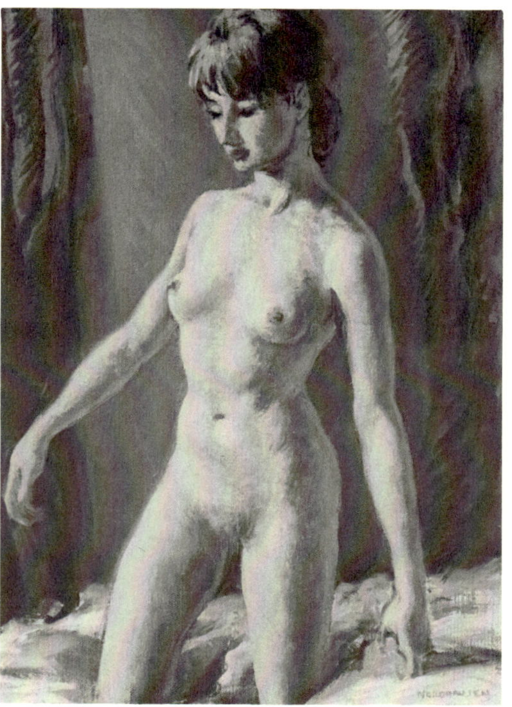

105. *Nude Kneeling*

1961
20″ x 16″
Oil on canvas

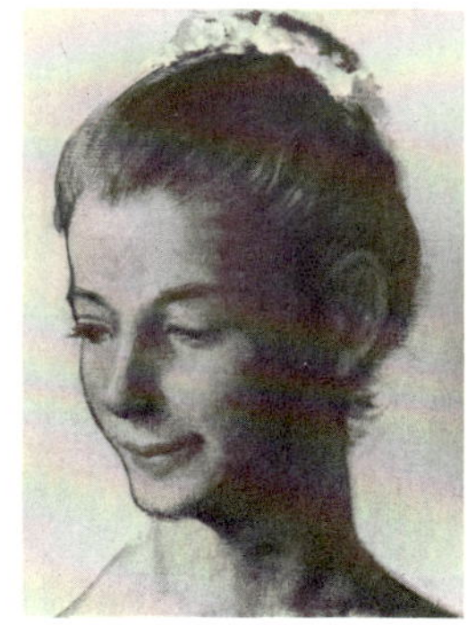

106. *Ballerina Head*

1963
48"x 24"
Oil on canvas
Collection: Syracuse University

1963
25"x 20"
Oil on canvas
Private collection

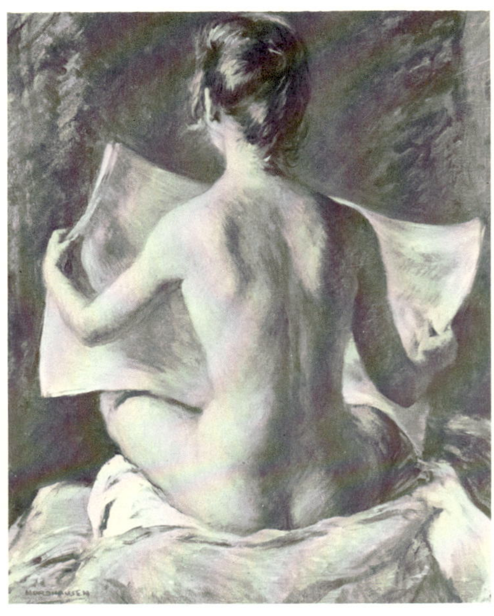

108. *Nude Reading*

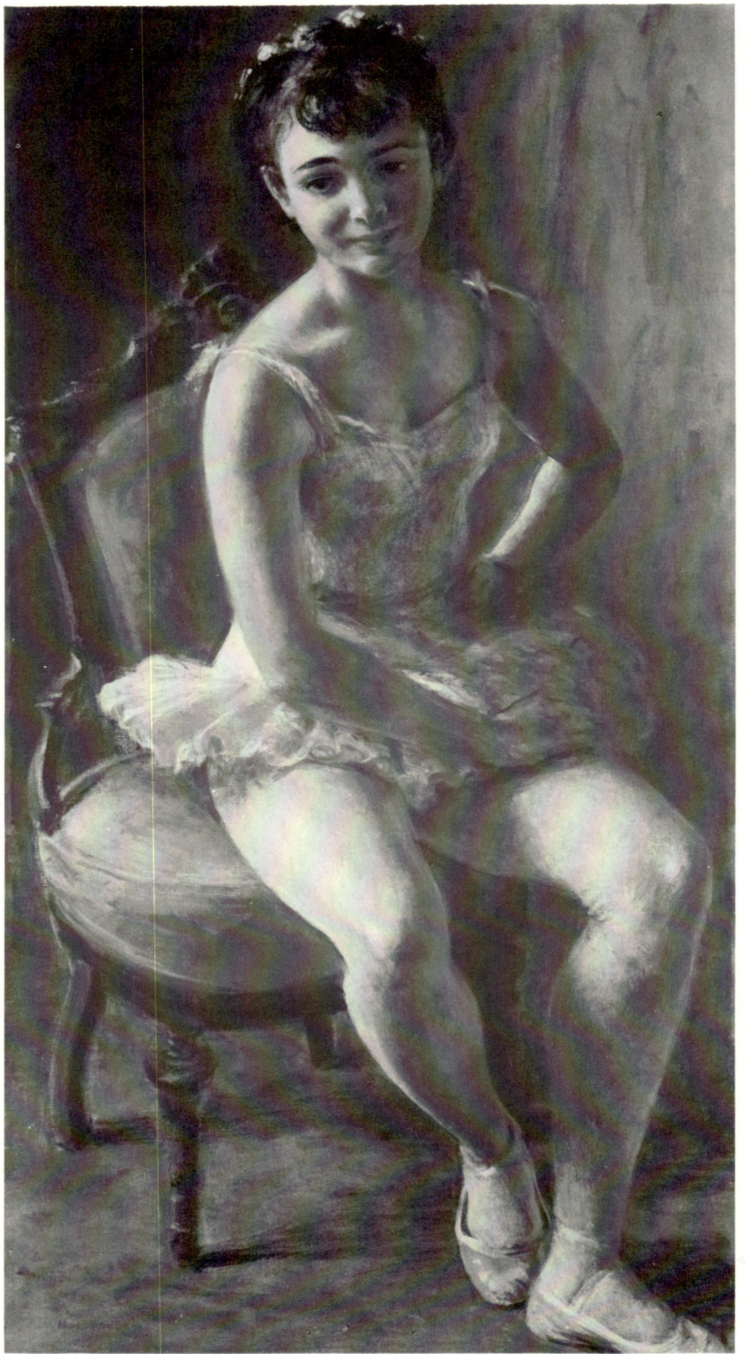

1963
12"x 16"
Oil on canvas
Matt Collection, New York City

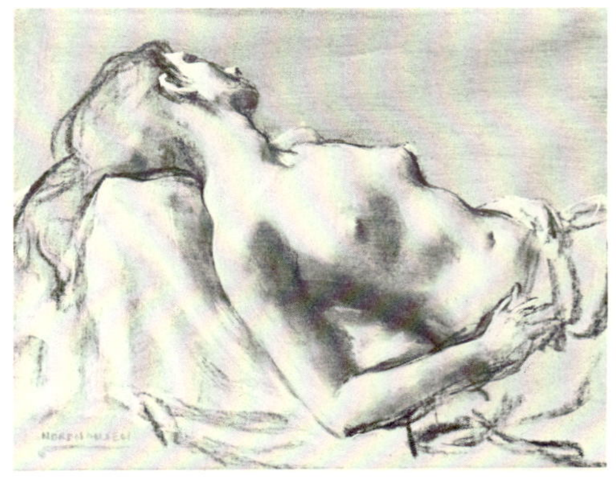

109. *Reclining Nude*

107. *Ballerina in Gold Chair*

1964
28"x 22"
Oil on canvas
Matt Collection, New York City

1968
25"x 20"
Oil on canvas

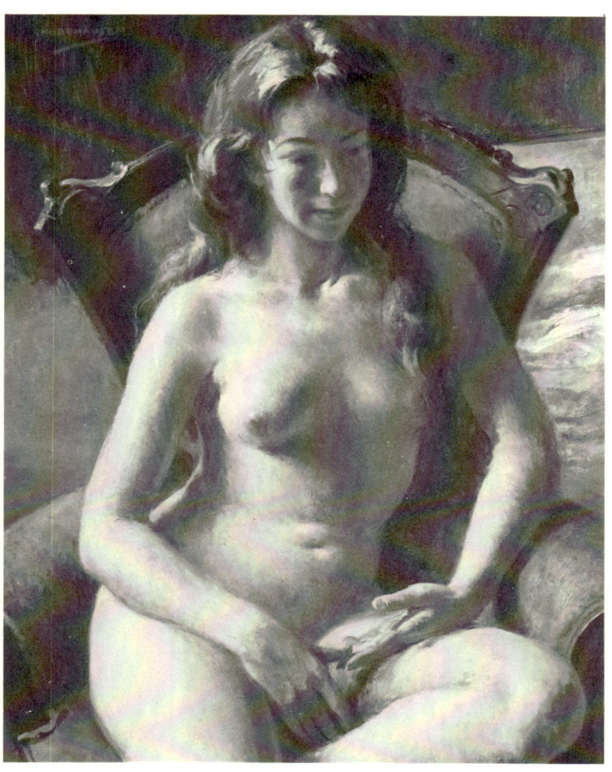

110. *Nude in Victorian Chair*

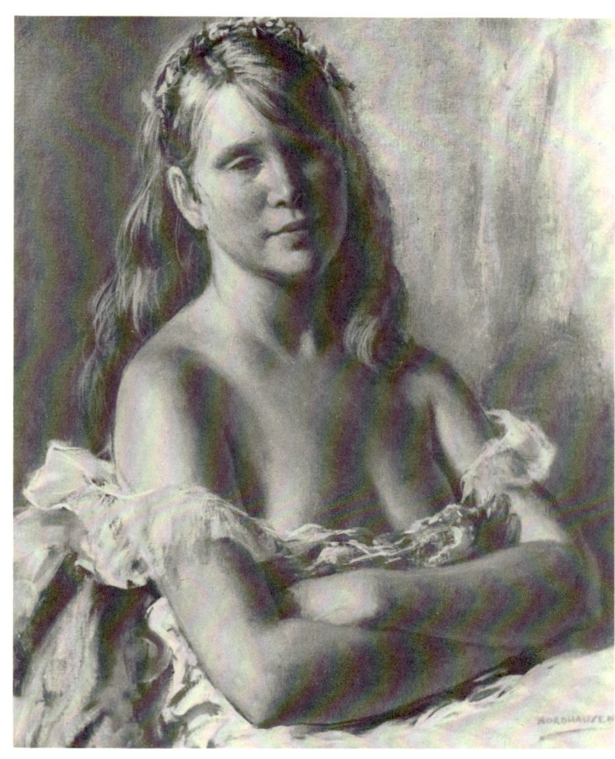

111. *Blond Primevera*

Drawing

ORDHAUSEN'S DRAWINGS over the years have numbered in the thousands. Many of them have been lost or destroyed, but many have been preserved and used either as sources of ideas for further study or for exhibition purposes. When asked to comment, Nordhausen will insist that drawing is everything, from the first mark on the blank paper to the final touch on the painting. Every stroke in the painting is basically a drawing. Drawing is a method of training the hand to record ideas and visions. It is the most spontaneous act of the artist's expression; it reveals the inner workings of the mind; it is like handwriting; and in fact, as has often been said, it *is* his handwriting.

More specifically, many of the drawings have a documentary value as a record of an object, scene, or event. Others are studies in the structure of objects, a figure, or a form. Or they are studies in the problems of visual language of line, light, and shade; the modeling of the form; and the space surrounding the form connecting one with another. Still others are records of ideas, sometimes as simple statements, at other times as experiments in developing a design or composition.

Aesthetically they cannot be divided into rigid categories, since their values and purposes are frequently blended. A drawing intended as an experiment or preliminary study for a painting may later be recognized as a unique and positive expression in its own right. The tentative idea revealed in a preliminary drawing is often more beautifully and directly expressed than in the finished painting.

In the discussion of style in drawings critics frequently rely on the traditional nineteenth-century polarization of concepts: the Classic (Ingres) with its more formal balance of figures and shapes, their clearly defined contours and subtle modeling, as opposed to the Romantic (Delacroix), with its free and emotional reaction to the object, as the spark from which all else flows. Nordhausen takes a somewhat middle position, as mentioned before, on the Realist approach of Courbet. His admiration for the old masters in drawing developed more in the direction of Goya with his power and uncanny skill in manipulating figures in an imaginary space. So, too, the drawings of Degas are examples of superb draftsmanship and the understanding of persons as expressive forms. From the painterly point of view he sees in the drawings of Renoir and Rodin a totality of concept in the forms that provide for the spectator a continuous and unconscious spiritual life.

Frequently excellence in drawing the figure is identified with knowledge of anatomy. Although Nordhausen had experienced that discipline (including memorizing the Latin names of muscles and bones), he insisted that such study was a means to an end rather than an end in itself.

"I believe the study of anatomy is fine," he has said, "as long as it does not interfere with the total simplified form. To know the detail well helps one to be able to lose it successfully or subtly suggest it." And then, in a comment he had often used to characterize his economic philosophy, he would add, "You can't lose a dollar unless you have it."

As part of the discipline to clarify this concept of the "total person," he has long used the method of modeling small figures in clay as did so many of the old masters such as Tintoretto and Degas, with

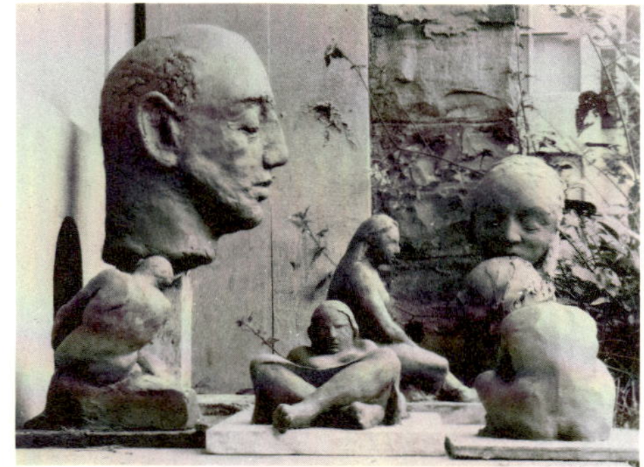

Nordhausen sculpture.

the emphasis placed largely on the solid single figure as a form rather than its movement or its composition into a group.

It has been said that there is no specifically American tradition or character in the drawings of our artists as there is in those of the French, English, or Germans. This Nordhausen flatly denies, pointing out that the figure studies of Thomas Eakins and Winslow Homer are strong, direct, unselfconscious, and convincing expressions of a distinctly American character. Among the American artists of his own time he admires the drawings of John Sloan and Robert Henri as well as those of Eugene Speicher, Leon Kroll, Bernard Karfiol, Walt Kuhn, and the Soyer brothers (particularly Raphael Soyer) as examples of great masters of the figure.

These ideas are not unique and have been expressed many times by contemporary art historians and critics. The important factor here, however, is that they are an integral part of Nordhausen's thinking and serve as a basis for understanding both his own distinctive character as an artist and his respect for others with comparable values and objectives.

This involves the "search for a basic philosophy," which was the theme of the Fifth Annual Conference on Art Education, sponsored by New York's Museum of Modern Art in April 1947 and published in a mimeographed report that same year. The session on drawing was led by an impressive panel of distinguished artists, educators, and critics, including Walter Gropius, Viktor Lowenfeld, Waldo Frank, Stanley William Hayter, Harry Sternberg, Alexander Kastellow,

and Henry Nordhausen.

Beginning with the concept of drawing as a fundamental human urge, Lowenfeld stressed its necessity for the growth of the child as an individual, whereby "the creative process rather than the end-product is the important factor." Waldo Frank characterized "our present way of life as anti-artistic in that it is machine-centered," with the result that we may make greater progress in material things but tend toward the "ultimate stunting and standardization of intellectual and emotional life." Art is essentially a human, man-centered activity, and the work of the artist and art teacher is a function of this philosophy of life.

Another phase of this artist-as-humanist concept was expressed by Walter Gropius with his emphasis on the need for human scale, specifically the human body as the yardstick for the design of man's visible surroundings—everything from great buildings to a simple chair.

The real question remained. How does one teach this man-centered creative activity? Considering that drawing is a fundamental urge common to everyone, it is also therefore a means of communication, a visual language. Whether one draws from objects or feeling, "the techniques of communication are teachable," said Stanley William Hayter. "The danger, however, is that together with these skills would also be imparted the personal limitations and biases of the teacher." He therefore advocated teaching "by provocation rather than didacticism."

Nordhausen's reply to this was that provocation was not enough; one has to learn not only what exists but what must be discovered. He cited

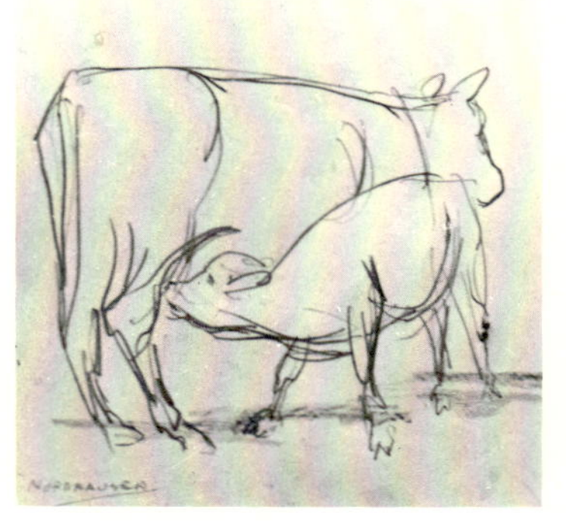

112. Cow and Calf

his own training in Munich as "good academic" but that whereas it offered technical information it frequently overlooked the unique potentialities of the individual. "All great painters were great draftsmen," he said, "but they used drawings as a means toward learning. . . . The danger in teaching drawing is the tendency toward imitation of the past rather than direct contact with reality and a reliance upon ready formulae rather than perceptive experience. . . . Drawing should be taught in a spirit of experiment: all forms of visual interpretation should be encouraged in order to furnish students with the experience necessary to creative power and the skill to interpret this experience successfully."

The review of Nordhausen's drawing reveals this learning process as well as his deep emotional commitment to people and their expressive moods. The drawings show his interest in the structure of objects, both the figure and the form, the concept of the object primarily as a total entity, a whole rather than an assemblage of parts. Whereas he believes in the study of anatomy, he insists it is not a matter of memorizing the names and shapes of the bones and muscles alone. Rather, it is the functional relationship between one form and another—the thrust and counter-thrust of muscular shapes from the shoulder to the back, for instance, or the thigh to the knee or the calf to the ankle. In the total figure the emphasis is on form, not contour; contour is seen as a transition around the form, rather than as a line, with its own flow or as a separation of the form from the surrounding space.

Nordhausen's techniques in drawing vary from a medium soft pencil to charcoal, pen and ink, red or black conté crayon, and red chalk, usually on a fine-grained, fully rag content paper. His general preference is for the conté crayon, whose slightly greasy content allows for rich and delicate gradations of tone, and, since it is less amenable to changes and erasures, demands greater clarity of concept and certainty of control. The luminous white of a high-quality paper provides the basis for an inner glow which gives the figure its form and vitality, but frequently he uses a single tone of either gray, warm sienna, or cool blue similar to the transparent prime used in his paintings. This use of a single tone can enhance and unify the mood of the drawing; it forms a basis from which he can work in the highlights with white tempera or modify the shadows with the black or red conté crayon.

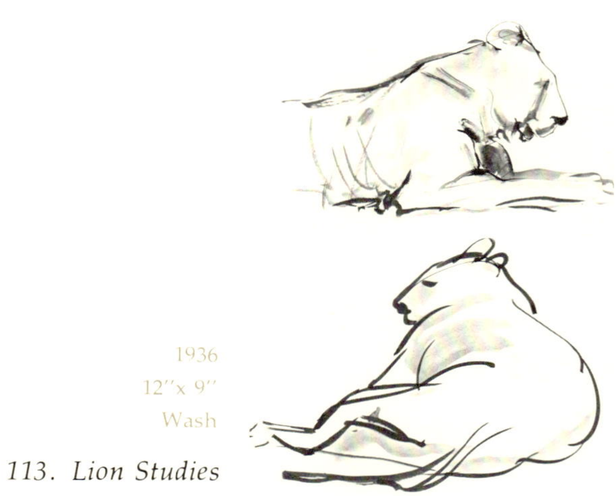

113. Lion Studies

1940
Size unknown
Conte crayon

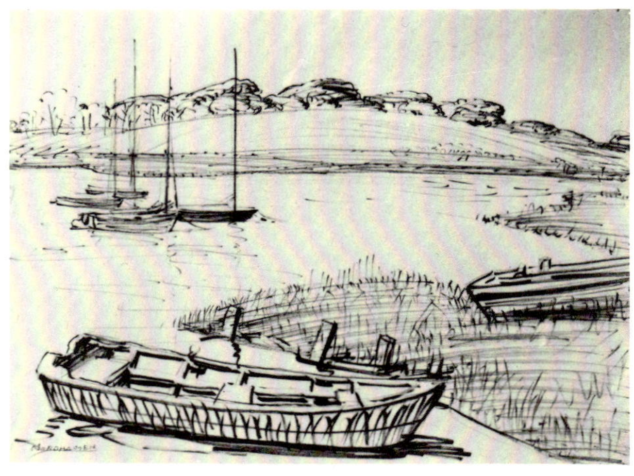

115. *Shoreline with Boats (Puerto Rico)*

1938
19"x 11"
Conte crayon

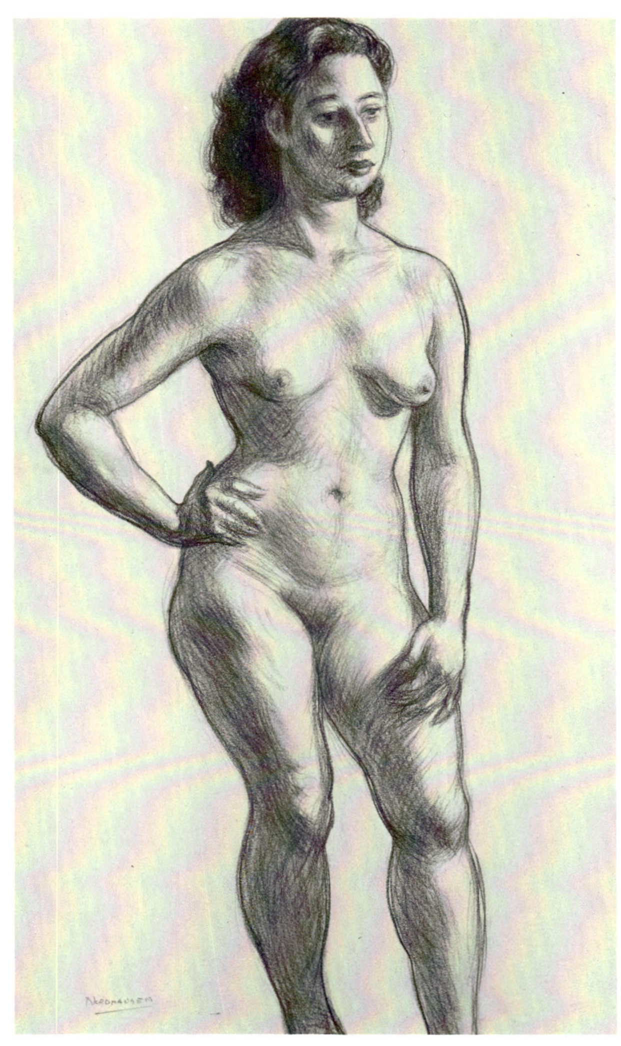

114. *Standing Nude*

1941
15"x 12"
Red conte crayon
Collection: Syracuse University

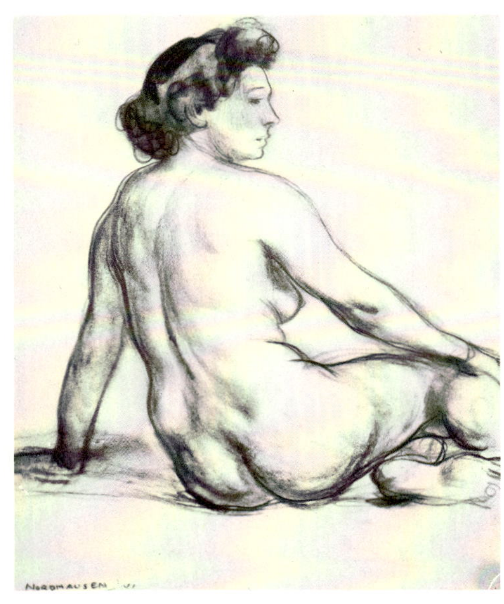

116. *Nude Back, Sitting*

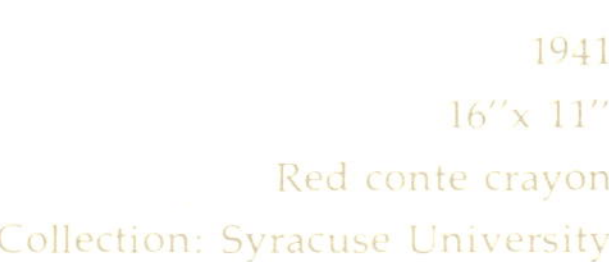

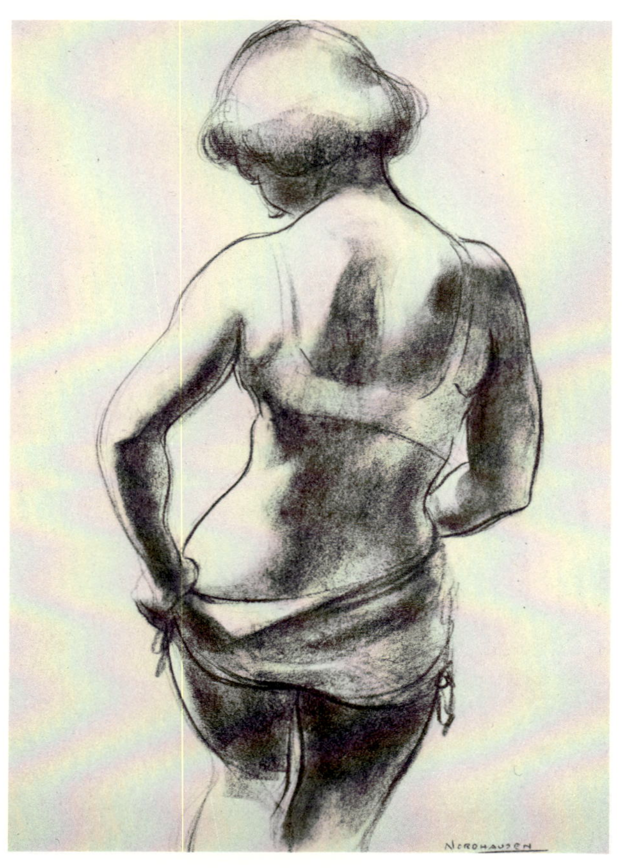

117. *Performer Dressing*

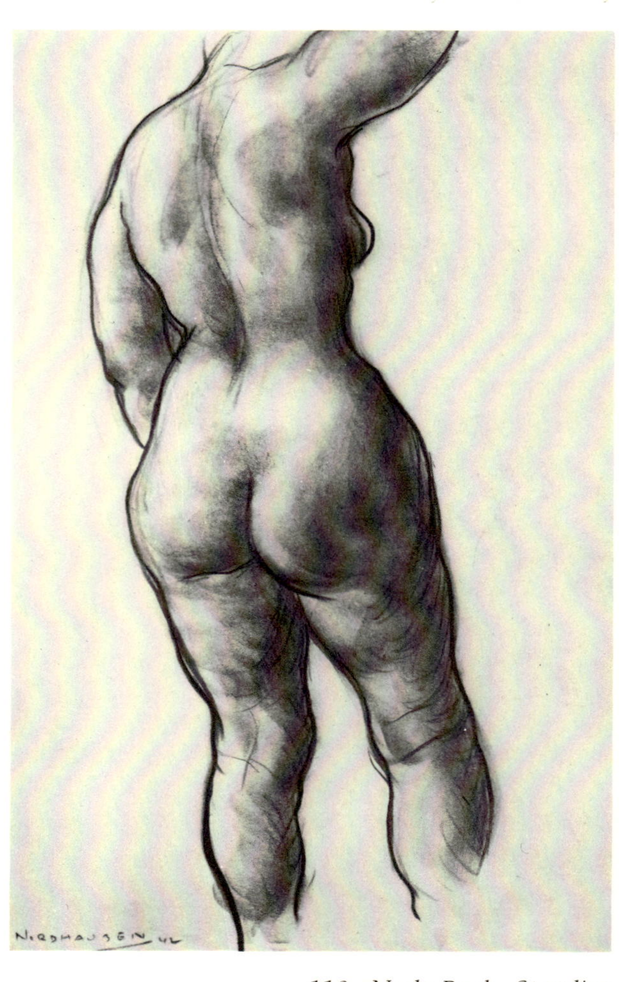

118. *Nude Back, Standing*

121. *Castello Saint Angelo*

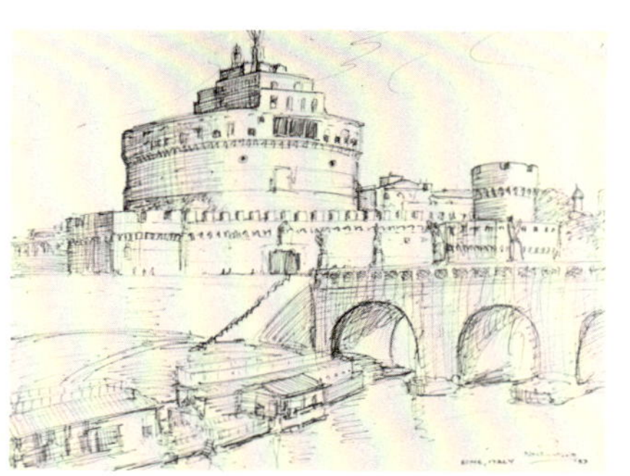

Nordhausen / 102

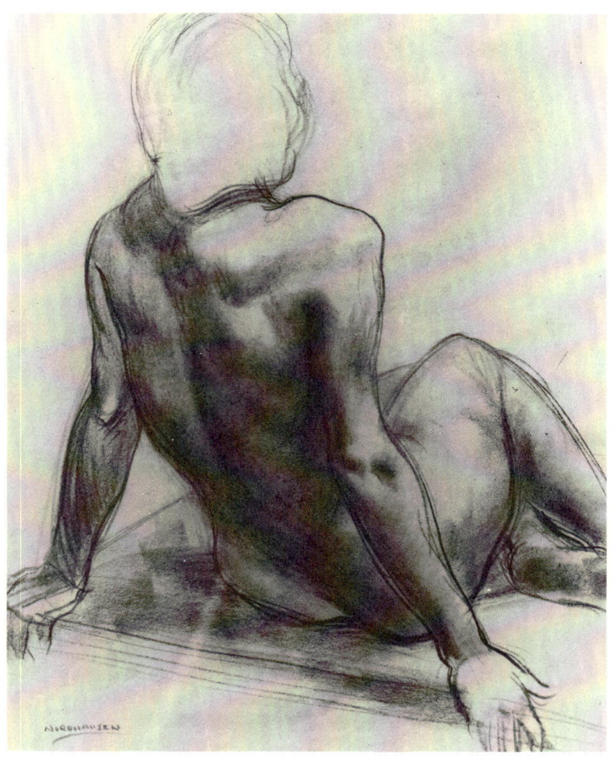

119. *Nude in Repose*

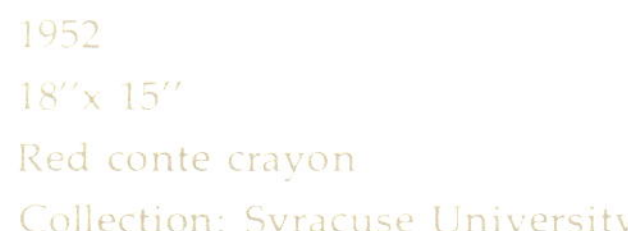
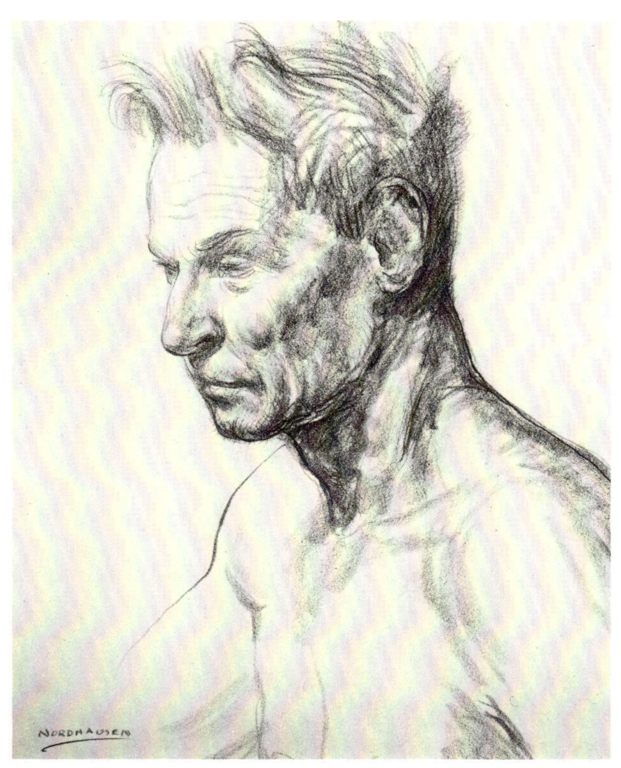

120. *Head of a Man*

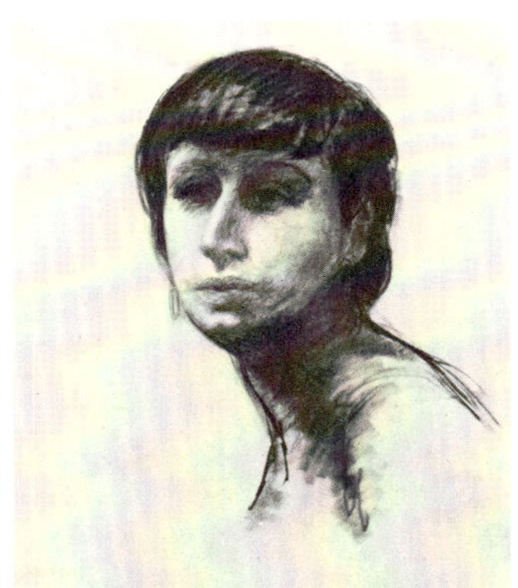

122. **Head Study**

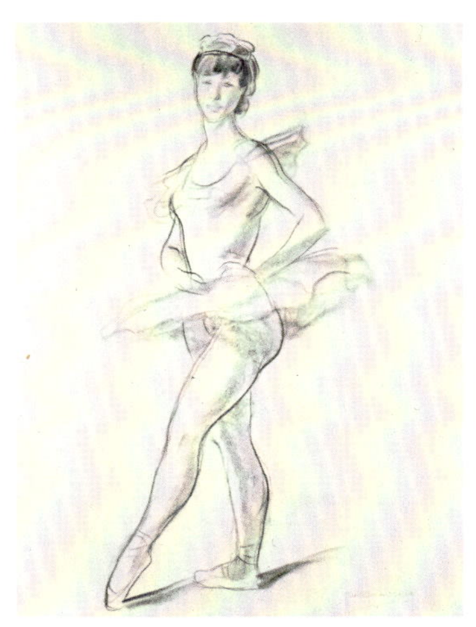

123. *Ballerina*

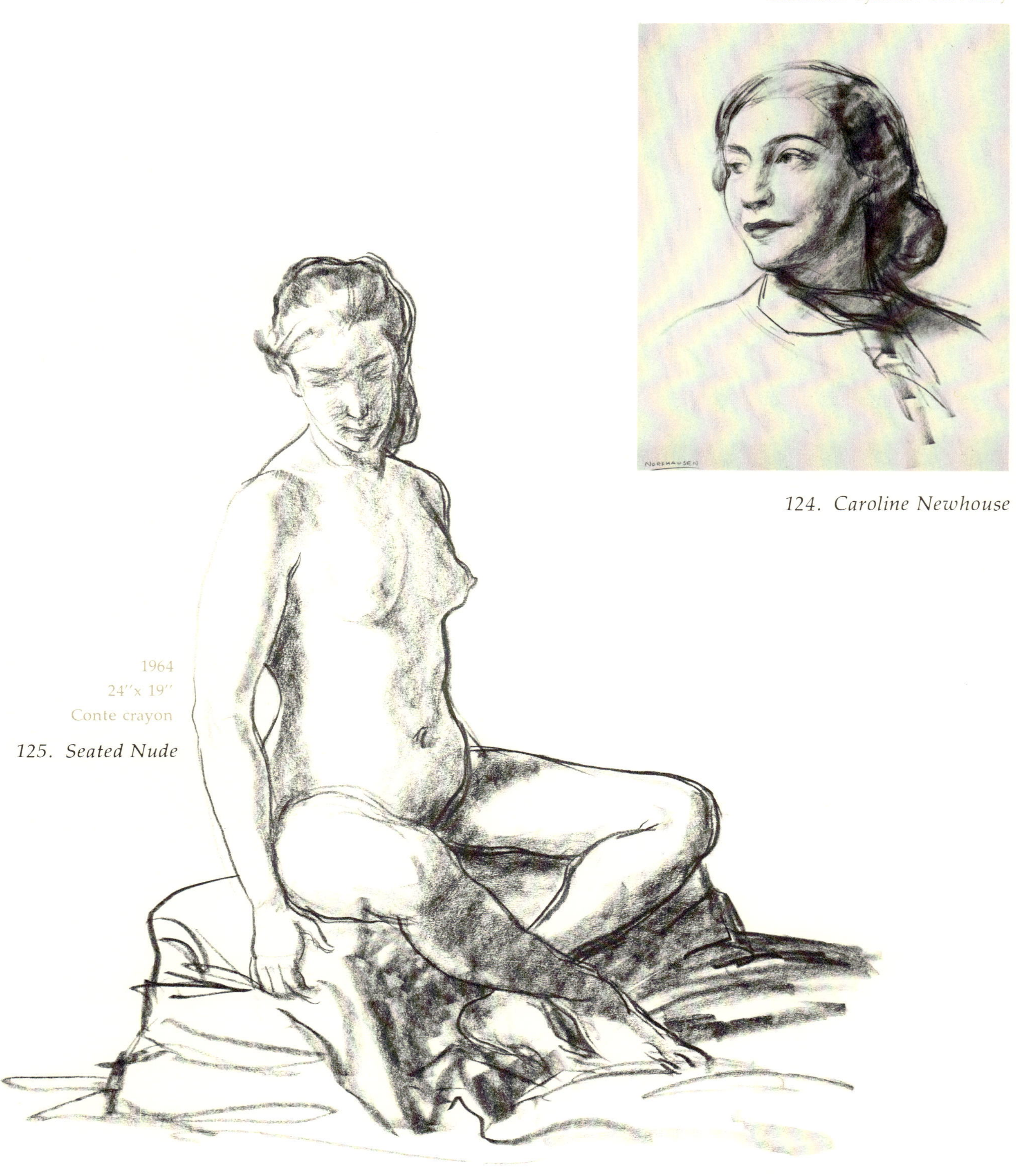

1963
19''x 15''
Red conte crayon
Collection: Syracuse University

124. *Caroline Newhouse*

1964
24''x 19''
Conte crayon

125. *Seated Nude*

1966
14″ x 16-½″
Brown conte crayon

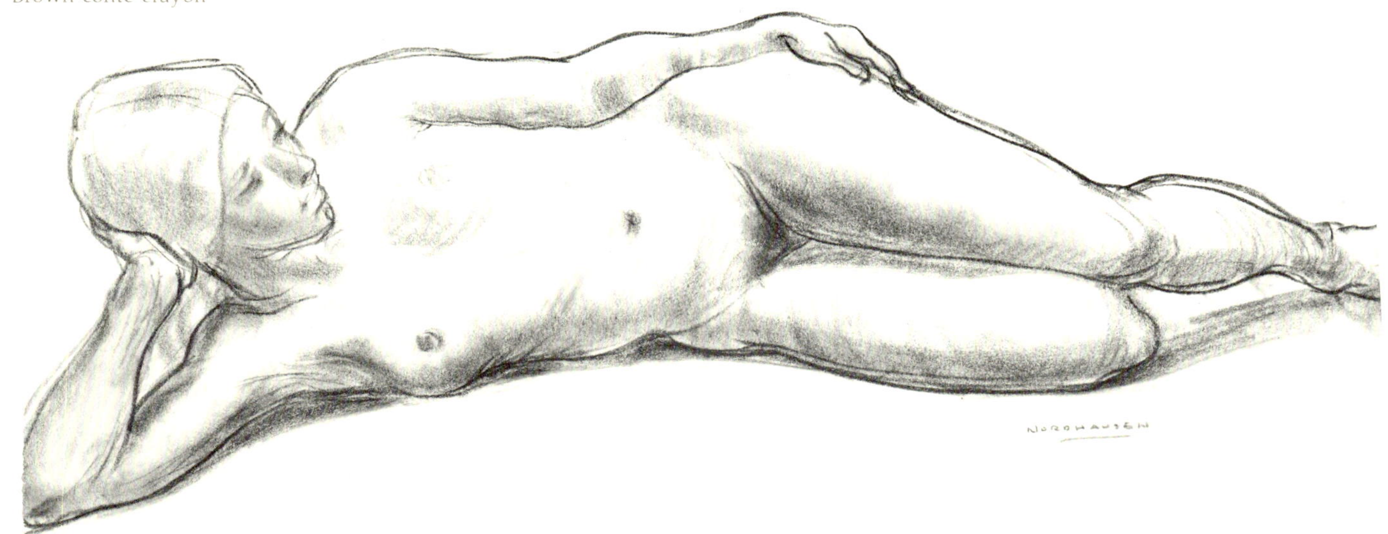

126. *Reclining Nude*

The Still Life

PAINTING A STILL LIFE has many advantages for the artist. The objects do not move; the forms can be as simple or complex as one wishes; the light and space conditions can be constant—and the still life can be an excellent opportunity for study and experiment. In addition, still lifes are always effective in the decoration of homes or office interiors.

As a pictorial representation of dead or inanimate objects, the theme has many interesting iconographical associations, from the things common to everyday life—flowers, fruit, vegetables, and hardware—to objects from the hunt, the kitchen, and the symbolic flowers in the Garden of Paradise. Of basic significance is the fact that through the interpretation of the artist, the object is no longer dead or inanimate—the *nature morte*—but acquires a new life of its own.

Since antiquity the still life has maintained a degree of popularity for the sheer beauty of recorded objects, its style varying from the free to the precise, even to the *trompe l'oeil* as a deliberate attempt to create the illusion of actuality. Beauty and illusion may be transformed into satire, as can be seen in the examples of soup cans, bottle tops, and Brillo boxes of contemporary Pop artists.

Nordhausen's interest in the still life is that of straight painting—involving no iconographical problems, no tricky illusionism, and no social satire. The use of objects and materials as contrast or complement to figures is evident in many of his nude and figure studies, and he has often remarked about the fascination inherent in such materials as silk, cotton, wool or velvet. The same technical and emotional fascination may be found in the forms and textures of apples and other fruits, the shiny green peppers and the patterned pineapple, as well as the intricate patterns of space that develop logically around them.

The flower still life has a particular attraction, not so much as an expression of seasonal mood, such as the freshness of spring or the lush exuberance of summer, but for the combined pleasure and discipline of color. Flowers in themselves have an immediate, universal appeal through colors that can be pure, subtle, complex, delicate, or lyrical. They have the advantage of previous arrangement, an established art in itself, but of necessity require an intense and sustained execution. As an exercise the flower still life sharpens the eye in the perception of its character and subtleties and it also quickens the mind in the search for desired effects as well as the hand in the execution of the painted canvas.

1939
12''x 16''
Oil on canvas

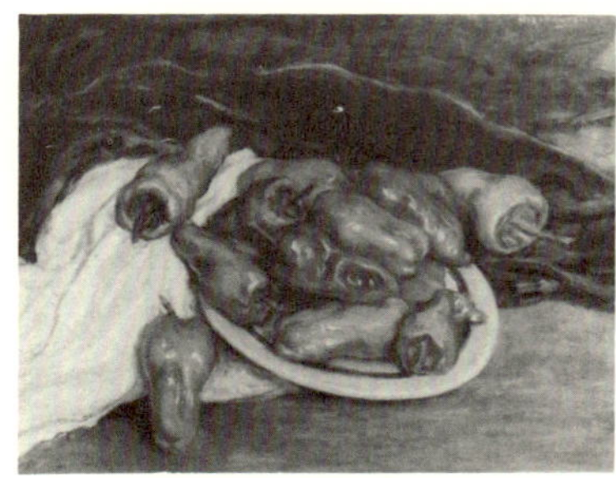

127. Green Peppers

1939
12"x 16"
Oil on canvas
Foley Collection, Columbus, Ga.

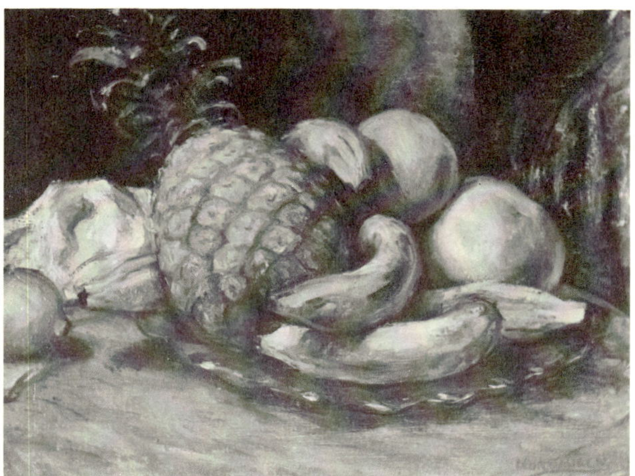

128. *Fruit*

1950
25"x 20"
Oil on canvas
Private collection

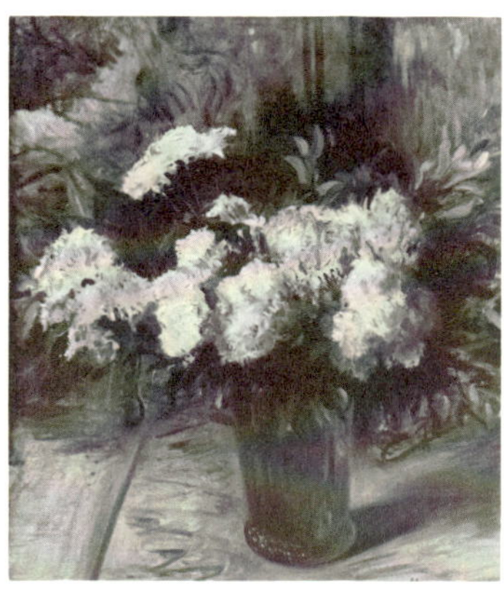

130. *Flowers in Glass Vase*

1946
25"x 20"
Oil on canvas
21 Club Collection, New York City

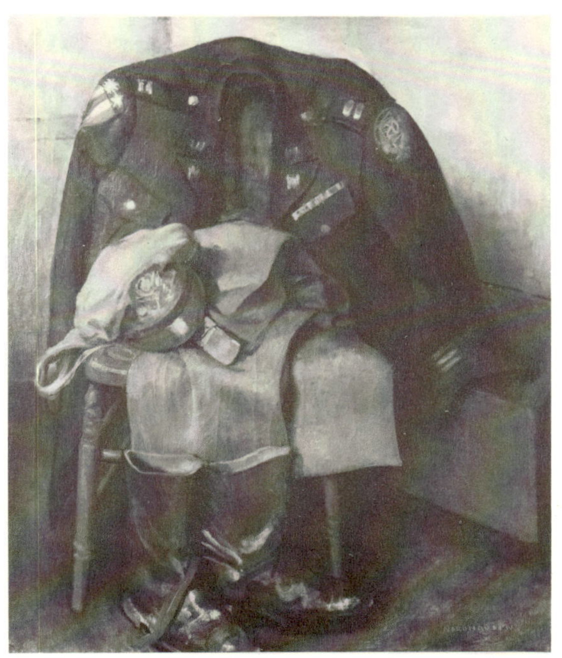

129. *Change of Life*

1977
25"x 20"
Oil on canvas

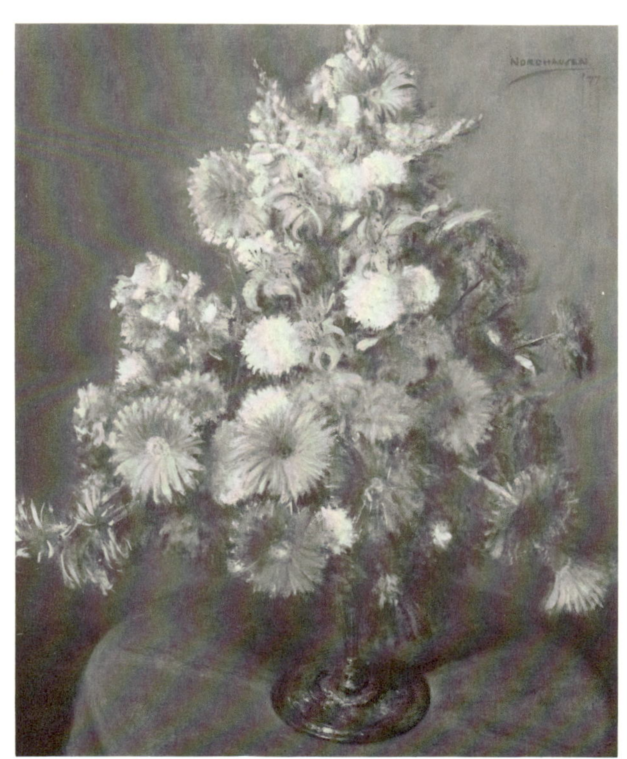

131. *Summer Flowers*

The Landscape

ORDHAUSEN'S LANDSCAPES, like his flower still lifes, have a certain verve and spontaneity, but they are different. The forms of nature, with its hills and rocks, groves of trees and buildings, are solid and eternal, but space when seen as the predominant feature, is filled with light, color, and movement that are constantly changing and must somehow be comprehended. Nordhausen's landscapes are painted outdoors on the site, usually in a single session. The objective in his selection of the site and the composition of its forms is to discover its basic character, that quality which distinguishes one particular setting or region from another.

In this search for the character and personality of a landscape there is a certain analogy to the artist's attitude noted in connection with his portrait and figure painting. But it is not the obvious literary device of portraying inanimate nature as having human feelings and character. It is more the direct probe of its multiple features to find the significant form that gives it permanence and meaning.

Nordhausen spent several summers in Peacham, Vermont, and was well aware of the tradition that is popularly known as the "Vermont Landscape." That tradition has its historical aspects: from the colonial emphasis on the description of its topographical characteristics to the nineteenth-century idealization of the "wilderness" as an expression of the beautiful and the sublime. The twentieth-century artist maintains his own highly personal and individual interpretation; but it is usually in response to the pastoral image of cultivated hills; a hill farm with its white house and red barns; and patterns of woodland, lake, and brook.

To Nordhausen these patterns are not manmade but are God-created in an ageless evolution of granite hills and valleys, beautiful in their varied and undulating contours and forms but harsh and relentless in their remote reality. The people seem to be affected by that granite reality; they are not a part of the landscape; the endlessly rolling forms predominate.

The Italian landscape is different. It has been lived in for millennia; the land and the people are warm, lovable, and outgoing. The villages seem to be part of the land as though they had been built together; their clearly organized forms and natural assertiveness in a unifying pattern of light reflect that humane character even though the figures are hardly noticeable in the composition. Similar distinctions are observable in the paintings of Maine's Monhegan Island with their bleak and forbidding rock formations; in the lush tropical atmosphere of the Puerto Rican landscapes; in the vast windswept spaces of the American West; and in the clean, orderly, romantic atmosphere and space in those of southern Germany.

1928
19''x 18''
Watercolor
Johnson Collection, Endicott, N.Y.

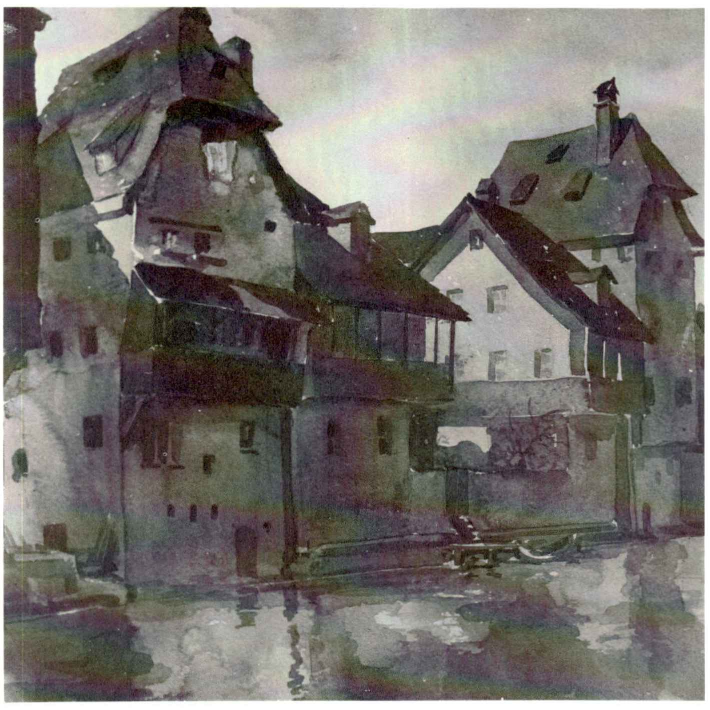

132. *Nürnberg*

1929
16''x 20''
Watercolor
Williams Collection, Columbus, Ga.

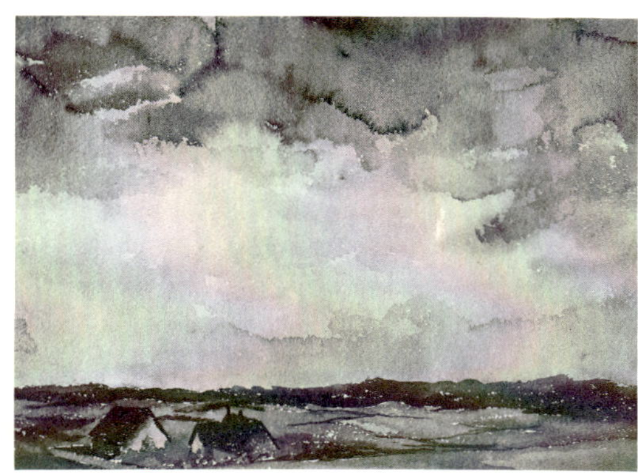

133. *Outside of Dinkelsbühl*

1936
16''x 20''
Oil on canvas
Private collection

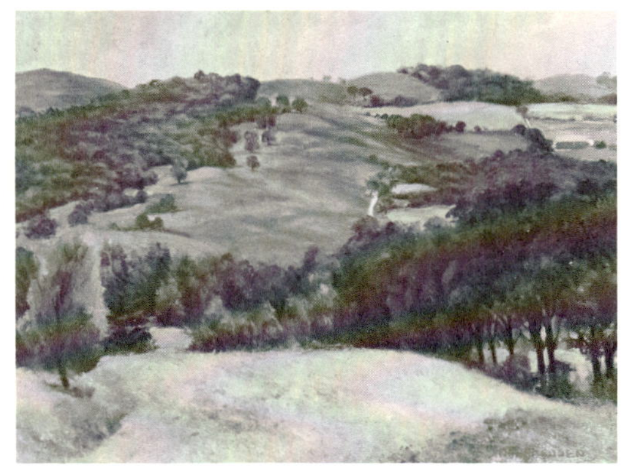

134. *Vermont Landscape*

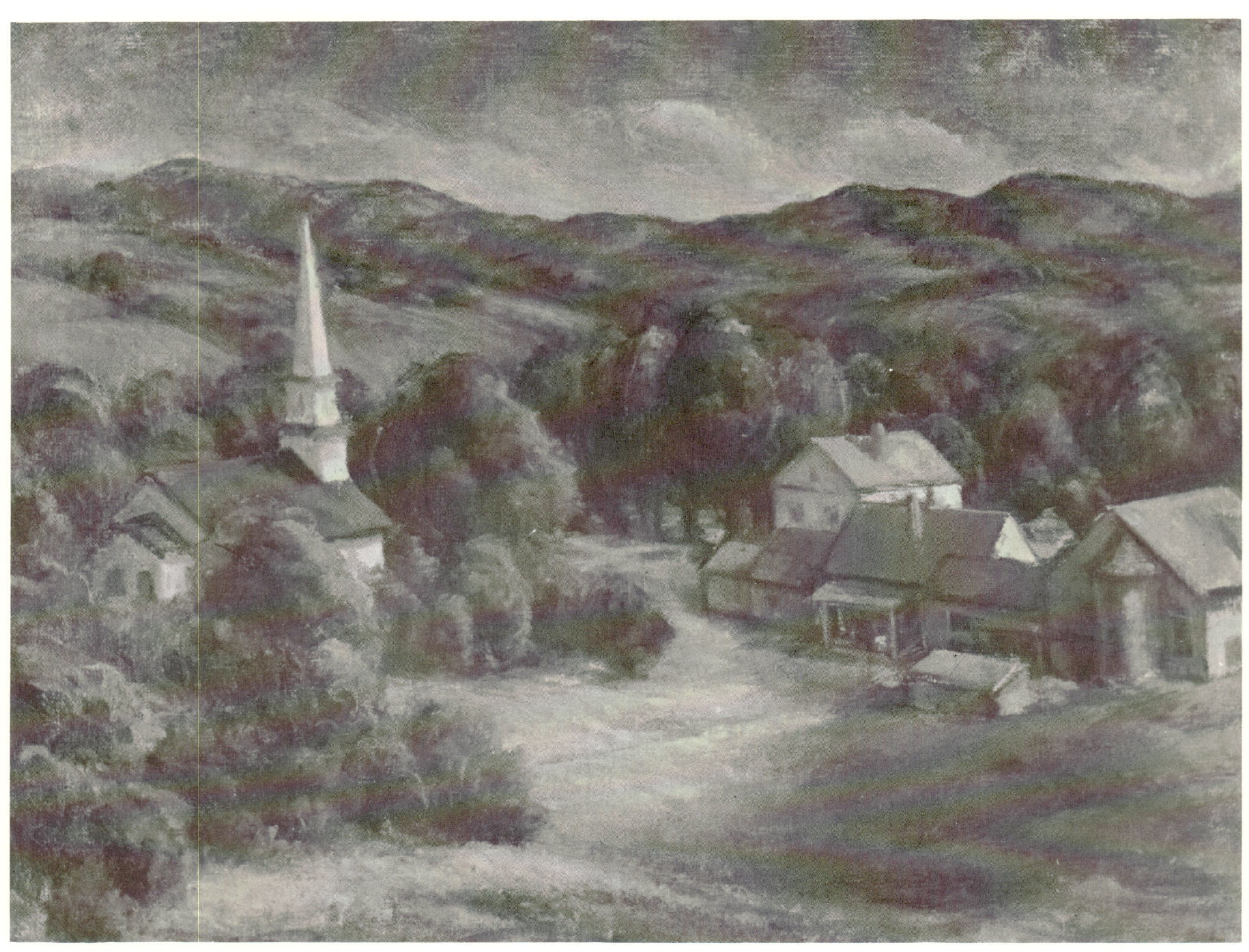

1937
20″x 24″
Oil on canvas
Private collection

135. *Peacham, Vermont*

1939
16″x 20″
Oil on canvas
Private collection

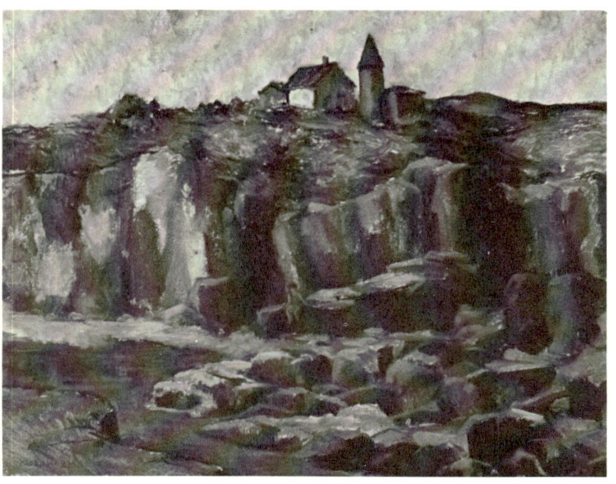

136. *Monhegan Island*

1948
16″x 20″
Watercolor

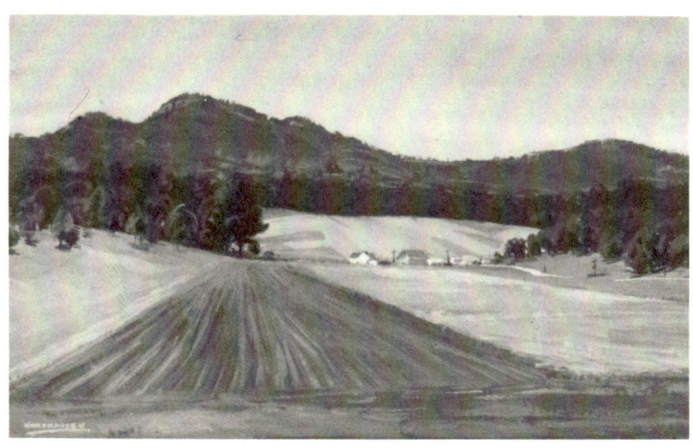

138. *Wyoming Landscape*

1940
16″x 20″
Watercolor

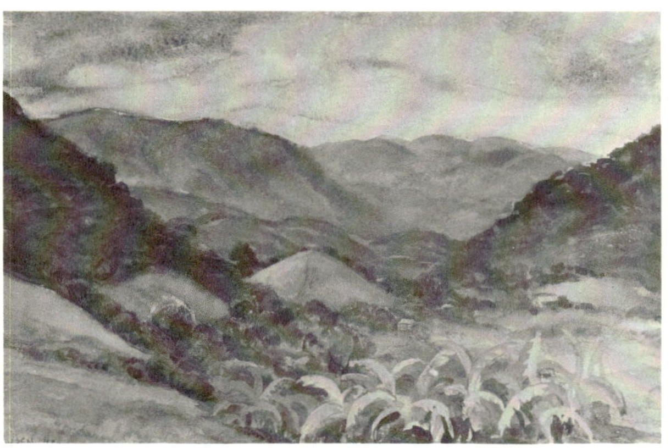

137. *Puerto Rico*

1948
16″x 20″
Watercolor
Edwards Collection, Columbus, Ga.

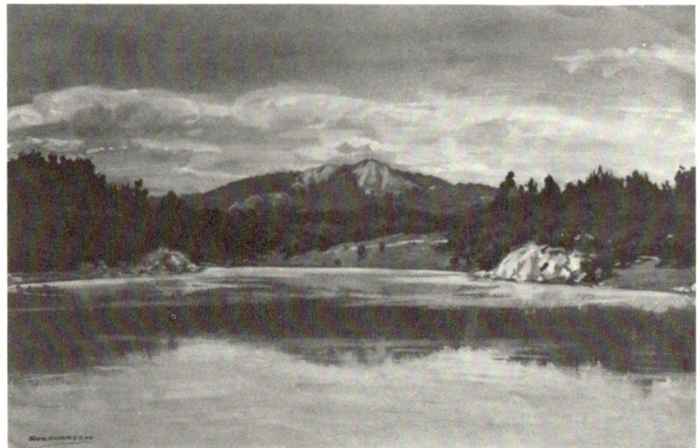

139. *Stockade Lake, South Dakota*

111 / *The Landscape*

1950
16″x 20″
Watercolor
Private collection

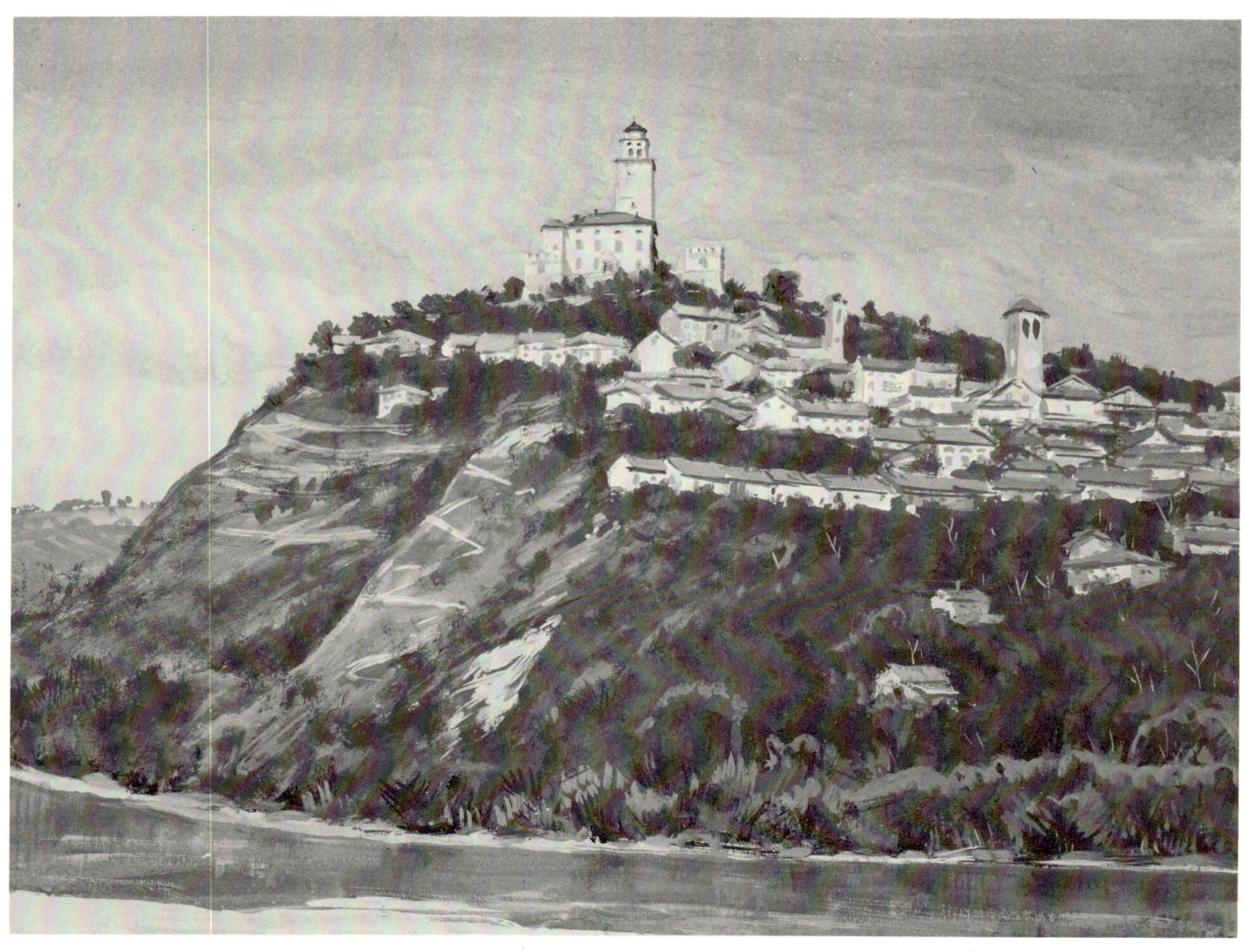

140. Montecastello

1962
16" x 20"
Watercolor
Private collection

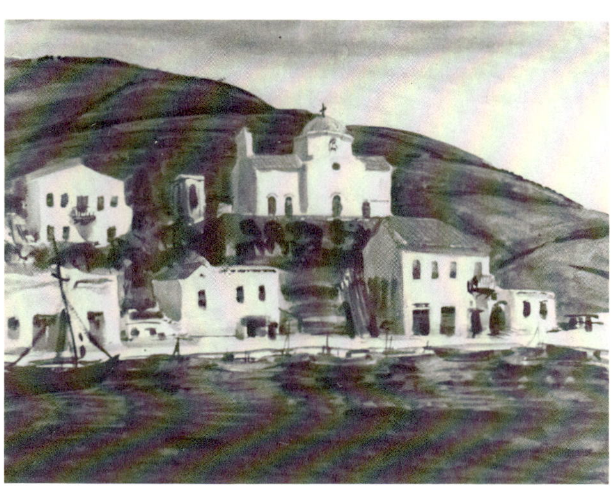

141. *Greek Island*

1962
16" x 20"
Watercolor
Private collection

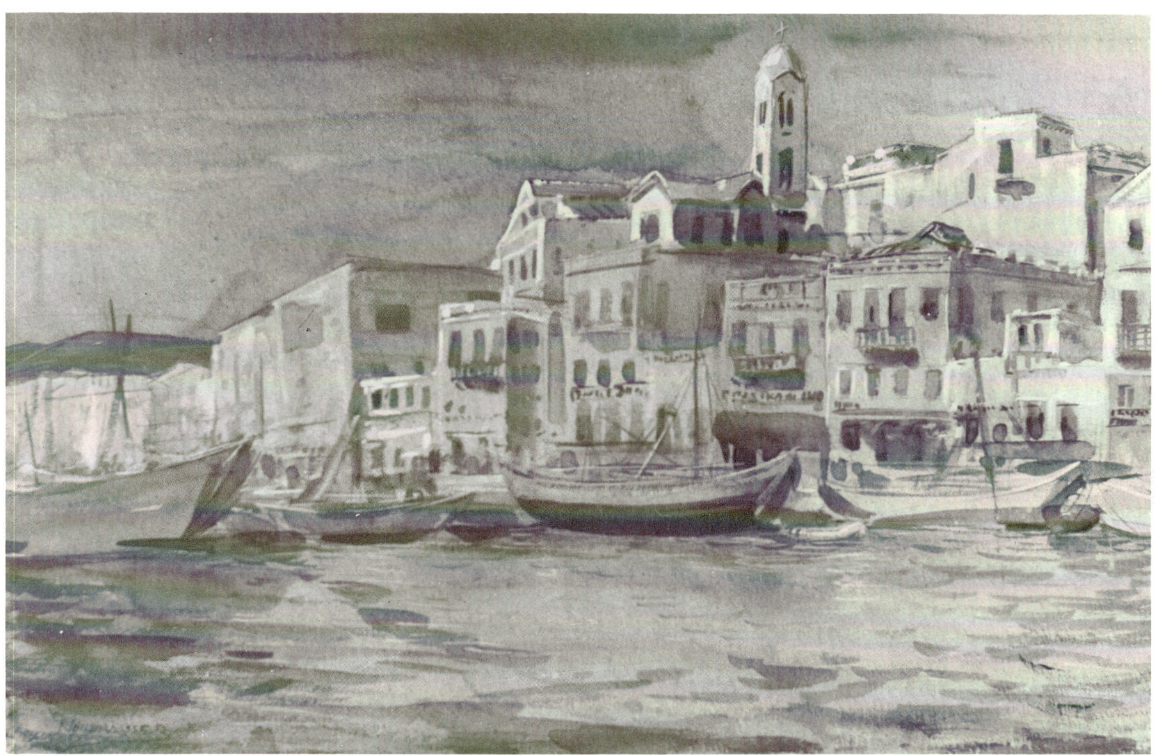

142. *Greek Island (Mikonos)*

NORDHAUSEN'S interest in prints, primarily etchings, was confined largely to the early 1930s after his second trip to Munich. He was intrigued by the technical discipline of the medium as well as by the possibilities of duplication of favorite motifs used in painting. Thus the *Man with a Cane* (143) and the *Landscape Near Dinkelsbühl* (148) are based on paintings done in Germany in 1929. Comparison of the painted portrait with the etching reveals the greater interest in light which the latter medium affords and the corresponding softening of the features and forms of the figure. In the case of the landscape, the primary concern for space in the watercolor has been similarly reinterpreted to emphasize the light and the romantic mood of twilight.

He developed the monotypes during the same period, but these were more often used for both study and exhibition purposes. The monotype (not to be confused with the typesetting machine patented by Tolbert Lanston in 1887) is a print medium which allows, by its very nature, only a single "pull" or print from the original plate. Actually, it is a medium combining features of both painting and printmaking, since it involves the brilliant and rich color qualities of the painting as well as the freedom to experiment and explore which are characteristic of the print media.

Although the monotype has not been a particularly popular medium in contemporary art,* it has a long history that includes the seventeenth-century Giovanni Benedetto Castiglione, William Blake, Auguste Renior, and Edgar Degas, as well as many Americans, such as Albert Sterner, Eugene Higgins, William Glackens, and Maurice Prendergast. William Merritt Chase had a special exhibit of his monotypes at the National Academy in 1881.

The process involves the direct painting in oil colors on a smooth metal plate or white opaque glass. It is then transferred by pressure, usually with a leather etcher's roller, to dampened paper, which results in an approximate duplication, in reverse, of the original. The paper is usually white or near white, of good, semiabsorbent quality, which is soaked in water and then placed between blotters to remove the excess surface water.

The brushes and oil paint are the same as those Nordhausen uses in regular painting on canvas. Sometimes he applies a thin brownish layer the previous day, which then dries and provides the common base tone similar to the colored prime

---

* A complete list of American museums which have monotypes in their collections, artists who produce them, and a full bibliography appeared in the Print Collectors' *Newsletter*, Vol. 9, no. 5 (November-December 1978). See also Ernest W. Watson's article, "The Monotypes of A. Henry Nordhausen," *American Artist*, Vol. 11, no. 6 (June 1947).

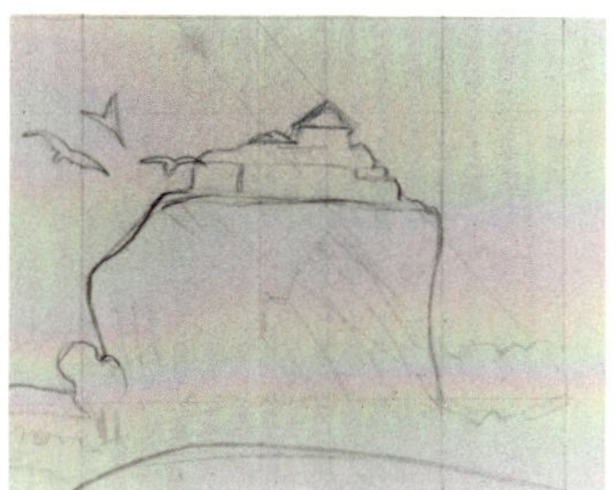 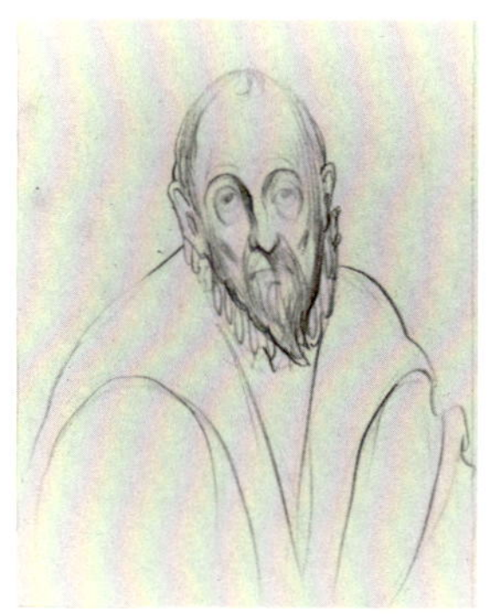 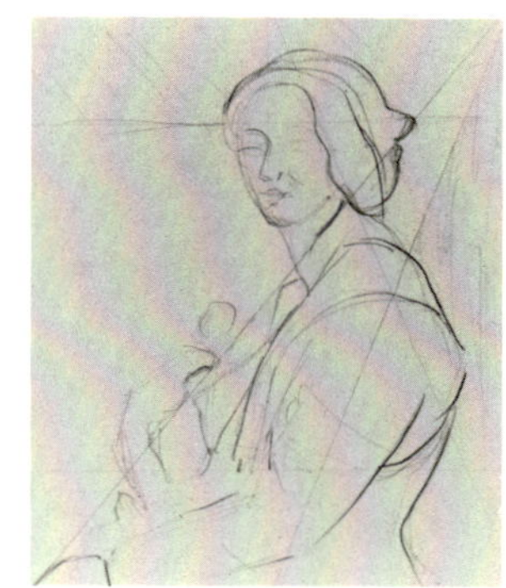

used on his canvases. In order to slow the drying and allow longer painting time, he often uses kerosene instead of turpentine as a medium. For an additional copy, the plate must be repainted, which might be in approximately the same form or revised, but in any case each new print is original and unique.

The print is not a perfect duplicate of the original image on the plate, a fact which accounts for its special charm and quality. Many unforeseen effects are produced by the pressure and printing process—a blending of juxtaposed colors and a blurring of edges, resulting in a unity of painterly tone. Yet the print retains much of the transparency of a watercolor in addition to the solidity of an oil painting.

Because of the ease and directness of the medium, Nordhausen uses monotypes somewhat as he does drawings, as studies or experiments in color and composition. Thus, there are standing nudes seen in various positions, seated figures, acrobats, and especially many circus groups and scenes. In 1932 he executed a series of analyses of old master paintings in the Metropolitan Museum, which resulted in an exhibition of some twenty-five monotypes in the Memorial Union Gallery of the University of Wisconsin in January 1933. The exhibition, designed primarily as part of the university's educational program, was cited in the introductory pamphlet as the work of an artist "who looks to the work of the Old Masters for solutions to the problems confronting him at his own easel."

While the local art history professor sniffed haughtily that "these are not good copies,"

Nordhausen's notes and preliminary drawings indicate that his interest was indeed focused on the aesthetic problem and the artist's solution to it rather than on making a literal "copy." Hence the Goya, *City on a Rock* (150), is analyzed as a composition with its overlapping squares and triangles planned with mathematical precision, its areas divided into geometric mean and extreme ratios in 3 : 5 proportion (i.e., the golden section), while the painting is executed in a free, spontaneous, almost reckless manner. The Corot, *Sibyl* (151), unfinished as it is, also has a beautifully designed, systematic foundation which accounts for its classic serenity. The Franz Hals, *Hille Babbe*, has warm underpainting and some rich glazing of color, but Nordhausen points out in his notes on one drawing: "His clever brush work at times destroys the convincing solidity" of the figure. Similarly, the Cezanne, *Man with a Straw Hat,* has a warm tone to the underpainting, which in contrast to the cool and high-keyed greenish yellow of the hat and touches of gray-green in the beard gives the painting much of its power and beauty. In El Greco's *Portrait of a Man* (152), the so-called Self-Portrait, he points out the series of vertical ovals throughout the design of the head and figure which make the painting almost a caricature, an observation which he stresses in the written notes, the pencil sketch, and the monotype. At the same time he notes the rich color in the underpainting and glazing.

All of these comments, visual and written, are not meant to be disrespectful of the great masters. They are, on the contrary, records of honest study, part of the process of "discovery," as Nordhausen once called it. The object of the study is not the subject of the painting but the means by which that unique and distinctive expression is achieved. To characterize these works as merely "studies in technique" is to miss the point, too, as the written comments, the drawings, and the monotypes themselves demonstrate.

It is useful to compare some of the monotype studies with similar compositions in the oil medium, such as the two monotypes of a Rubens-like model undressing (153/154), one seen from the front, the other from the rear, with the pair of oil paintings (75/76) of the same subject. Or again, some of the clown compositions *Clown Talk* (156) and *Clown with Hat* (87) appear to have been preliminary studies for the paintings. In each case the freedom and spontaneity of the monotype is readily apparent. In other examples such as the shimmering *Burlesque Dancers* (57) and the *Flying Trapeze* (68), the sense of tension and excitement seems best conveyed through the monotype medium alone.

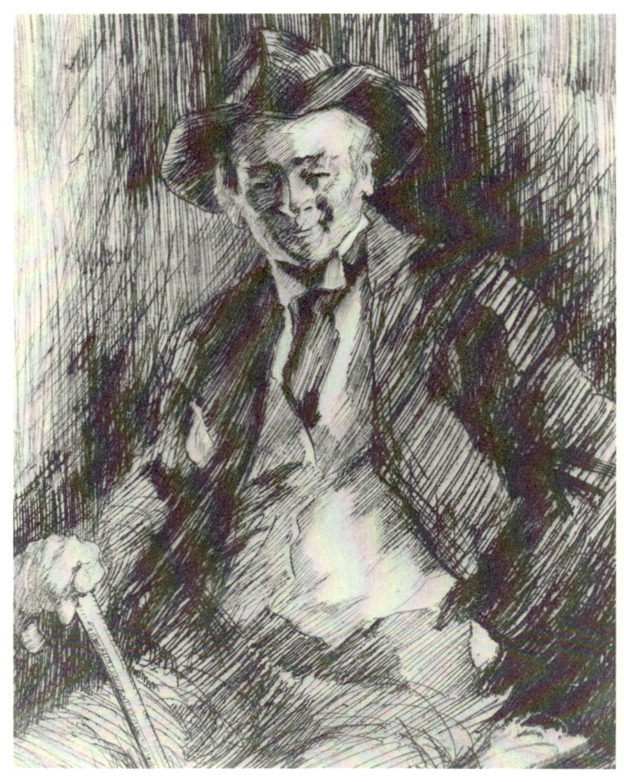

143. *Man with a Cane*

1929
6"x 4-1/2"
Etching

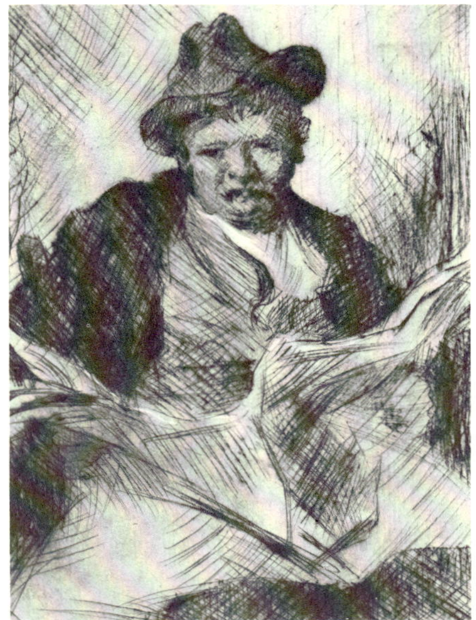

144. *Bavarian with Newspaper*

1929
6-1/4"x 5-1/2"
Etching

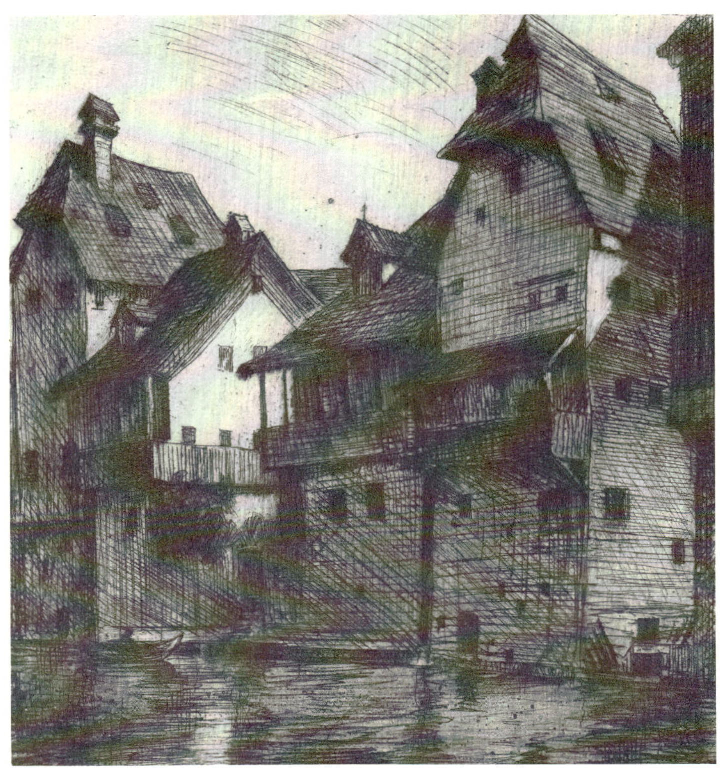

146. *Houses in Nürnberg*

1929
5-3/4"x 4-1/4"
Etching

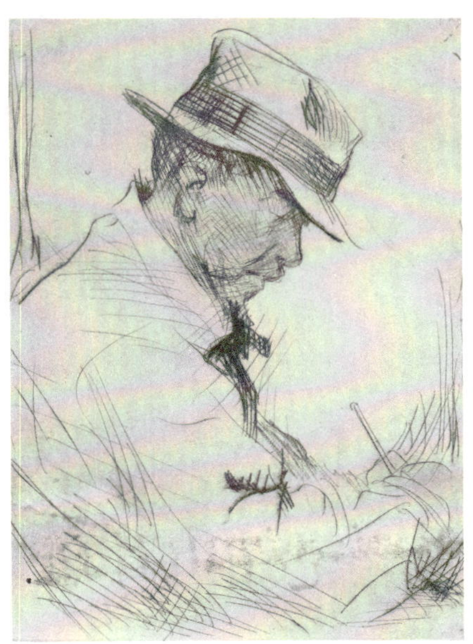

145. *Wilhelm Funk*

117 / *Prints and Monotypes*

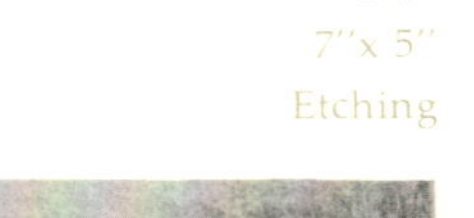

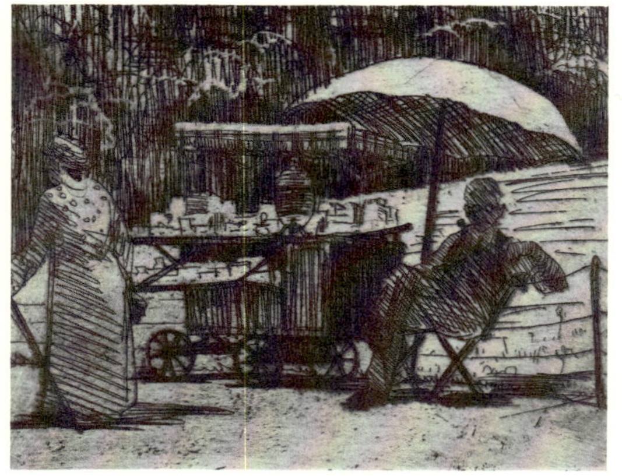

147. *Munich, Englishe Garten*

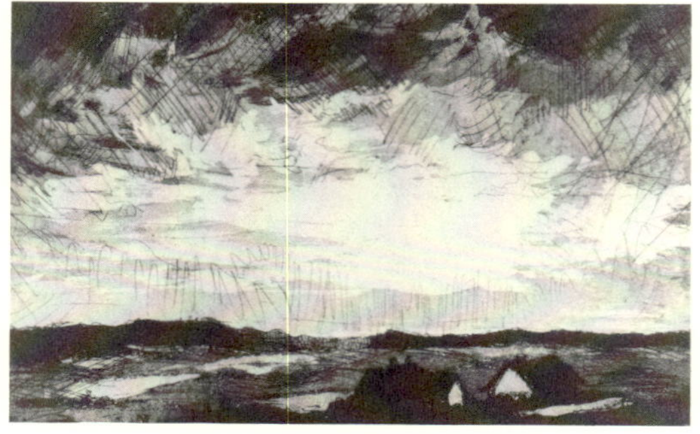

148. *Landscape near Dinkelsbühl*

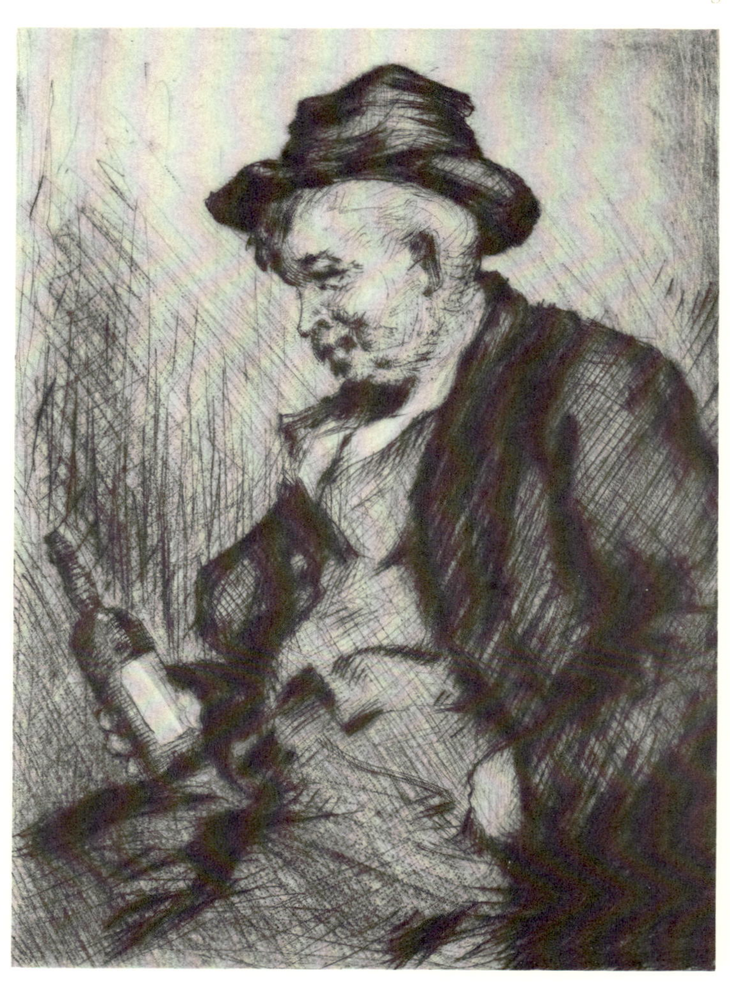

149. *Man with Bottle*

1932
22″ x 16″
Monotype

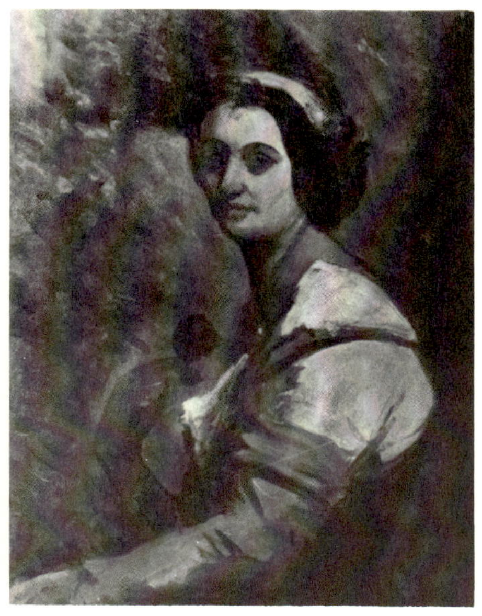

151. *Sibyl (after Corot)*

1932
17″ x 25″
Monotype

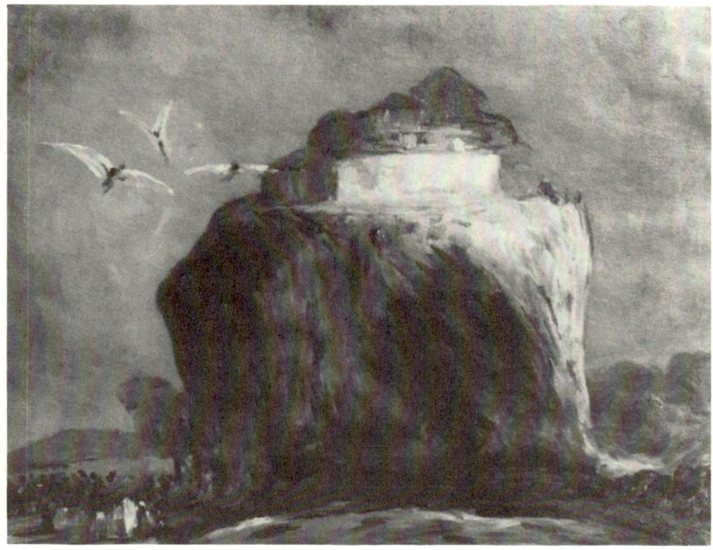

150. *City on a Rock (after Goya)*

1932
20″ x 16″
Monotype

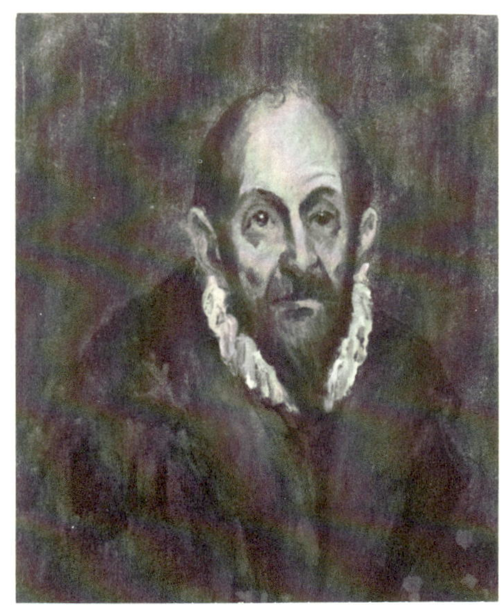

152. *Self Portrait (El Greco)*

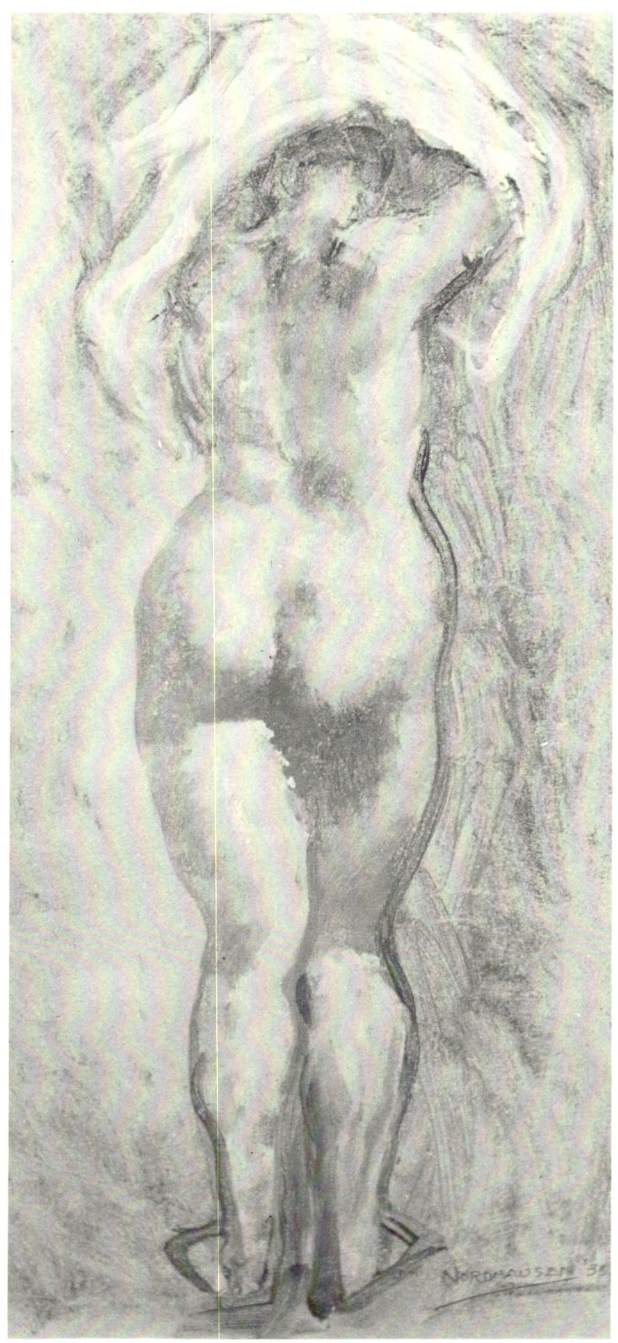

153. *Nude Undressing*

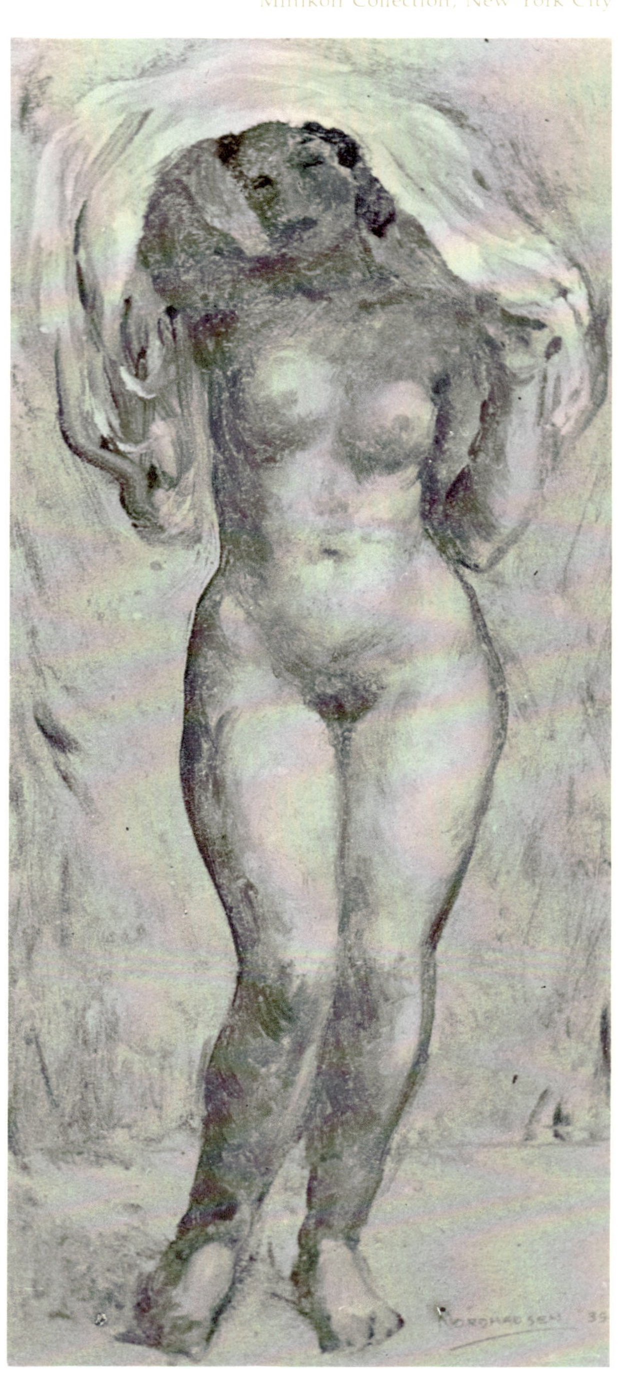

154. *Nude Undressing*

1937
18"x 14"
Monotype

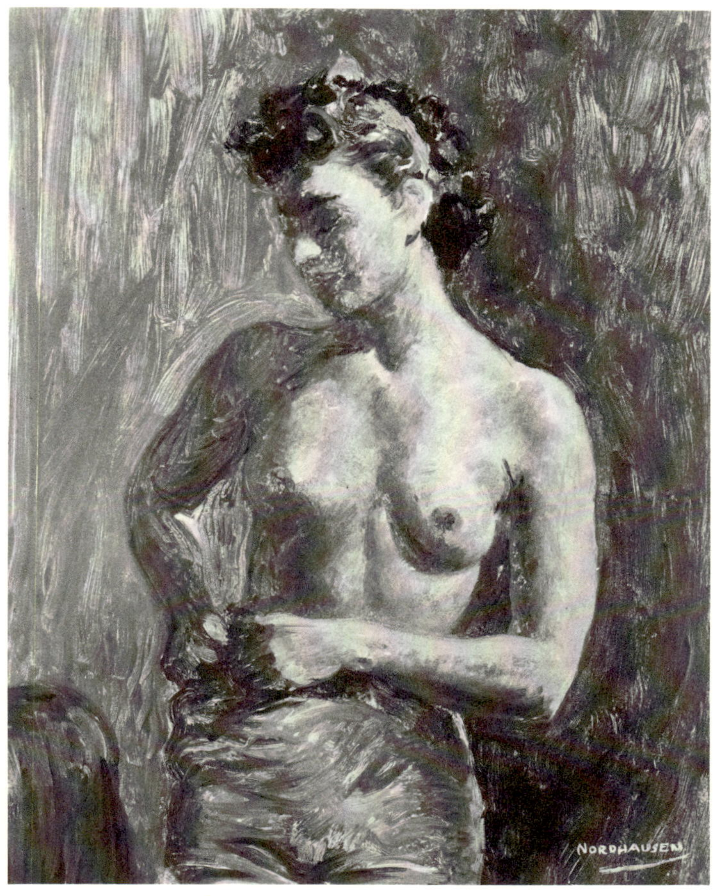

155. *Nude Undressing*

1939
16"x 12"
Monotype
Private collection

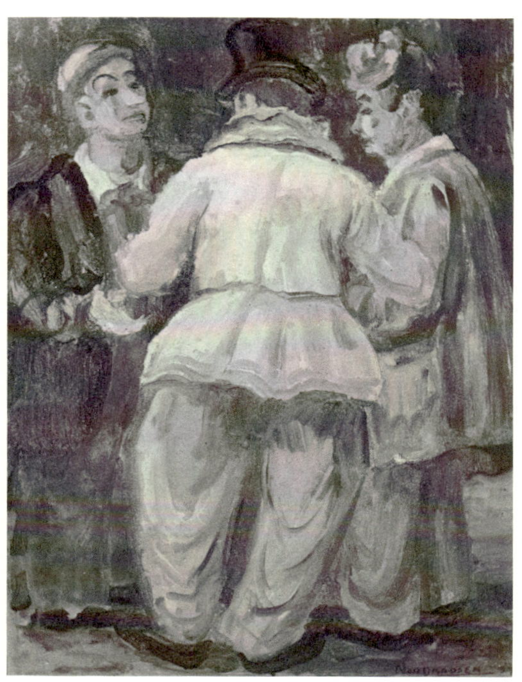

156. *Clown Talk*

The Portrait

W HY THE PORTRAIT?" is a simple question, to which there is an equally simple answer, namely, to preserve the likeness of an individual. But the extension of the question involves a wide variety of associations and requirements that makes the art of portraiture one of the most challenging and frustrating problems in the contemporary artist's repertory.

The representation of the physical or psychological image in a permanent form involves a number of basic factors: the passive representation of the subject as opposed to its creative interpretation; the subject as a specific and unique individual as opposed to its function as a symbol of authority, social rank, or moral character; or again the exploitation either by artist or by subject or by both for a variety of business and promotional purposes, as opposed to the modest seclusion of the work in the owner's home or office.

The solution to these problems has been established in a wide variety of traditional styles, from the Renaissance style of Raphael and Titian, to the Baroque of Rubens and Rembrandt, and the nineteenth-century variations we know as Classicism, Romanticism, Realism, and the multitude of experimental interpretations characteristic of the modern styles.

To Nordhausen and the artists of his generation, these options were available everywhere in the museums, and, as we have seen, Nordhausen's commitment was to the direct and honest realism of Courbet as interpreted by the masters of his Munich apprenticeship. For him the subject takes precedence over artistic inventiveness; it was not to be glorified or idealized but should assert itself through the artist's image with truth as well as personal conviction.

This is all well and good when dealing with a hired model or a volunteer subject where the artist has only himself to please. The commissioned portrait is something different, for in this case the artist does not choose the subject but the client chooses him. Since there is usually a substantial fee involved, the subject or the sponsoring group must be fully satisfied; if not, the project is a failure. Of course many of these "failures" become artistic successes. For example, Sargent's famous portrait of *Madame X*, which was refused by the client, then achieved great notoriety and success at the Paris Salon of 1884 and is now one of the historic masterpieces of the Metropolitan Museum in New York.

In a sense, therefore, commissioned portraiture is a form of commercial art, but in Nordhausen's case it is an integral part of the artist's total and unique character. His attitude toward the problem is best explained in an article entitled "The Business of Portrait Painting" by Katherine Sproehnle which he had kept in his files and used in a number of lectures and demonstrations through the years.*

The occasion was an interview with the famous Spanish painter Ignacio Zuloaga, who in February 1925 had just completed a highly successful exhibition at the Reinhardt Gallery in New York. To the question, "How do you feel when you are painting a portrait?" Zuloaga answered gloomily, "I feel just sick, sick." He had little cause to complain,

* *Saturday Evening Post,* April 11, 1925.

however, since his minimum price was $15,000, and he could choose whom he wanted to paint. "But," he insisted, "I paint for myself—for an exact likeness there is the photograph. For me to work forty years to become a photographer, that isn't much. People change, and if you have an exact likeness at one certain time, a few years later you have nothing. It should be a good picture; and it is character, not likeness, that matters."

By contrast, the author quoted Arthur Halmi, at that time a popular painter of fashionable women. "If a woman is beautiful," he said, "she should be painted that way; if she is not so beautiful she should be painted to get the best out of her." Then, citing the typical woman's quest for beauty through fashionable clothes, cosmetics, hairstyle, and proper exercise, he added, "What is more reasonable than that they should want to be made attractive in pictures to hang in their houses?"

The article recited a number of the standard complaints. One New York matron telephoned the painter Boris Gregoriev after she had had her portrait in her home for over a month: "I don't like the left eye . . . and neither does my husband. My butler saw it and wouldn't have recognized me. Will you please change it?" The artist replied firmly, "No, that's the way I saw you, and still see you." Sargent once defined a portrait as "a picture of somebody with something wrong with the mouth." Nordhausen frequently complained that there are so many people to please, not only the sitter, but the family, their friends, the maid, and the cook—they all have an opinion. "A portrait," he said, "is commonly expected to do everything for a sitter that nature has been unable to do."

Nevertheless, since Nordhausen first undertook the commissioned portrait as a major effort in 1947—that of the ninety-six-year-old Confederate Gen. John W. Moore—he has completed well over five hundred portraits which were considered reasonably successful from both the clients' and the artist's point of view. They represent a wide variety of people of all types—housewives, businessmen, sportsmen, debutantes, generals, admirals, politicians, educators, actors, and clergymen—who are portrayed, not so much as vaunted "men and women of distinction," but as people of character. The recognizable attributes of social or professional rank are there—the white gown of the debutante, the military uniform, or the academic robe—as are the physical and stylistic characteristics of the subject, but these are integrated by that strange combination of the artist's eye, hand, and perceptive intelligence.

The process was described as a kind of "interview" by Hilton Kramer in his thoughtful review of an exhibition of portrait drawings at the Museum of Modern Art, where the "artist and subject are seen to face each other on equal terms . . . in which certain details of character and personal history are vividly revealed. . . . An effective portrait always leaves us with a sense of mysteries beyond the immediately visible."*

This sense of mystery is what Nordhausen had in mind when he referred to the poetic quality of a work of art: "The lens of the camera records mechanically and coldly, but the artist's eye re-

*© 1978 by The New York Times Company. Reprinted by permission.

cords an impression, enhanced by the imagination, which may account for the poetry in art."

Thus it is with the understanding and genial skill of the interviewer that Nordhausen paints the portrait. He does not try to make something out of the subject but lets the subject speak for himself. Contrary to the haughty disdain for the photographer expressed by Zuloaga and many of the "fine" artists of the older generation, Nordhausen sees basically no difference between the problems of the portrait painter and the photographer, except of course the medium. The composition, the use of light, form (i.e., volume), animation (movement), likeness, and character expression are all major concerns of the artist, regardless of whether he is using the brush or the camera.

Indeed, artists have used the photograph since the time of Louis Daguerre, both as reference material and as actual image, even to the extent of the direct copy. At the initial sitting, Nordhausen frequently takes a number of photographs of the subject—sometimes dozens of details of hands, profiles, *en face* views, the total figure from various sides, even drapery and costume details. While he is doing this he notes the characteristic attitudes, movements, and positions the sitter takes which are distinctly his own. Then he works out his ideas of design and composition with this material before the next sitting, when he begins work on the actual canvas.

"I watch the posture of the subject," Nordhausen has said, "the movement of hands, body or head that seem to be the typical gesture of that particular person so as to determine what features should be emphasized. Perhaps it will be a profile view, or full face, or a three-quarter view, or again seen more from above, from the sides, or head-on. A reflected light cast into the shadow often helps explain certain features of form and character. In the case of a profile or a head facing right or left, I usually allow more space in the direction where the head is looking. Photographs and sketches can be used to plan the composition or fine lines of directions to the head."

The crucial decisions are made by the end of the first sitting, which is usually the most interesting session for both artist and subject. This involves the photographs, various sketches, and usually a lively discussion—depending on the person and his response to the artist's questions, stories, jokes, or observations—aimed at a relaxed posture and the often hidden characteristics that make up the personality. The size and shape of the canvas, the proportions of the head and figure, the placement of the lights, and the character of the color are determined not only by the model but also by the setting for which the portrait is intended, whether it is the intimacy of the home, the formality of an office or board room, or the massive open space of a museum or public building. A further consideration is the size and character of other paintings, including portraits, with which it is to be hung.

Nordhausen explains it this way: "some artists and many teachers recommend that the head in a portrait be painted under life-size about eight and a half to eight and three-quarters inches from the top of the head to the bottom of the chin. Such rules or measurements cannot be rigidly followed. If a portrait has to be limited in size to fit into a small wall area the figure of necessity has to be painted

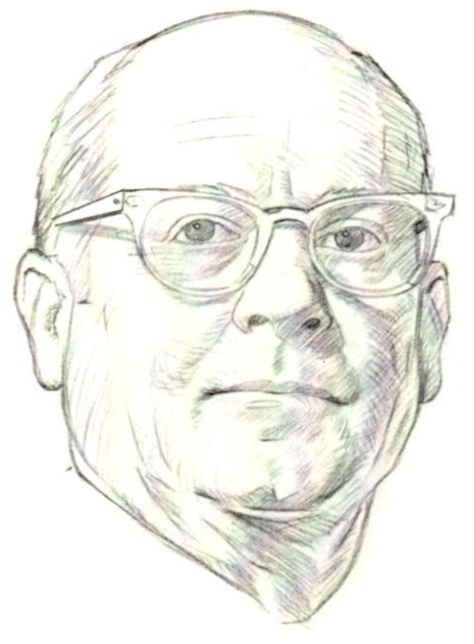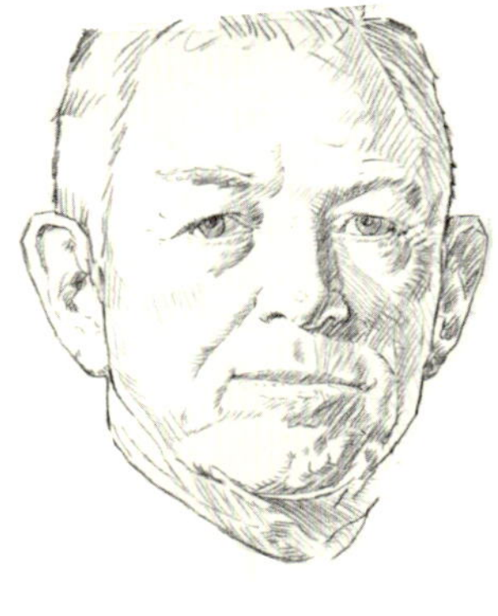

Preliminary portrait studies.

under life-size if most of it is to be included and the canvas is smaller. However, if the portrait is to be hung well over eye level or will hang with other portraits that are over life-size, it is best to paint the portrait well over life-size. One must also be aware of the color of the other portraits as well as that of the wall or room in developing his design."

Once these problems are thought through, either during the first sitting or in the preliminary studies worked out by the artist afterward, he is ready for the second sitting. The subject is drawn in with charcoal on the prepared white canvas, usually a medium smooth linen with an oil ground and then coated with a thin film of shellac and alcohol fixative to protect the drawing from successive layers of paint. The entire canvas is then covered with a transparent color or prime, which is dark enough to give a single unifying tone to the succeeding color composition but light enough so that the drawing shows through and the canvas retains its luminosity.

Depending on the color plan of the painting, this prime coat is composed either of raw umber or of a combination of raw umber and terra verte, blue or burnt sienna, diluted with a painting medium (usually equal parts of linseed oil, turpentine, and damar varnish). As the later colors are built up, this basic tone, tending either toward the warm with the tannish burnt sienna, or the cool with the blue or terra verte, provides a rich, unifying common denominator to the composition. Nordhausen's preference in both portrait and figure composition is the combination of raw umber and terra verte, which has a warm but slightly greenish overtone he feels has the greatest color subtlety and variation.

Next, the large forms with their lights and half tones are wiped out with a soft paint rag. Sometimes these can be varied, experimented with, and changed, since at this point the prime is still wet and can be brushed in or wiped out as the artist pleases. Then the light and half-light areas are built up with the casein white, which, since it is an emulsion and soluble in oil or water, will firmly adhere to the wet film of oil and medium. The casein is applied in two or three thin coats, not a single heavy one, to insure its proper drying and thorough adhesion. The old masters used egg and white lead for this purpose. "They understood," Nordhausen often repeats, "The importance of good underpainting; how it adds to the solidity, permanence and luminosity of the final painting so that it does not tend to darken but becomes richer and more luminous with age."

By the time of the third sitting the underpainting has thoroughly dried; and the casein white areas, since the paint is matt and absorbent, is lightly varnished over to preserve the reflective luminosity of the base in the later colors as they are added. In varnishing the matt casein areas a glazing color may be added, depending on the type of flesh color of the particular sitter, which then makes a better base on which to work. Nordhausen constantly stresses the importance of the large masses and forms rather than the outline of the figure, so that, beginning with the head and hands, these light areas are built up almost in the manner of sculpture, with a heavy application of paint with either a palette knife or a loaded brush to insure a sense of solid structure.

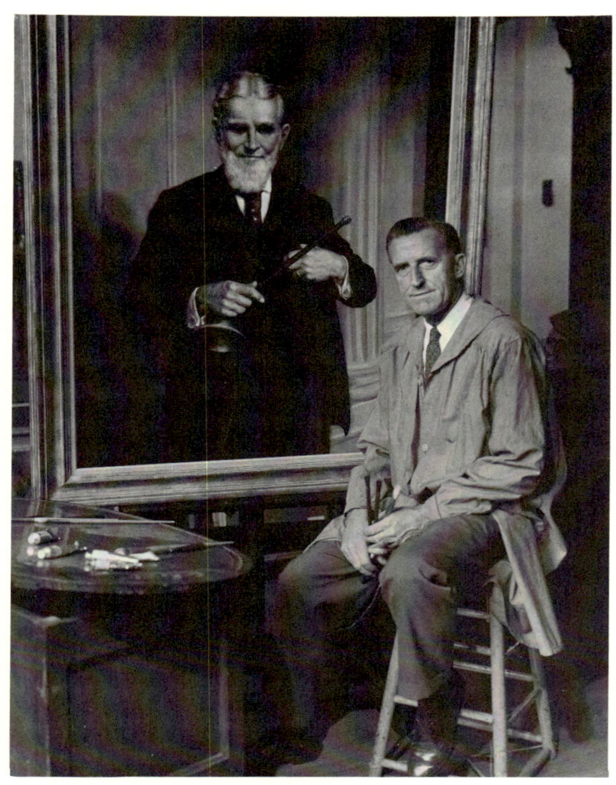

Sometimes at this point Nordhausen begins the applications of glazes of color, that is, the pigment with turpentine, oil, and damar varnish, whereby the juxtaposition of hue, the transparencies of successive layers, and brilliance of the underlying white produce the subtle and elusive optical grays so beautifully managed by the old masters. Nordhausen frequently points out the subtle optical grays in the figure paintings of Peter Paul Rubens, particularly in the cool and silvery transitions from a warm shadow to the rich flesh tones of the lights.

The portrait continues with the secondary and successive areas, drapery, costume, and background, with, as Max Doerner used to stress in his techniques class, a consistent emphasis on the "luminosity of color and the solidity of form."

The modeled white and the glazed color are the principal means to this end: "No color can be made more brilliant in its varied tones of light and dark," Nordhausen once said, "than a glazed one, particularly over white . . . paint in full rich oil color, using the impasto, the scumbling, the glazes, and some of the fine qualities of the underpainting. Such a procedure, properly handled, can lead to a painting that is sound, luminous, rich in texture, and fine in subtle nuances."

In Nordhausen's experience there have been surprisingly few outright rejections of the finished portrait. If somehow he has not been able to establish a rapport with, or comprehend the character of, the sitter, it is he who has made the decision to discontinue the work, often early in the process, and has either destroyed the canvas or painted it over for use on something else. In several cases a sponsoring group has not been able to raise the money for payment, and he has kept the portrait for exhibition purposes; eventually, someone buys it anyway. The best indication of success, however, is the fact that most of the clients have become lasting and devoted friends, and the correspondence reveals not only letters of appreciation but a continuing dialogue of mutual interests and affection.

One such letter, from a knowledgeable and affectionate patron and friend in the early years, was written by Frank Alvah Parsons, then president of the New York School of Fine and Applied Arts and his teacher in both studio and classes on the history of art.

"There are two ways in which men believe a work of art may be produced," he wrote. "One results in the form or body of a thing without life or soul, the other is the expression of the artist's conception of spirit and soul and the body as a means of conveying this expression to others.

"You have shown in the portrait you have done for me the latter of these two methods in no uncertain terms. From the very moment we came together for the first sitting, I felt you rather than saw you putting your whole soul into the recognition of and expressing the best things you could find to express. . . .

"Besides the portrait itself, which I shall value more than I can tell you, there is a feeling that comes with it of your interest, your enthusiasm and the affectionate endeavor which every man appreciates more than any object itself" (January 25, 1927).

A more complicated problem appears when the client wants a portrait of a deceased person. This was the situation when Nordhausen was commissioned by Syracuse University in 1976 to paint portraits of the two principal donors, Mr. and Mrs. Ernest Stevenson Bird, for the new Bird Library. Mr. Bird had died only a short time before. There were no official photographs available, only a few inadequate snapshots which his widow managed to collect. Obviously, the reconstruction of the appearance, let alone the personality of a deceased person, is something that could not be done by a photographer.

Using the techniques of a police reporter, the artist tried a number of sketches from the fuzzy snapshots, then proceeded to gather all the information he could from the subject's family and friends—everything from the color of the subject's eyes and hair, his habits, conversation, expressions, height and weight, and his clothes and the way he wore them.

With more sketches and comments from those who knew the subject, he proceeded in his Georgia studio, using as an initial model a friend of similar age and size. Without further comment or discussion, the finished portrait was installed, along with that of Mrs. Bird, in a special room in the new library. At the dedication, in the presence of Mrs. Bird, the university officials, other patrons, and friends of the family, the appropriate speeches were made and the covering curtains were pulled to one side. There was an awful moment of silence; then suddenly a soft, half-choked voice was heard—Mrs. Bird's: "My God, that's my husband," followed by another, "There is Steve!" and the applause indicated the successful completion of the artist's mission.

The attempt to immortalize an individual with a commissioned portrait presents other problems. Either because of delay on the part of corporation or university officials or reluctance on the part of the subject, the request for a portrait often does not come until the subject is a tired and crotchety old man instead of the dynamic executive or scholar he may once have been. So the artist, if possible, is obliged to reconstruct the original character and personality as best he can.

In most cases, Nordhausen has been able to accomplish an honest and direct portrayal of the subject as he sees it to the satisfaction of all concerned. The portrait of Gen. John W. Moore, who hated Yankees (Nordhausen's New York accent is always clearly perceptible), and at the age of ninety-six was still leading Confederate soldiers against the northern invaders, is depicted as a strong but sympathetic character. That of Annie Louise MacLeod, painted in her Florida retirement, reveals the kindly elegance and scholarly insight that distinguished her career as dean of the College of Home Economics at Syracuse University. So it is with the wide variety of people and personalities of all ages and types from exuberant youngsters on their good behavior to the bearded grandfather with his old-fashioned hearing aid. They are honest and straightforward characterizations—and most important, they are good paintings as well.

Social acceptance has long been of considerable importance—and sometimes a problem—for the artist in America, particularly the portrait painter. 1959 marked a change in the pattern of Nordhausen's career in this respect when an exhibition of work by New York painters, including several figure studies by Nordhausen, was held at the Columbus Museum of Arts and Sciences. Impressed by what he called "the sensitivity and sound craftsmanship," and the color which "enhances these necessary qualities but is not insistent in itself," the director, Edward S. Shorter, invited the artist to lecture and give a painting demonstration on the art of portraiture for the museum membership.

The success of this performance led to extensive entertainment and introduction to a wide circle of enthusiastic friends and supporters largely under the guidance of Ethel Chandler Williams, a Museum trustee who had long been prominent in Columbus society. Through her influence, there developed a large number of portrait commissions and the sale of many easel paintings, including ballet and circus figures, still lifes, and landscapes. In 1960 Nordhausen established a studio in the heart of downtown Columbus, and a few years later the Museum was able to mount an exhibition of sixty portraits of Columbus celebrities he had painted during this brief period. This exhibition, in turn, led to further commissions in other cities of Georgia, Alabama, South Carolina, and Virginia, and his continuing success prompted the remark during a recent television interview that "Columbus discovered America in 1492, but I discovered Columbus in 1959."

The technical procedure as described here —from the prepared canvas to the drawing, the prime, the laying in of the whites for the forms, the multiple glazes, and the final color composition —is essentially the same in all of Nordhausen's painting in the oil medium, whether the subject is a still life, a landscape, or a complicated figure composition. It is included in the discussion of portraiture because it demonstrates the close association of the technical problems of painting, drawing, and design with the aesthetic problems of color and composition and the more subtle and complicated psychological problems of the subject and the ultimate purpose of the work of art.

Nordhausen's interest in the personality and character of the subject in portraiture is an obvious and necessary part of the project, but the same concern was observed in the figure studies, the ballet dancers, the circus clowns, and even in such "impersonal" themes as the landscapes and the still lifes. Each model, whether a ballet dancer or clown, a friend, or a professional model hired through an agency, was a subject of intense study as an individual, which accounts in part for the reoccurrence of the same model in not one but often a series of paintings with their intriguing variations in expressive character.

It is this thorough integration of the various technical, aesthetic, and iconographical problems into a totality of expression that places Nordhausen in a unique position among the artists of our time. The lofty disdain frequently revealed in comments about a given artist as merely a technician or merely an illustrator, a realist, or again, an imitator of historical styles, has often created a misunderstanding by focusing attention on only one facet of the artist's work.

With his persistent and outgoing enthusiasm, wide range of ideas and activity, and substantial body of work accomplished over a sixty-year period, Nordhausen has demonstrated that an artist can indeed survive the fragmenting pressures of modern times and that the standards and artistic quality of the old masters can be maintained today as they have been in the past.

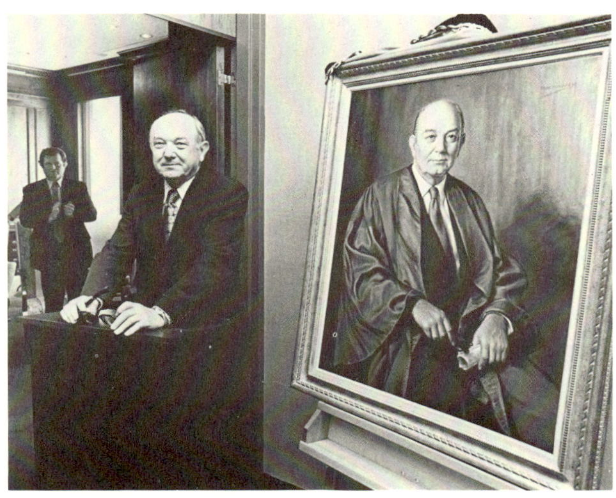

Unveiling of portrait of former Secretary of State Dean Rusk at the University of Georgia on May 4, 1974. Senator Edward Kennedy is at the left rear.

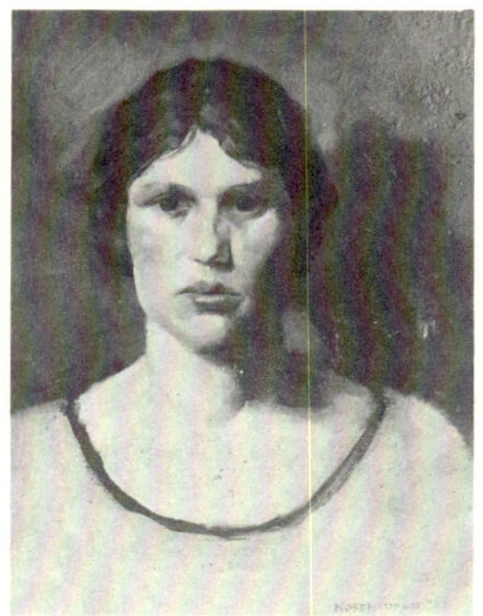

157. *Head of a Woman*

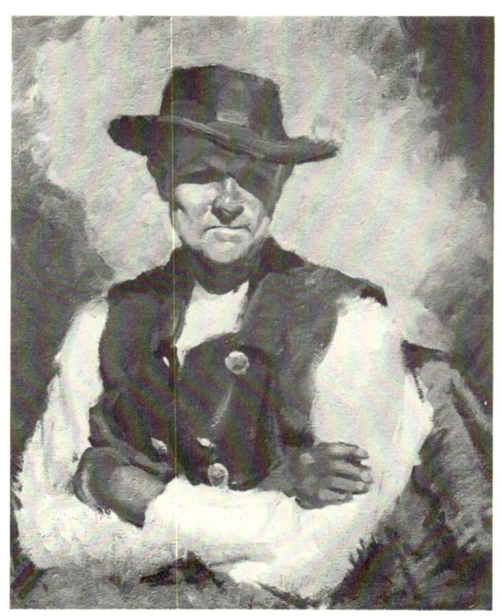

158. *Bavarian Peasant in Sunshine*

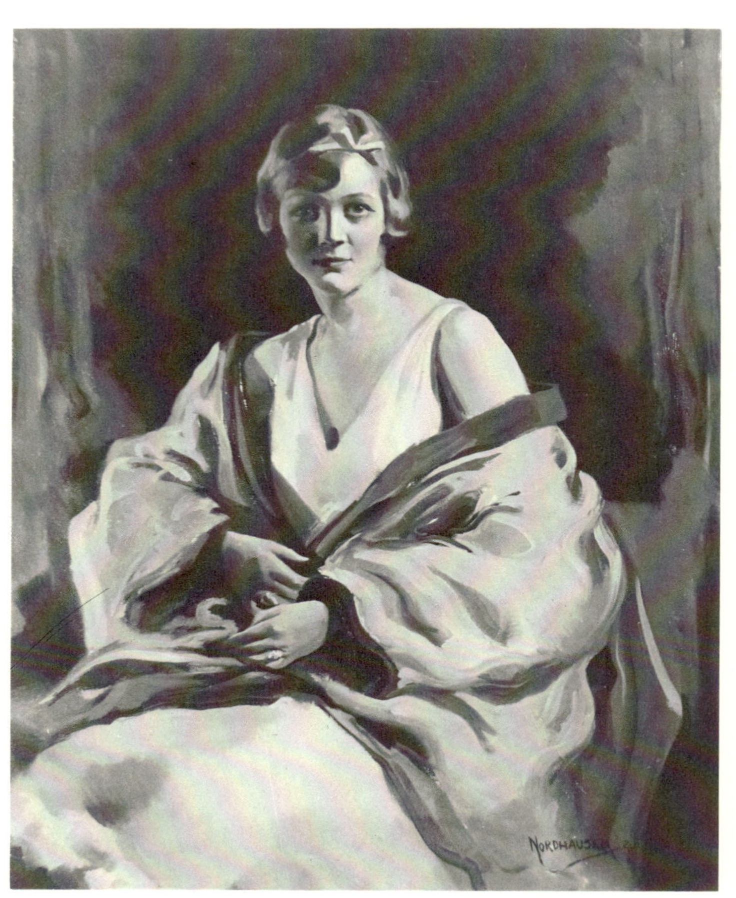

159. *Queenie Smith*

1926
40" x 30"
Oil on canvas
Private collection

1926
40" x 30"
Oil on canvas
Private collection

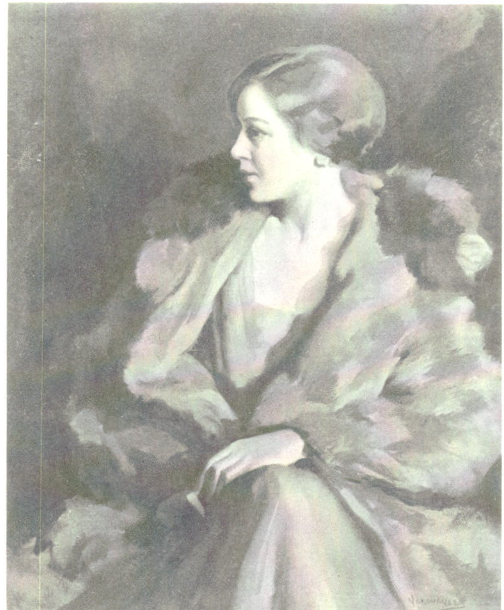

160. *Miss Betty Hunner*

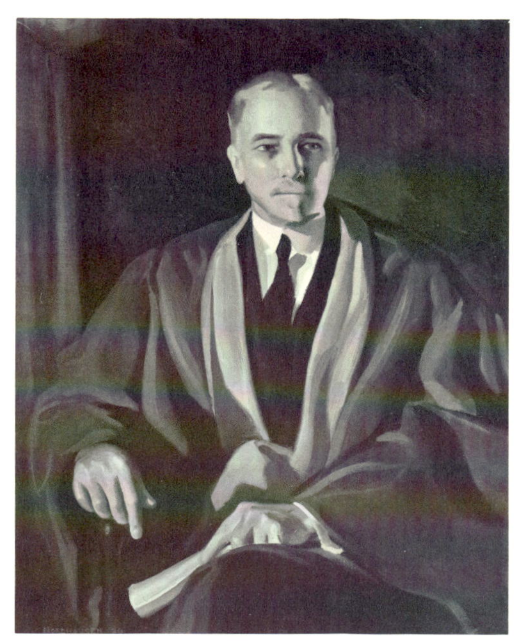

161. *Dr. Guy L. Hunner*

1926
36" x 28"
Oil on canvas

1926
36" x 28"
Oil on canvas

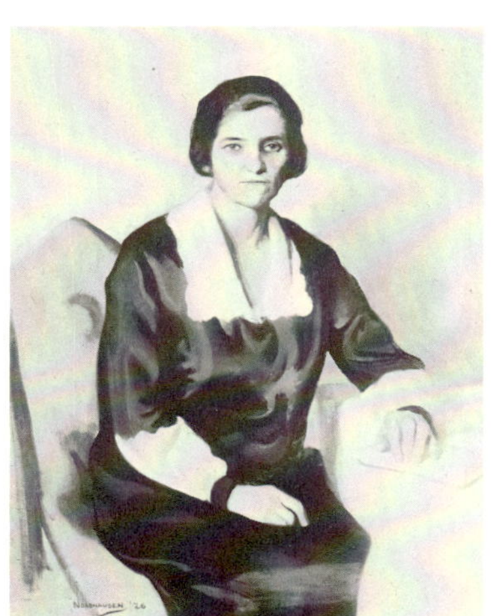

162. *Mother*

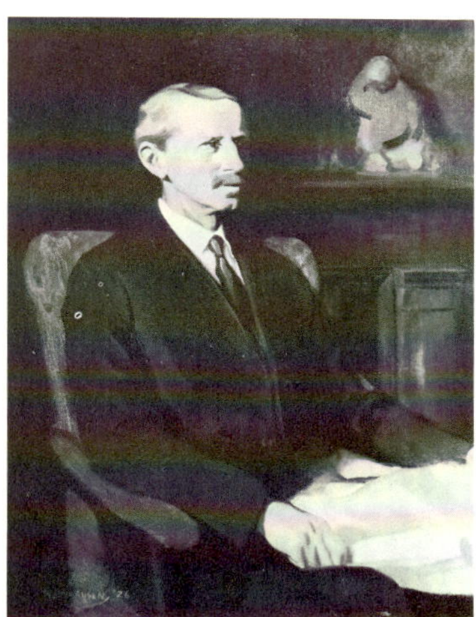

163. *Father*

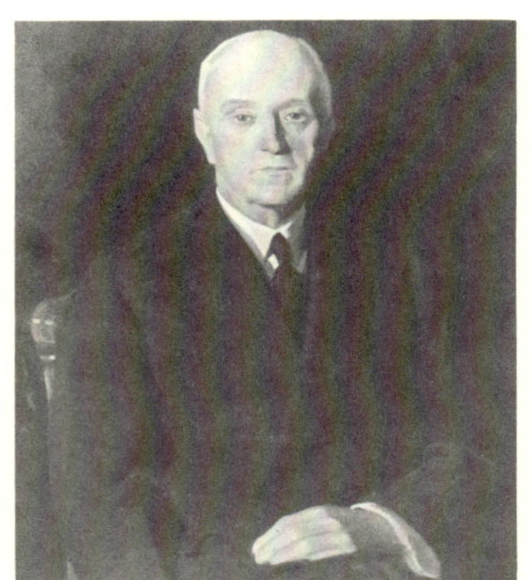

165. *Frank Alvah Parsons*

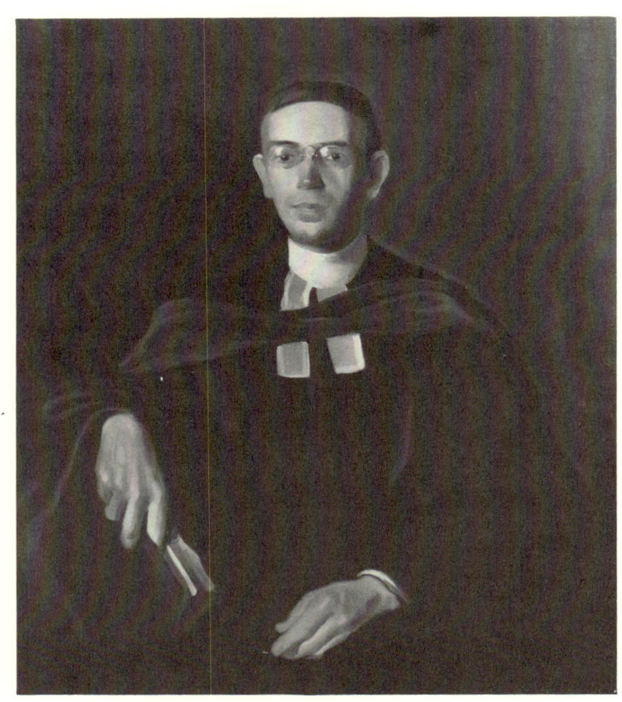

164. *The Reverend L. M. Johnston*

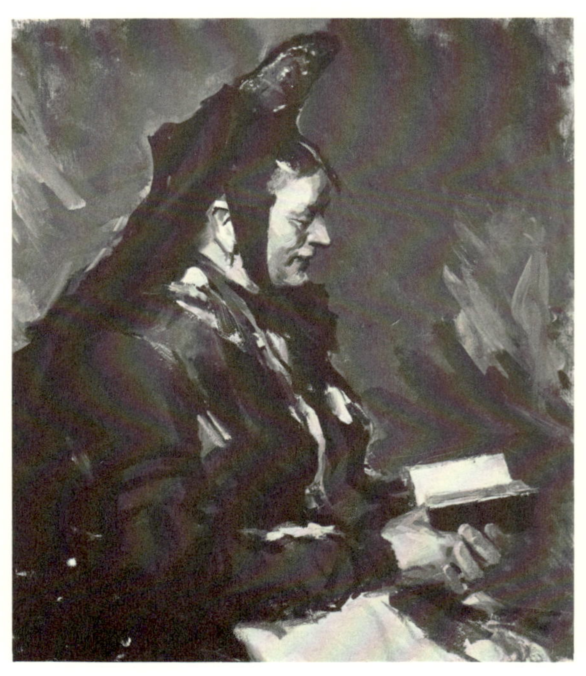

166. *Bavarian Peasant*

Nordhausen / 132

1929
40″x 30″
Oil on canvas

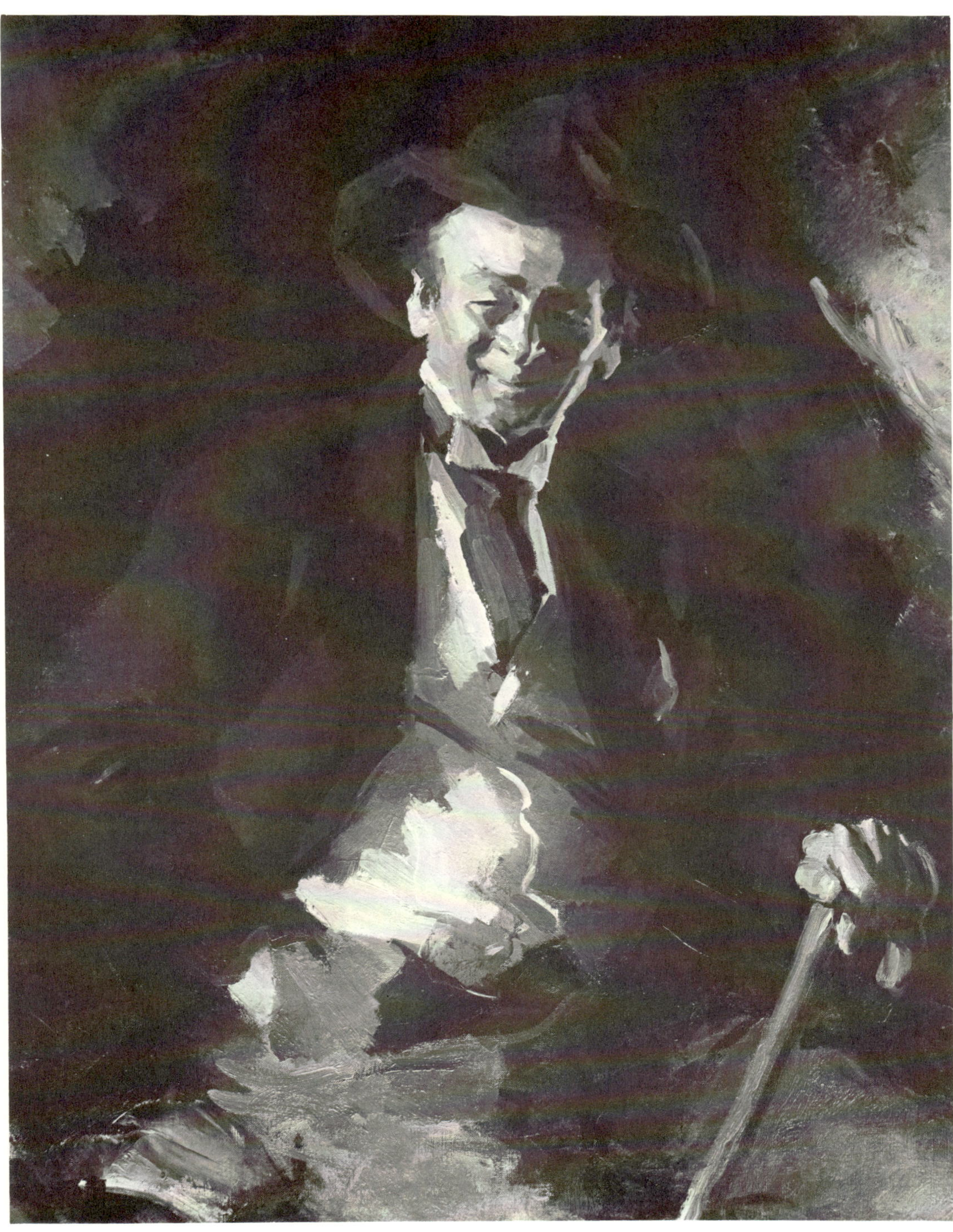

167. *Man with a Cane (the Poet)*

1929
40″x 32″
Oil on canvas
Private collection

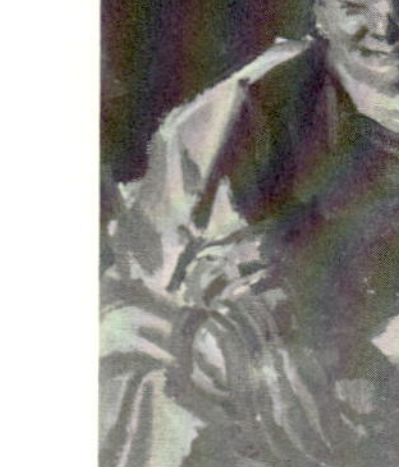

169. Woman with Jug

1929
20″x 16″
Oil on canvas
Private collection

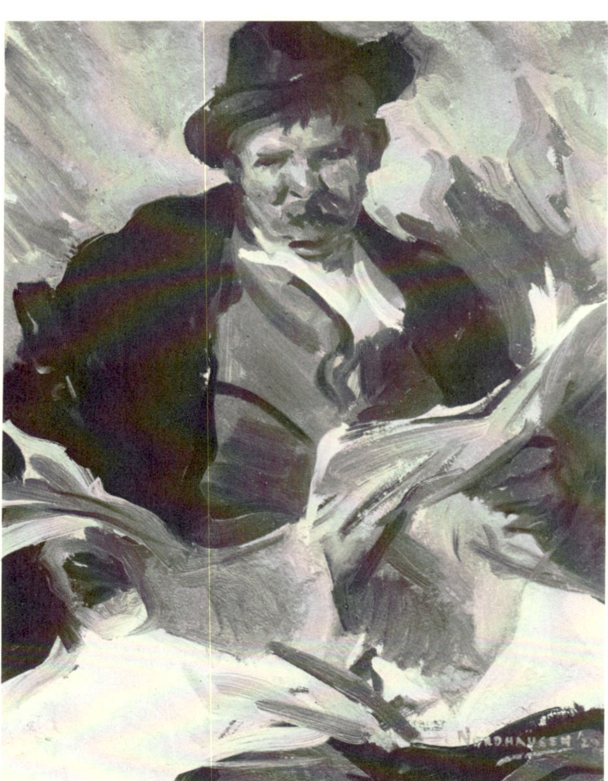

168. Bavarian with Newspaper

1929
30″x 24″
Oil on canvas

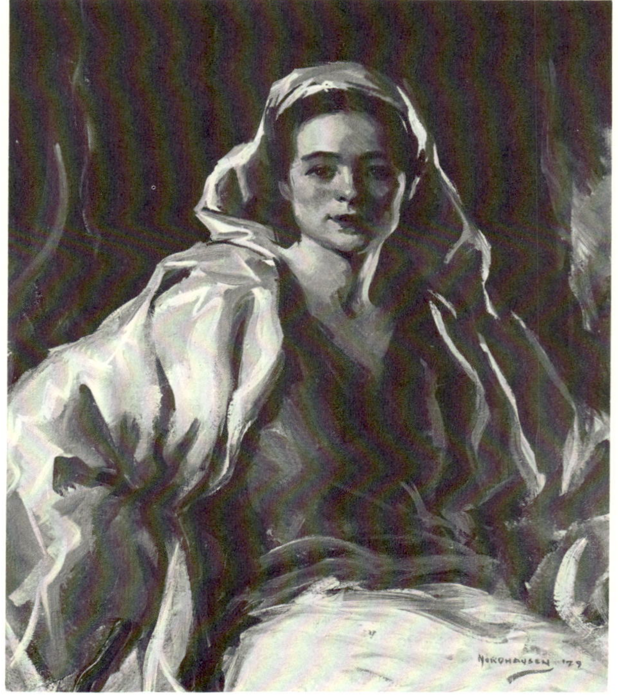

170. The Gold Shawl

1929
30″x 24″
Oil on canvas

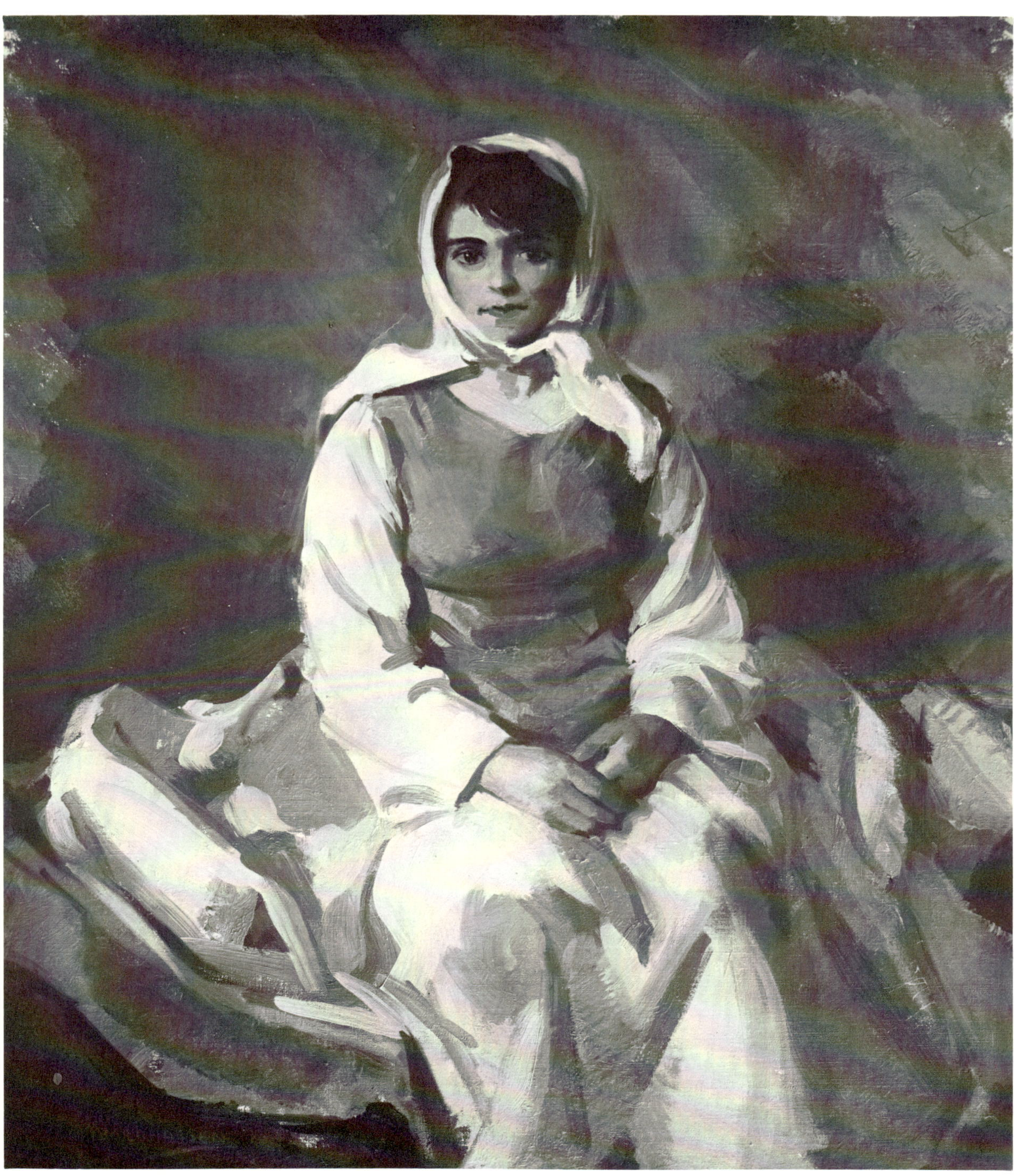

171. *Girl in Costume (Susie)*

1929
37"x 28"
Oil on canvas
Private collection

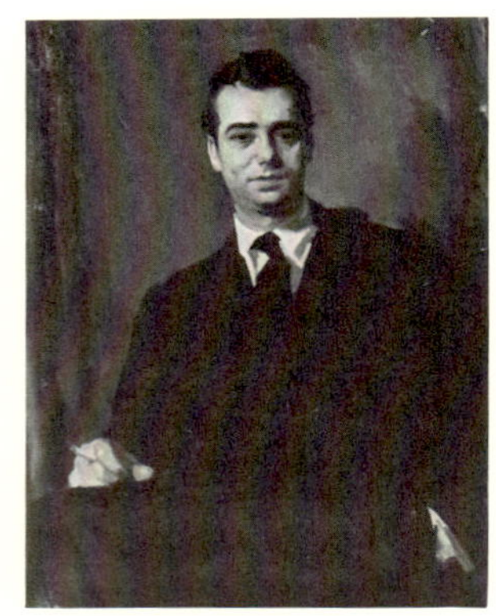

173. *Edwin Malone*

1929
28"x 22"
Oil on canvas
Schmeckebier Collection, Lyme, N.H.

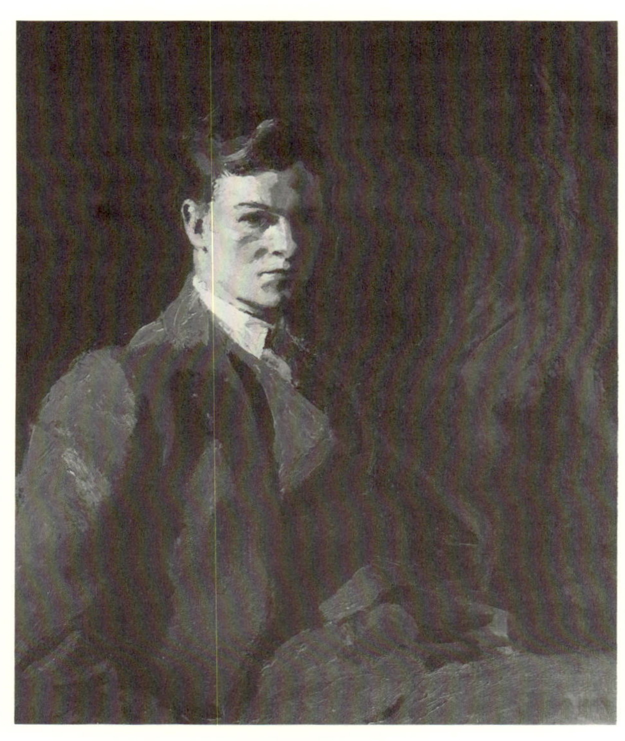

172. *Laurence Schmeckebier*

1930
38"x 32"
Oil on canvas
Collection: Georgia Institute of Technology

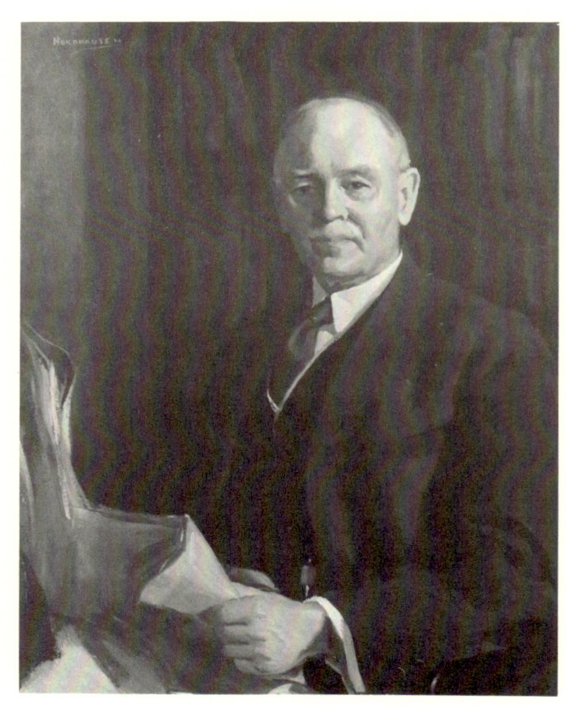

174. *President Martin Luther Brittain*

1930
30"x 24"
Oil on canvas
Stolen from the Georgia Institute of Technology

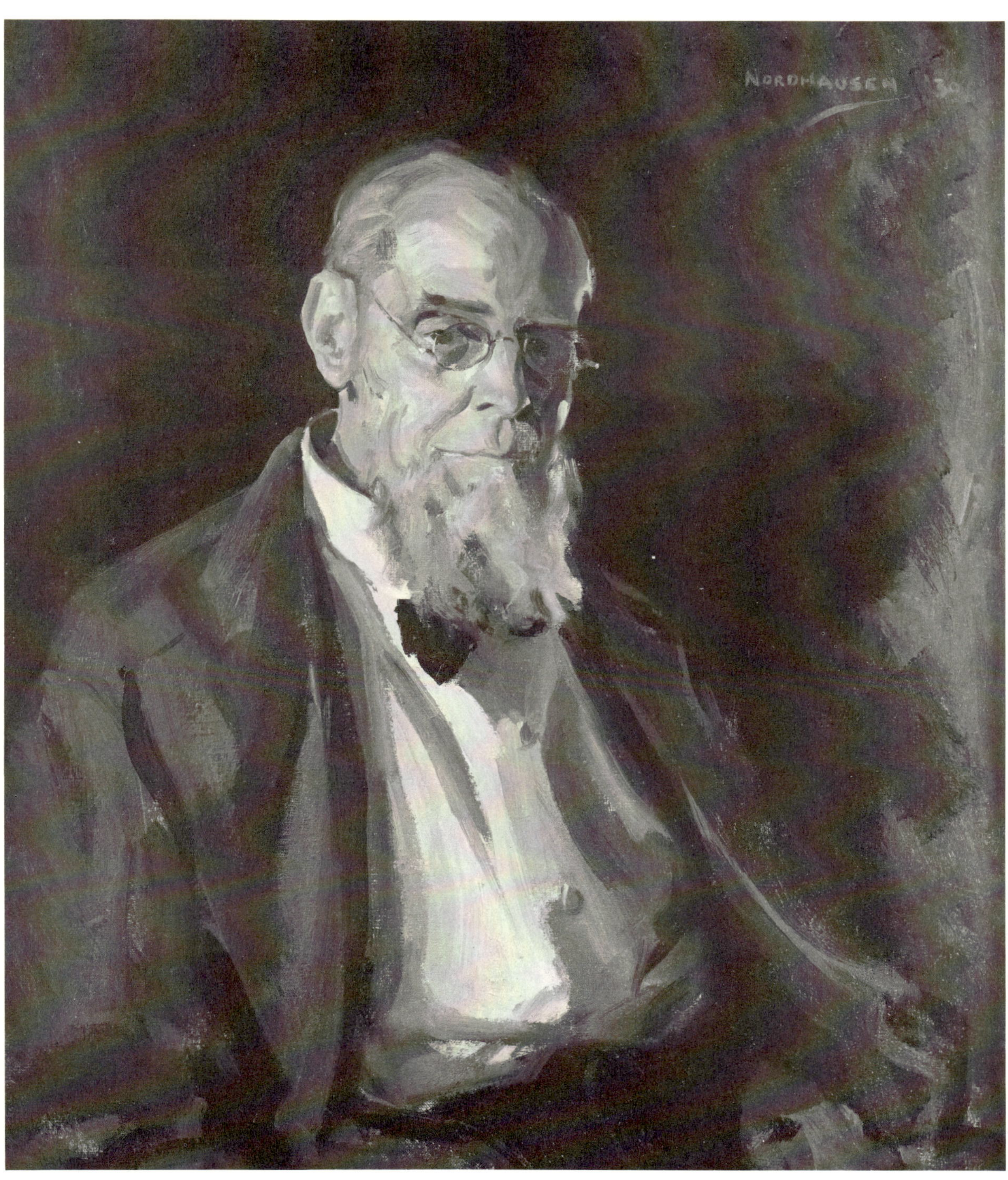

175. *Professor Heneker (Uncle Heinie)*

1939
22″ x 18″
Oil on canvas

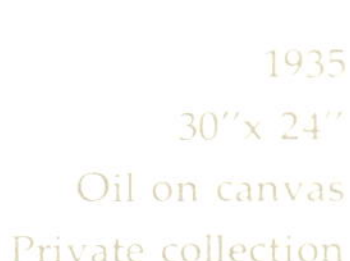

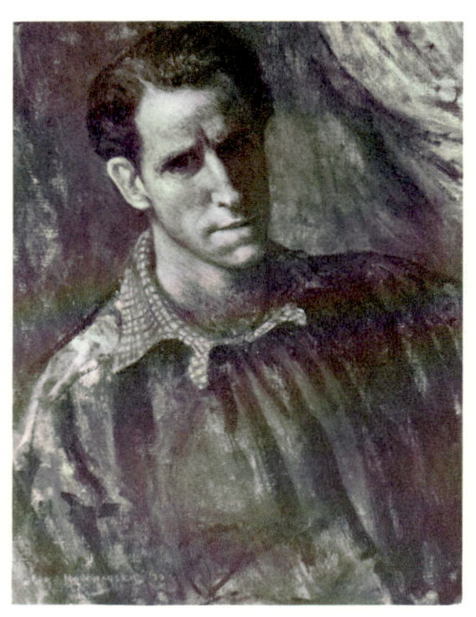

177. *Self Portrait*

1935
30″ x 24″
Oil on canvas
Private collection

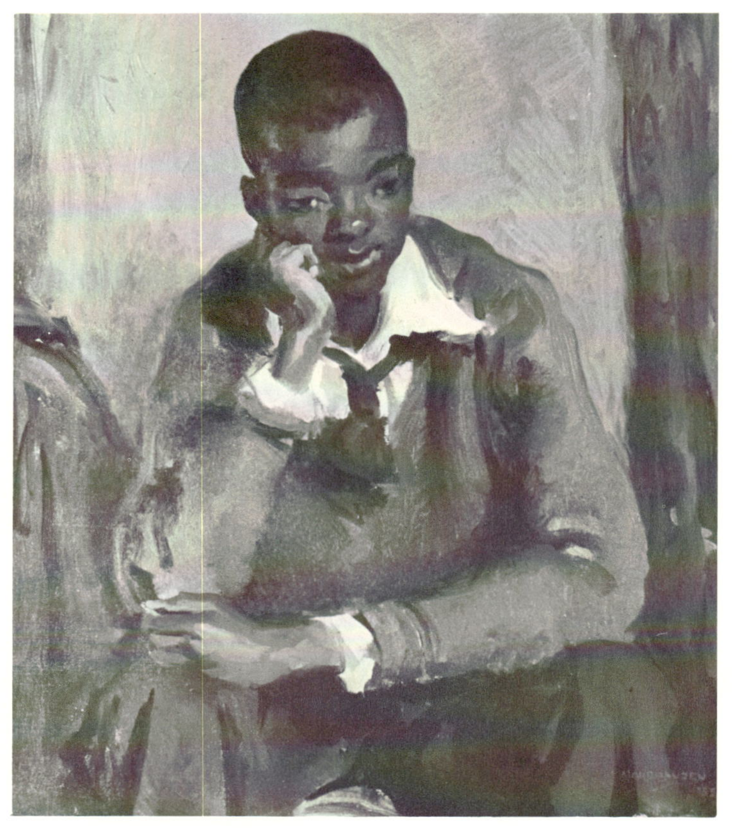

176. *Negro Boy*

1940
20″ x 16″
Oil on canvas
Kriendler Collection, New York City

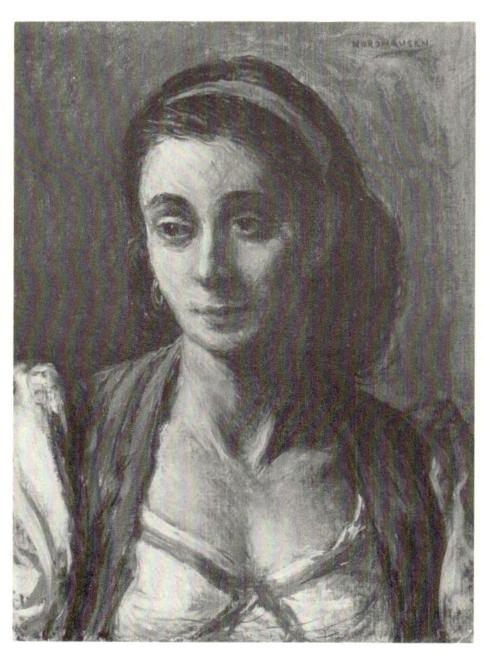

178. *Gypsy Girl*

1940
24" x 20"
Oil on canvas
Pepsi Cola "Paintings of the Year" Award, 1948
Kelbl Collection, New York City

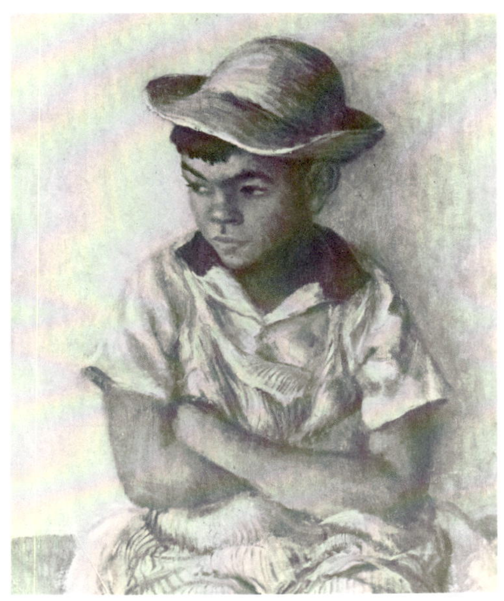

179. *Puerto Rican Boy*

1947
30" x 28"
Oil on canvas
Collection: Virginia Military Institute

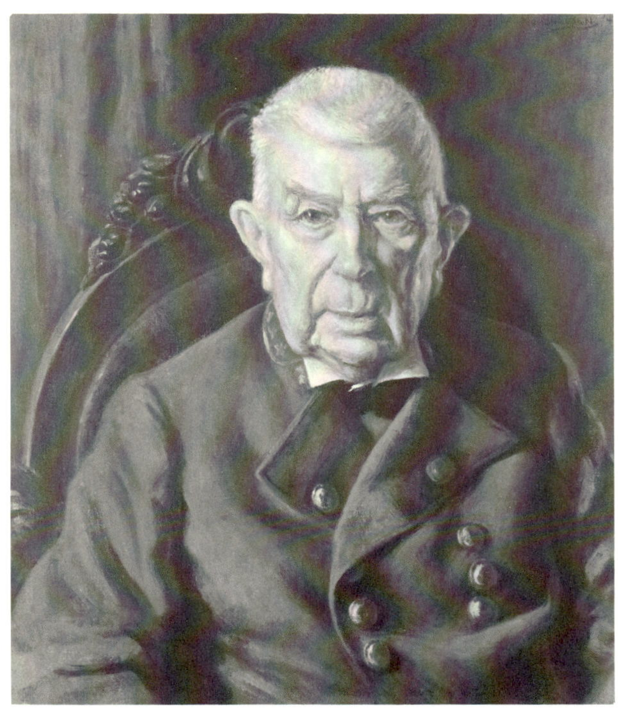

181. *General John W. Moore*

1940
24" x 18"
Oil on canvas
Private collection

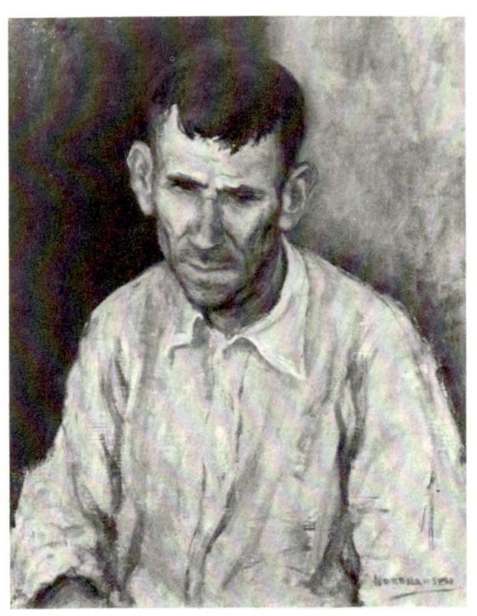

180. *Blind Man, Puerto Rico*

139 / *The Portrait*

1950
20″ x 16″
Oil on board

1950
25″ x 20″
Oil on canvas

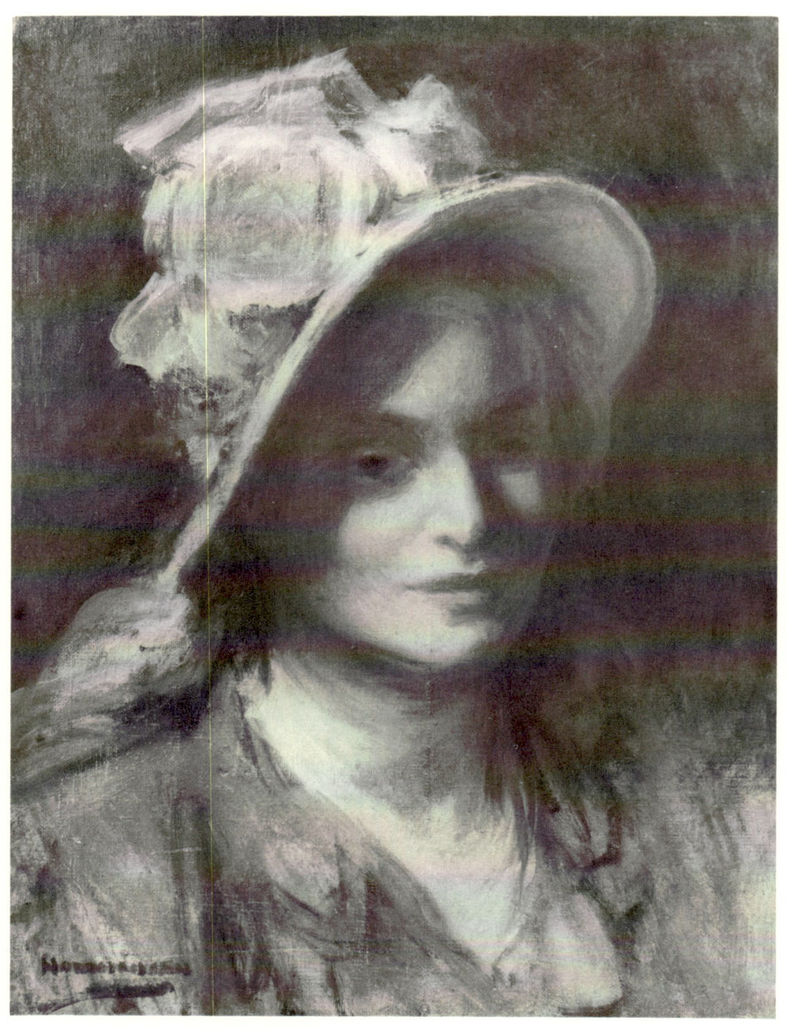

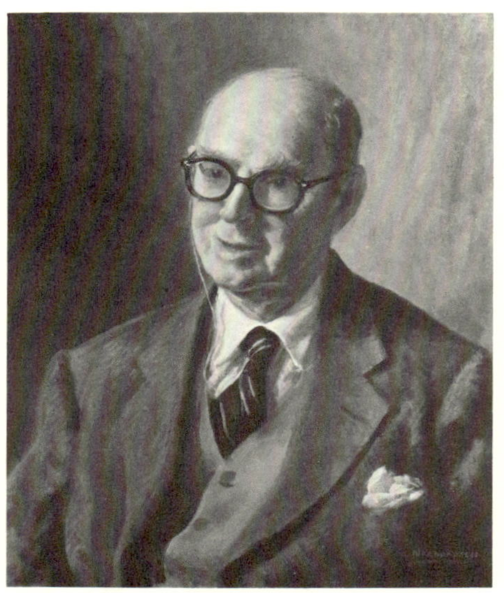

183. *Harrison Cady*

1951
30″ x 24″
Oil on canvas

182. *The New Hat*

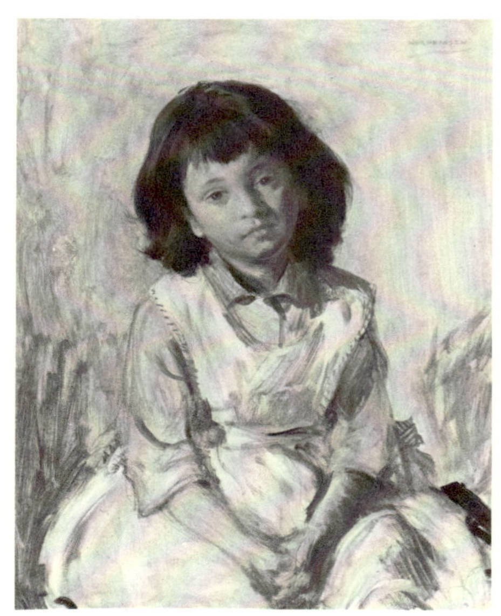

184. *Forget Me Not*

1952
20" x 16"
Oil on canvas
Rayvid Collection, Mount Vernon, N.Y.

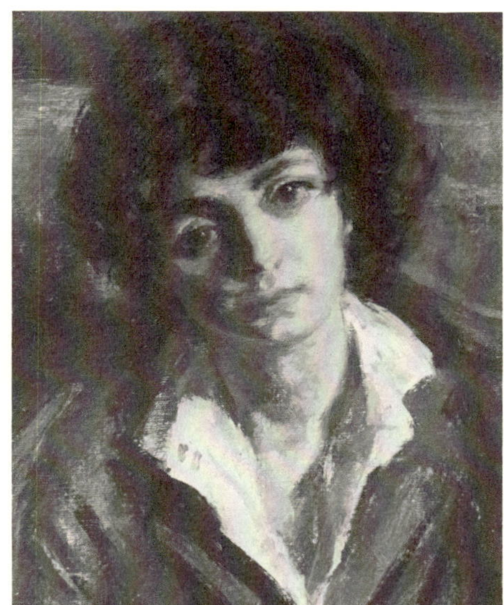

185. *Florentine Girl*

1952
20" x 16"
Oil on canvas

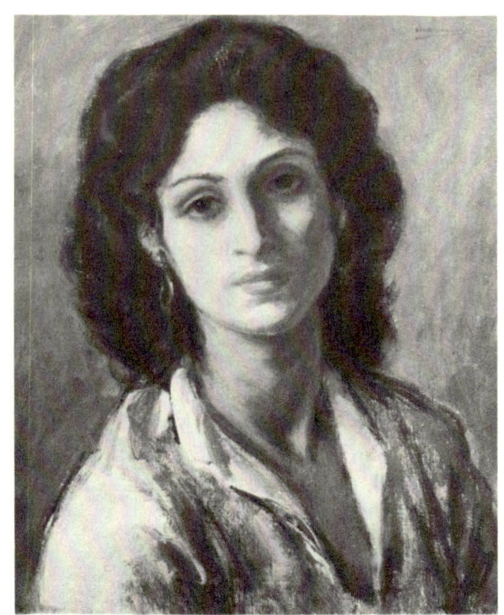

186. *Sardinian Girl*

1956
24" x 20"
Oil on canvas
Collection: Columbus Museum of Arts and Sciences

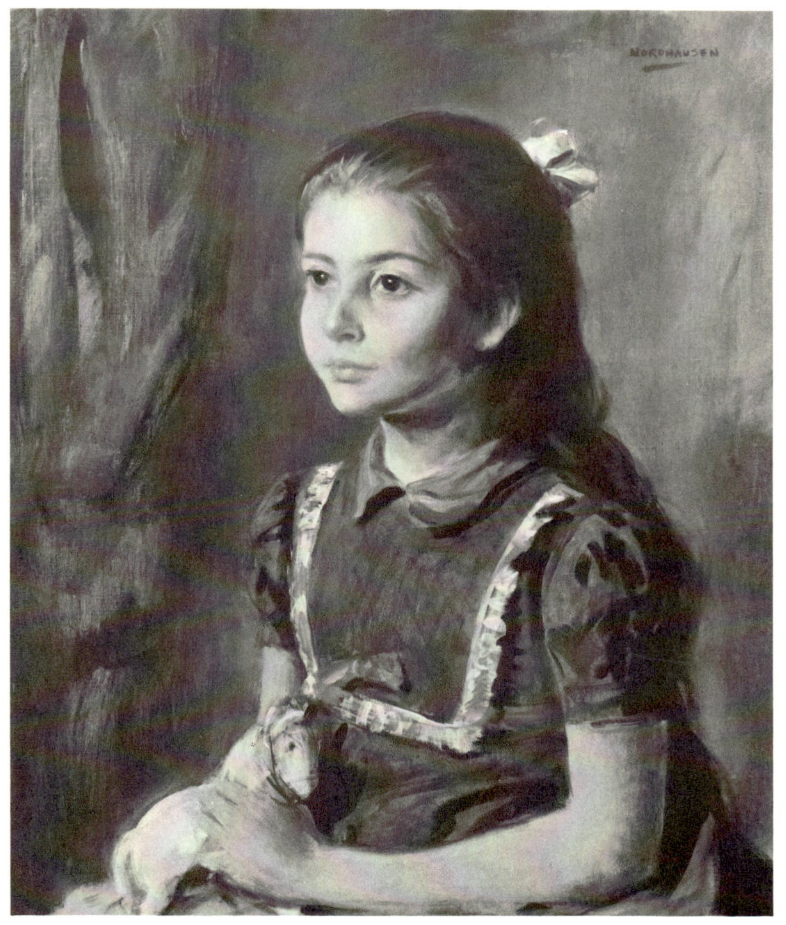

187. *Jean*

141 / *The Portrait*

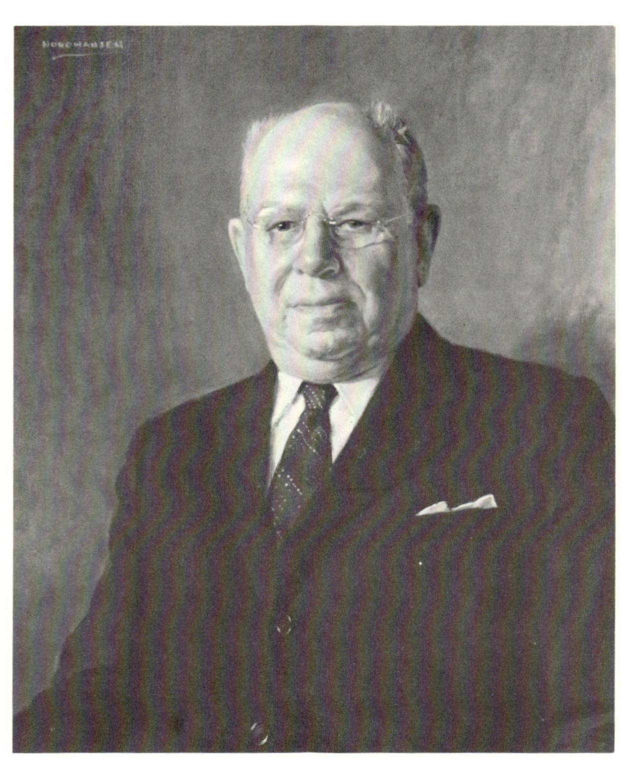

189. *Irwin Rothschild*

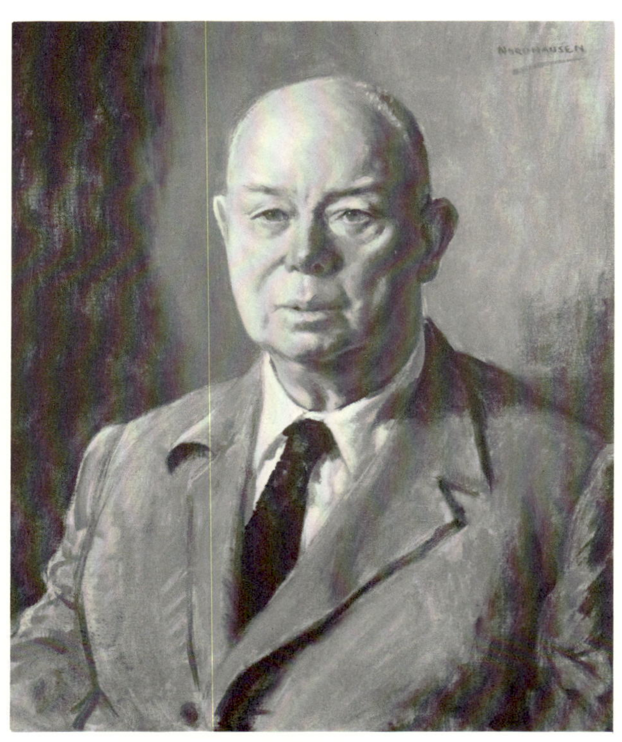

188. *Jean Renoir*

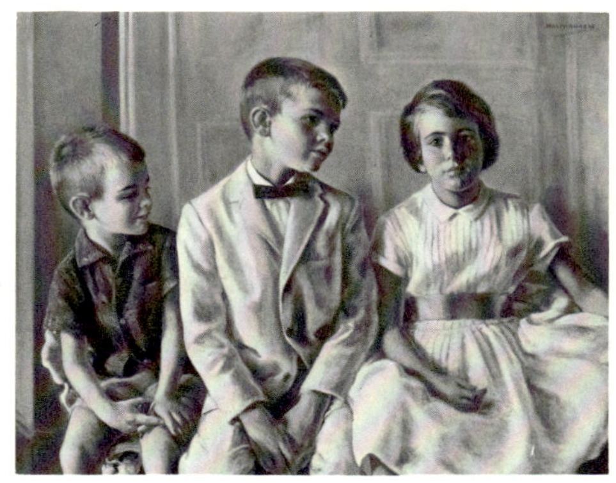

190. *The Foley Children*

1960
40"x 30"
Oil on canvas
Feighner Collection, Columbus, Ga.

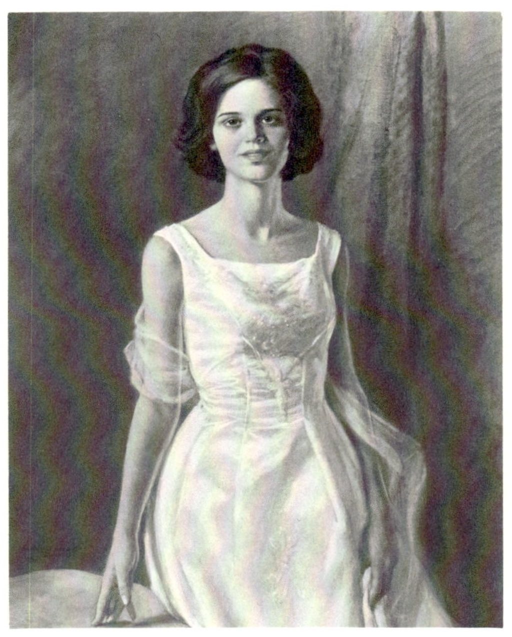

191. *Miss Celia Gary*

1960
36"x 30"
Oil on canvas
Passailaigue Collection, Columbus, Ga.

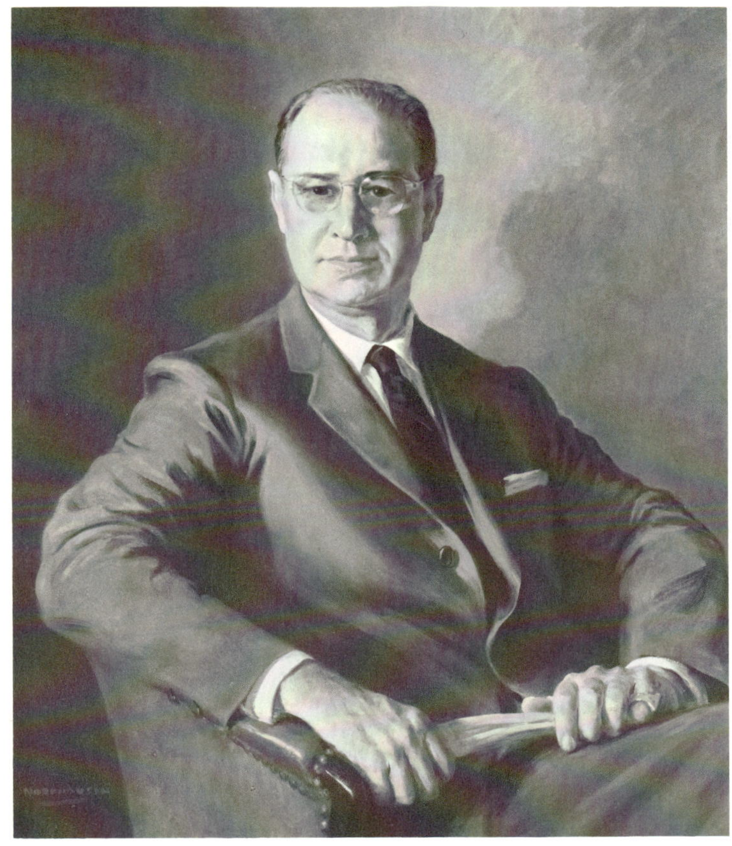

192. *Jack Passailaigue*

1965
40"x 32"
Oil on canvas
Taylor Collection, Atlanta, Ga.

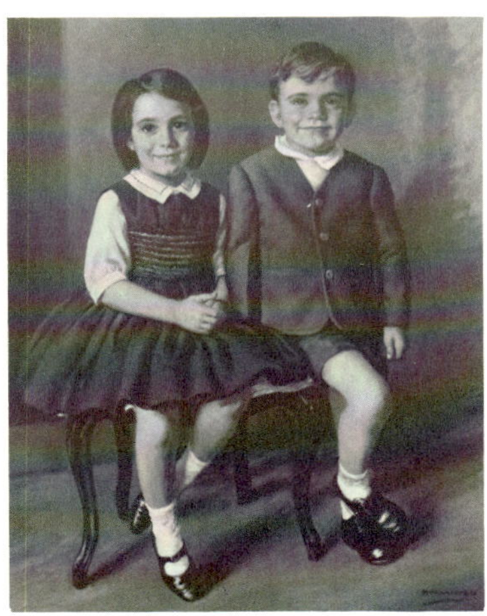

193. *The Taylor Children*

143 / *The Portrait*

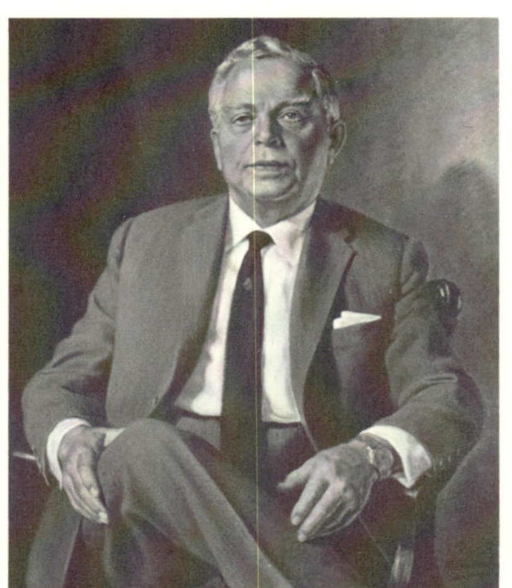

194. Samuel I. Newhouse

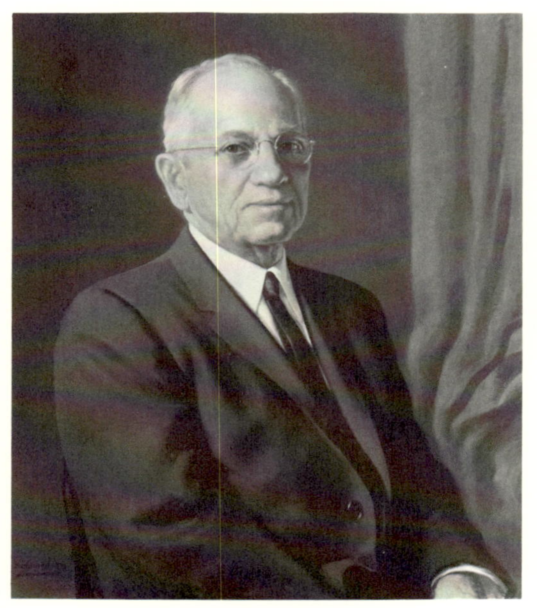

195. D. Abbott Turner

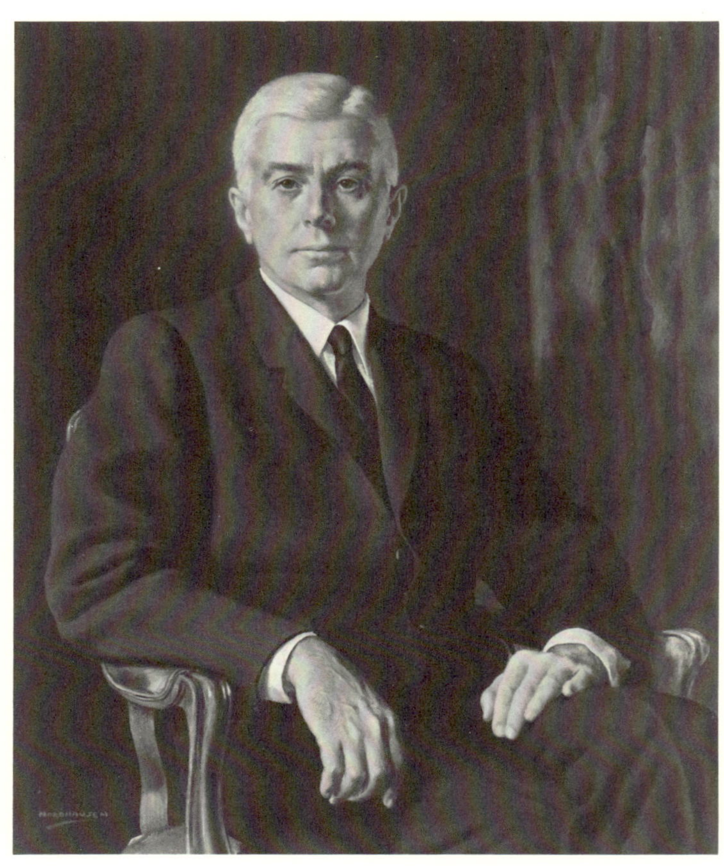

196. William T. Young

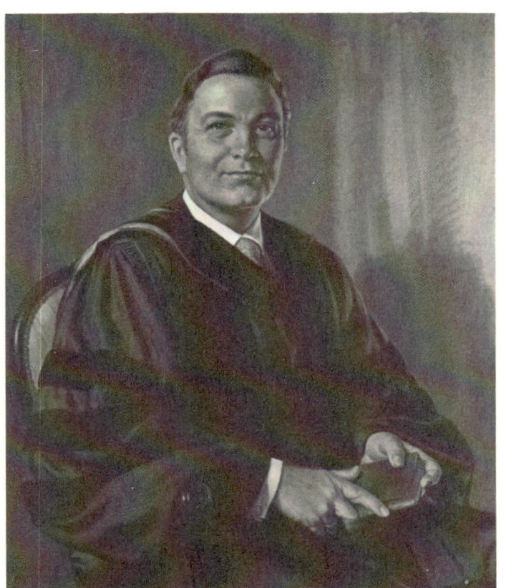

197. *Dr. Othell Hand*

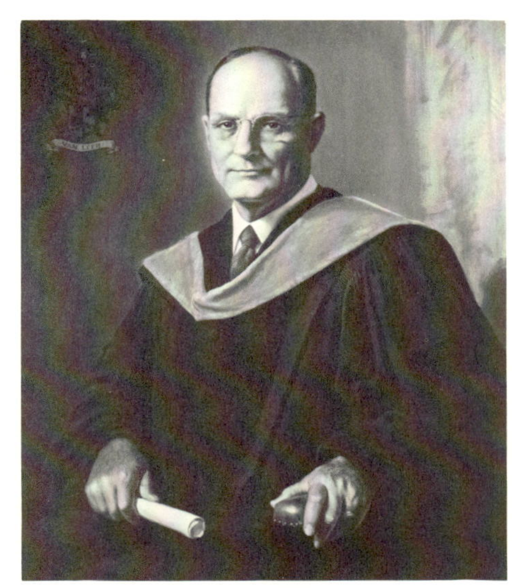

199. *Colonel Blake Ragsdale Van Leer*

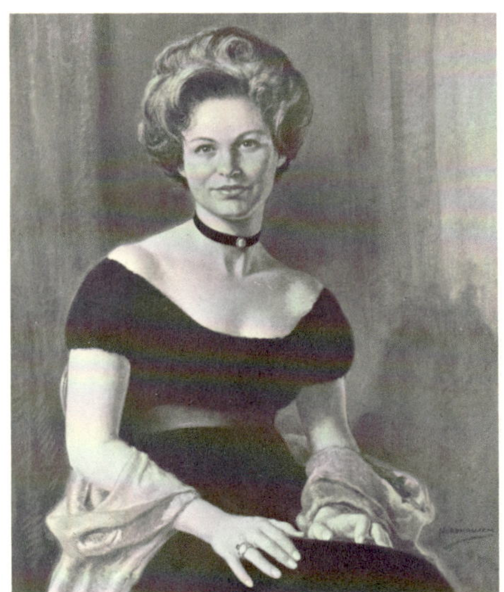

198. *Mrs. George E. Lipscomb*

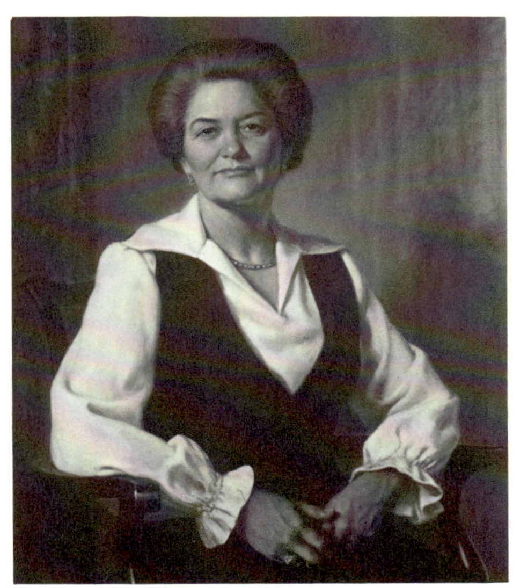

200. *Mrs. Nathaniel Hardin*

1974
42″ x 32″
Oil on canvas
Hawkins Collection, Columbus, Ga.

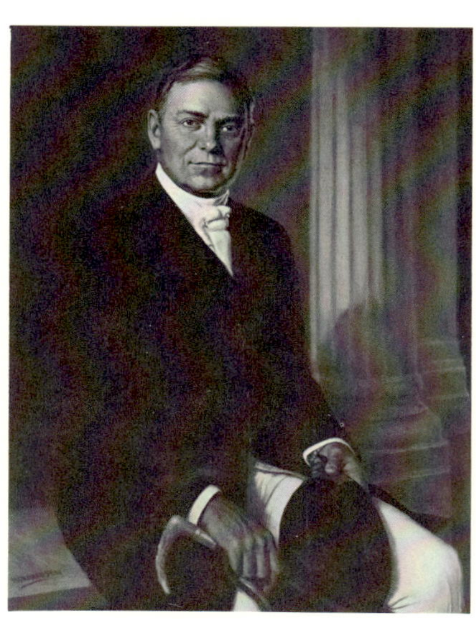

202. *Fitzgerald Hudson*

1973
38″ x 30″
Oil on canvas
Collection: University of Georgia

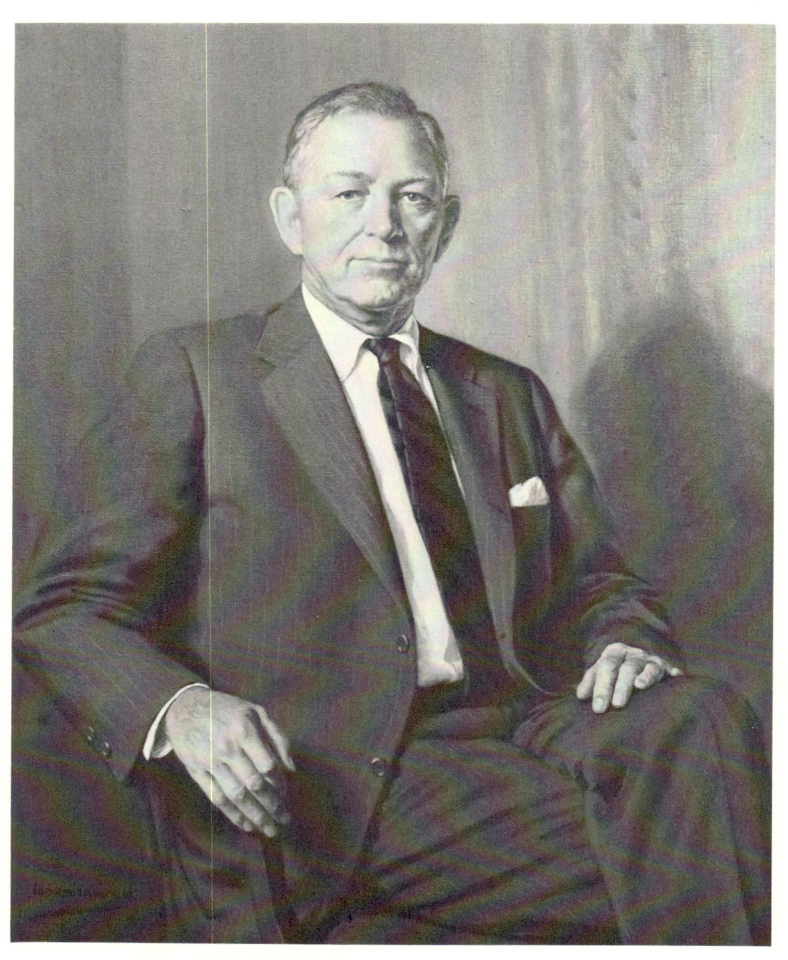

201. *Philip H. Alston, Jr.*

1975
38″ x 30″
Oil on canvas
Collection: Litho-Krome Co., Columbus, Ga.

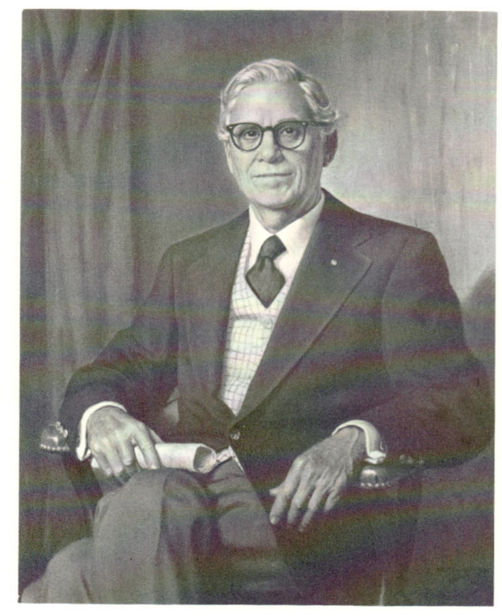

203. *J. Thomas Morgan, Jr.*

1977
38" x 30"
Oil on canvas
Collection: St. Lawrence University

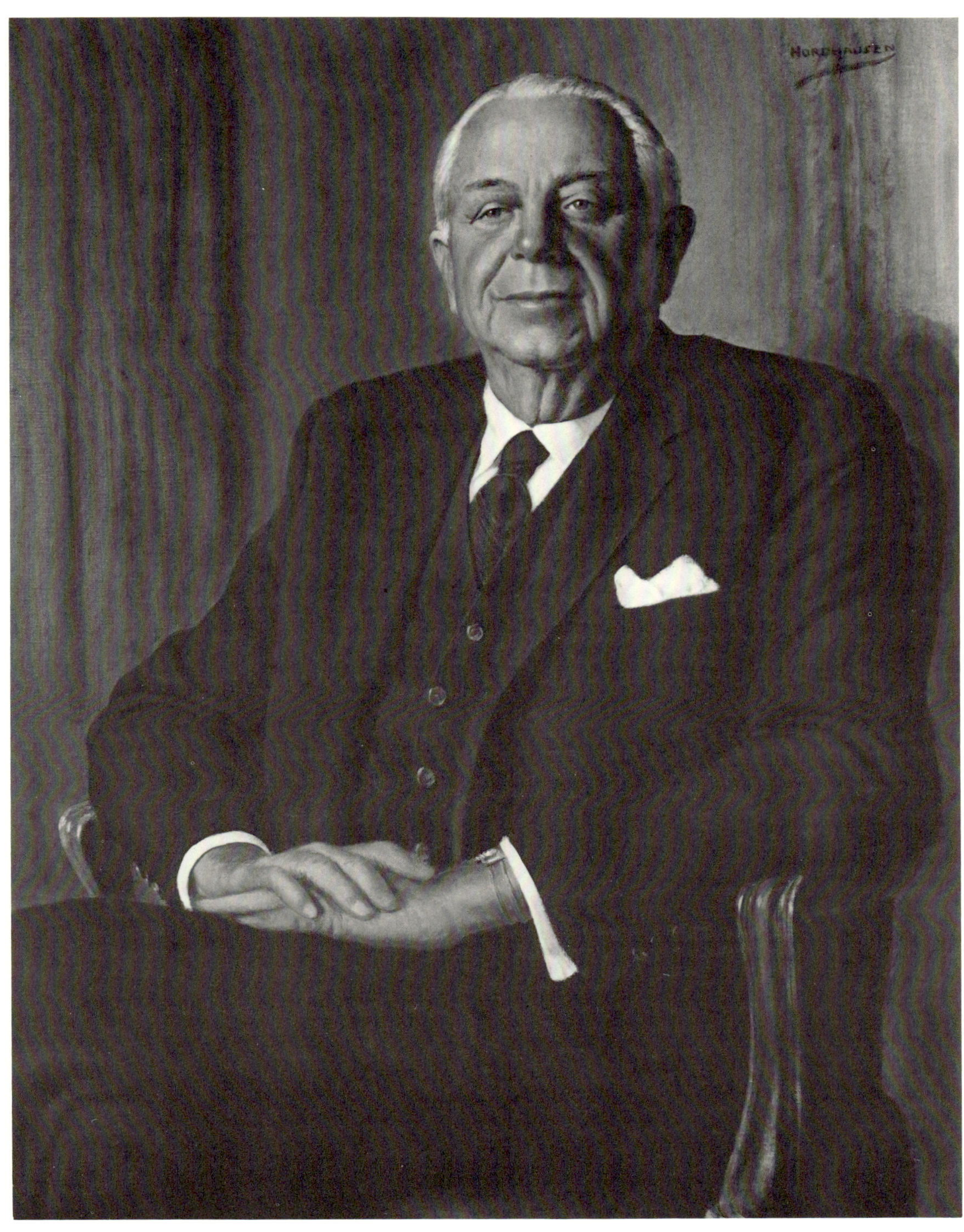

204. *Arthur Torrey*

1977
38''x 30''
Oil on canvas
Re Collection, Neponset, N.Y.

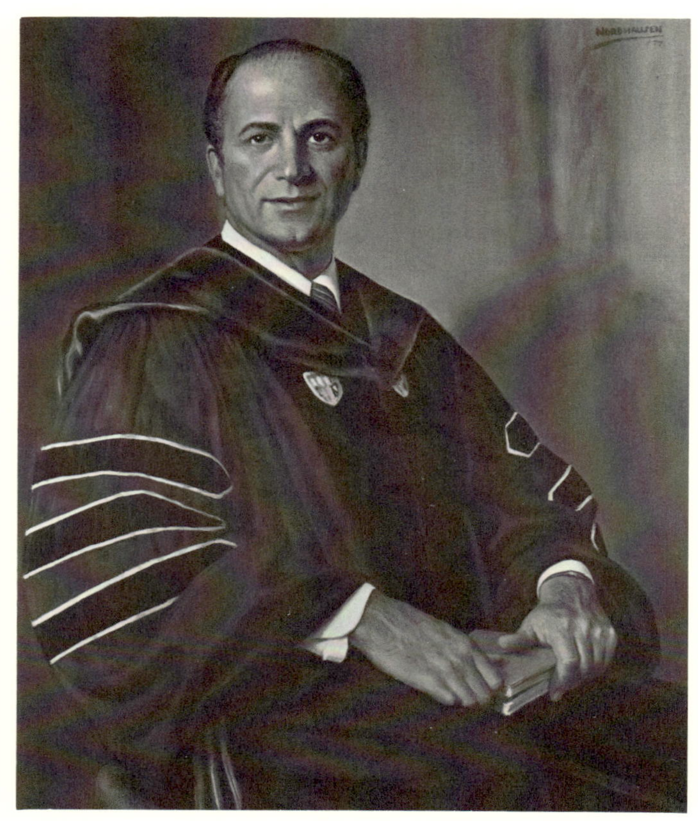

205. *Chief Justice Edward D. Re*

NORDHAUSEN

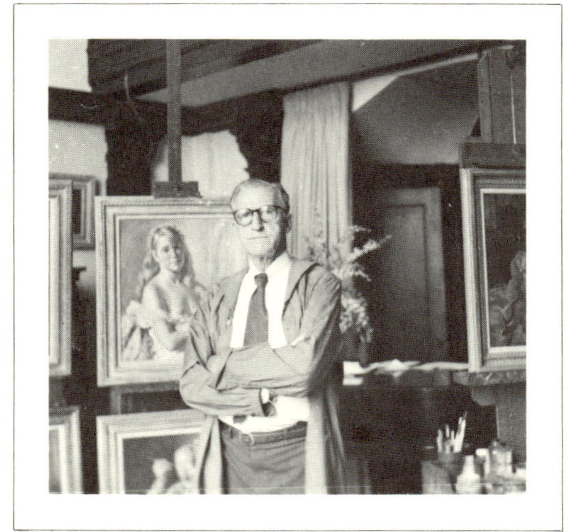

Chronology

Permanent Collections

Plates and Illustrations

Index

1901

Born January 25th in Hoboken, New Jersey. Family later moved to the Bronx, New York City, where he attended public school.

1910

Family bought summer boarding house in Lake Huntington in the Catskills of Sullivan County, New York. Attended one-room schoolhouse there.

1913

Returned to the Bronx; attended Public School No. 27.

1915

Attended Morris High School, then dropped out for two years to work, first in a law office, then as clerk in an insurance office.

1917

Returned to high school, this time Stuyvesant Technical High School, and developed interest in art through a German instructor, Henry Fritz. Worked weekends and holidays in a grocery store and delivered newspapers for the "Bronx Home News." Completed the four-year course in three years and received a scholarship sponsored by the School Art League of New York City.

1920

Entered New York School of Fine and Applied Arts (later Parsons School of Design). Studied painting with Howard Giles, drawing with Harry B. Baker. Spent summers as taxi driver in the Catskills which enabled him to finance further art studies.

1922

Went to Munich, Germany, to study at the Academy of Fine Arts under Hugo Freiherr von Habermann and Max Doerner. Also had independent study with Wilhelm Funk. Attended evening life and sketch classes at Hans Hofmann's and Heymann's art schools and regular courses in commercial design and layout, as well as graphics with Olaf Gulbranssen at the Kunstgewerbeschule. Traveled through France, Italy and Germany.

1925

Returned to New York and spent the next three years as a free-lance artist doing commercial work, stage design and figure painting.

1927

First one-man show, an exhibition of twenty-five paintings, including portraits, landscapes and still-lifes, done in Munich and New York, held at the Maryland Institute, Baltimore. Elected to membership in the Salmagundi Club; awarded first prize in its annual painting competition.

1928

Tiffany Foundation Scholarship, Oyster Bay, Long Island, enabled study with Gifford Beal. Returned to Munich for a year's independent study principally in portrait and figure painting. Continued private instruction with Wilhelm Funk and evening sketch classes in both Hofmann and Heymann schools.

1929

Returned to New York and established professional studio in the Gainsborough Studios on Central Park South; later (1931) moved to more modest studio apartment at 46 East 9th Street.

1929

Married Miriam Bernstein, one of founders of Flora Mir Candy Shops, and was responsible for the unique design and artistic character of the early units of this famous chain.

1930

First one-man exhibition, High Museum of Art, Atlanta, Georgia.

1931

New Haven Paint and Clay Club award for figure painting for "Girl with the Red Shawl." Taught art classes of all types from poster design to general drawing and painting in various institutions, including Roerich Institute, Morris High School and the New York School of Industrial Art.

1932

Fellowship awarded by the Spencer Trask Foundation (Yaddo), Saratoga Springs, New York.

1933, 1934

MacDowell Colony Fellowships, Peterborough, New Hampshire.

1936, 1937

Summer visits to Peacham, Vermont.

1938

Springfield (Mass.) Art League Award for figure painting.

1939

Joseph S. Isidore Prize for "Eda."

1940

Trip to Puerto Rico; painted landscapes and native types.

1941

Enlisted as private in the regular army; sent to Camp Croft (infantry) then to Fort Belvoir (engineers, camouflage), graduated from officer training as 2nd lieutenant, and transferred to radar with special training at Massachusetts Institute of Technology under Professor William Shockley.

1943

Promoted to captain and transferred to Air Force as Chief of Radar Intelligence and served in the China-Burma-India theater with 20th Air Force under General Curtis LeMay. Awarded a number of citations and eight battle stars.

1946

After discharge from the service, spent six months painting the circus with Ringling Brothers-Barnum & Bailey in Sarasota, Florida.

1946, 1947

Part-time study in philosophy and art history at the New School for Social Research, New York.

1947

Audubon Artists Award for "Nude on Mulberry Couch."

1948

Trip to Wyoming. Special Award in the Pepsi-Cola "Paintings of the Year" exhibition for "Puerto Rican Boy."

1948

C. H. Griffith Award for "Black Lace Gown."

1949

Mischa Lempert Prize for "Thoughtful Youth." Ranger Fund Purchase Award, for "Circus Friends" at the 123rd Annual Exhibition of the National Academy. Visited Mexico.

1950

Jack Kreindler Memorial Award for portrait study "Sara Mulligan."

1951

Four months in northern Italy painting landscapes. Allied Artists of America Gold Medal Award for best figure painting, "Natalia."

1952

Moved to professional studio in Hotel des Artistes, West 67th Street. One-man show of Italian landscapes at the Grand Central Galleries, New York.

1953, 1954

Year spent in Italy, mostly at Florence where he had a studio and in Calabria, doing landscapes and figure studies.

1956

Salmagundi Club Award for "Italian Girl in Purple."

1957

The Ted Kautsky Memorial Award by the American Watercolor Society for "Seated Nude."

1958

The Digby W. Chandler Award for "Clarisse" at the annual Salmagundi Club exhibition.

1959-1963

President of the Salmagundi Club. Effected reorganization from a private, professionally oriented group of artists to a charitable organization devoted to education and public service. Instituted among other programs a special project with the United States Navy known as Naval Art Cooperation and Liaison (N.A.C.A.L.) which sent American artists all over the world to depict naval achievements.

1960

Established second studio in Columbus, Georgia, for the increasing number of portrait commissions in the Georgia area.

1961

Louis E. Seley Award for "Seated Ballerina."

1962

Assignment to Greece and the Mediterranean with the Sixth Fleet mostly painting seascapes; tour of the Scandinavian countries.

1963

U.S. Navy Meritorious Award; the Salmagundi Club Medal for distinguished service; Wall Street Art Association Award for "Musical Clowns" at its Annual Spring Show.

1968

Philip I. Ross, Inc. Award for "Karyn" at Salmagundi Club Annual Spring Show.

1973

Benjamin West Clinedinst Memorial Medal for Distinguished Achievement in Painting awarded by Artists Fellowship, Inc.

1974

Gwynne Lennon award for "The 1890 Costume" at the annual Salmagundi Club exhibition.

1978

Death of Mir of a heart attack in New York. Marriage to Ethel Chandler Williams who for many years had been active in Columbus society, particularly in the Junior League and as a member of the board of the Columbus Museum of Arts and Sciences.

1980

Major retrospective exhibition of monotypes at the Columbus Museum of Arts and Sciences.

American College, Athens, Greece
Cleveland Museum of Art, Cleveland, Ohio
College of the City of New York, New York City
Columbus College, Columbus, Georgia
Columbus Museum of Arts and Sciences, Columbus, Georgia
William Connor Foundation, Connecticut
Cornell University, Herbert F. Johnson Museum of Art, Ithaca, New York
Darlington School, Rome, Georgia
Emory University, Decatur, Georgia
Georgia Institute of Technology, Atlanta, Georgia
Long Island University, Brooklyn, New York
Mercer College, Macon, Georgia
New Britain Museum of Art, New Britain, Connecticut
The Pentagon, Washington, D.C.
C. W. Post College, Brookville, New York
St. Lawrence University, Canton, New York
Salmagundi Club, New York City
Agnes Scott College, Decatur, Georgia
Shorter College, Rome, Georgia
Springer Opera House, Columbus, Georgia
Syracuse University, Syracuse, New York
Three Arts Theatre, Columbus, Georgia
U. S. Embassy, Lisbon, Portugal
University of Florida, Gainsville, Florida
University of Georgia, Athens, Georgia
University of North Carolina, Chapel Hill, North Carolina
University of South Carolina, Columbus, South Carolina
Virginia Military Institute, Richmond, Virginia

Plates and Illustrations

*Plates and illustrations are arranged chronologically within each
separate section of this volume, and the former are numbered sequentially as they
appear throughout the book. In the list of plates immediately below, the plate number
is followed by the title of the work, date of completion, ownership, and the page
on which it appears. Where no reference is made to ownership, the work
is in the private collection of the artist. All plate titles and
collections are also cross-referenced in the index.*

PLATES

I. *The Art of A. Henry Nordhausen*

1. **Boy in the Sun** / 1923, **12**
2. **Girl in White Shawl** / 1923 / Private collection, **13**
3. **Madam Leander** / 1923 / Private collection, **14**
4. **Miss Else Thieme** / 1924 / Private collection, **16**
5. **Man with Red Beard** / 1924, **17**
6. **Miss Irene Bordoni** / 1925 / Private collection, **19**
7. **Girl in Costume (Lillian Bliss)** / 1925 / Bliss Family Collection, **22**
8. **Teddy** / 1929, **24**
9. **Little Girl with Doll** / 1929 / Hearn Collection, **26**
10. **Child in Garden** / 1929 / Private collection, **28**

II. *Color Portfolio*

11. **Head of Woman** / 1923, **34**
12. **Baby Gwenn** / 1930, **35**
13. **Red Headed Nude** / 1938, **36**
14. **Clown Making Up** / 1938, **37**
15. **Clown with Green Bow** / 1938, **37**
16. **Nude Back, Seated** / 1940, **38**
17. **Nude on Mulberry Couch** / 1947 / Collection: Syracuse University, **39**
18. **Clarisse** / 1948, **40**
19. **Portrait of the Artist's Mother** / 1950, **41**
20. **Natalia** / 1950, **42**
21. **Natalia Half Nude** / 1950, **43**
22. **Natalia Nude** / 1950, **43**
23. **General Withers A. Burress** / 1952 / Collection: Virginia Military Institute, **44**
24. **Okhee Chae** / 1954 / Yashitoni Collection, **45**
25. **The Bathers** / 1955, **46**
26. **Girl in Pinafore** / 1956, **47**
27. **Seated Ballerina** / 1957 / Collection: College of the City of New York, **48**
28. **Autumn Flowers** / 1958 / Woodruff Collection, **49**
29. **Tying Her Ballet Slipper** / 1958 / Collection: Columbus Museum of Arts and Sciences, **50**
30. **Ballerina** / 1958 / Huff Collection, **51**
31. **1870 Costume with Parasol** / 1958 / Glenn Collection, **52**
32. **Dean Annie Louise MacLeod** / 1958 / Collection: Syracuse University, **53**
33. **Admiral Arleigh Burke** / 1961 / Collection: The Pentagon, **54**
34. **Byzantine Church, Aegina, Greece** / 1962 / Chrissoveloni Collection, **55**
35. **Nude on Purple Couch** / 1965, **55**

36. **Ben Hurt Hardaway III** / 1967 / Hardaway Collection, **56**
37. **Nude with Hat** / 1967 / Foley Collection, **57**
38. **The 1890 Costume** / 1968 / Williams Collection, **58**
39. **1890 Costume Standing, Back** / 1967, **59**
40. **Ready to Go On** / 1968 / Passailaigue Collection, **60**
41. **Seated Ballet Figure (The Red Rose)** / 1970, **61**
42. **Tying Her Slipper** / 1970 / Desind Collection, **62**
43. **Self Portrait** / 1971 / Collection: Salmagundi Club, **63**
44. **Professor Dean Rusk** / 1974 / Collection: University of Georgia, **64**

III. *Figure Painting*

45. **Nude** / 1924 / Private collection, **70**
46. **Venus and the Devil** / 1924 / Private collection, **70**
47. **Seated Nude, Back** / 1925 / Turner Collection, **70**
48. **Nude** / 1928 / Private collection, **71**
49. **Nude** / 1929 / Private collection, **71**
50. **Susanna and the Elders** / 1930, **71**
51. **Woman Reading** / 1930, **72**
52. **Girl in Peasant Costume** / 1930 / Mink Collection, **72**
53. **Girl with the Red Shawl** / 1930 / Esther Gold Collection, **73**
54. **The Old Fashioned Blouse** / 1934 / Millman Collection, **74**
55. **Girl with Puffed Sleeves** / 1934 / Rayvid Collection, **74**
56. **Burlesque Figure** / 1934 / Destroyed in fire, **75**
57. **Burlesque Dancers** / 1934, **75**
58. **Burlesque Bump** / 1935 / Private collection, **75**
59. **Injured Performer** / 1935 / Private collection, **76**
60. **Half Nude** / 1935 / Mink Collection, **76**
61. **Seated Half Nude** / 1935 / Private collection, **76**
62. **Clowns Resting** / 1935 / New Britain Museum of Art, **77**
63. **Circus Friends** / 1935 / University of South Carolina, **77**
64. **Circus People** / 1936 / Private collection, **78**
65. **Nude Fixing Hair** / 1936 / Private collection, **78**
66. **Nude Back, Seated** / 1936 / Rogers Collection, **78**
67. **Musical Clowns** / 1936, **79**
68. **Flying Trapeze** / 1936 / Williams Collection, **79**
69. **Bareback Riders** / 1936 / Taylor Collection, **80**
70. **Bareback Riders** / 1936 / Private collection, **80**
71. **Circus Folks** / 1936 / Riley Collection, **80**
72. **Balancing Act** / 1936, **81**
73. **Flying Trapeze** / 1936, **81**
74. **Burlesque** / 1937, **81**
75. **Standing Nude, Back** / 1937 / Destroyed in fire, **82**
76. **Standing Nude, Front** / 1937 / Destroyed in fire, **82**
77. **Seated Nude** / 1937 / Private collection, **83**
78. **Indonesian Ballerina** / 1937 / Matt Collection, **84**
79. **Indonesian Ballerina (Durine Dieters)** / 1937 / Shorter Collection, **85**
80. **Ballet Dancer (Eda)** / 1938 / Collection: William Connor Foundation, **85**

81. **Ballerina Resting** / 1938 / Private collection, **85**
82. **Old Fashioned Blouse (Sera)** / 1938, **86**
83. **Mother and Child** / 1938 / Williams Collection, **86**
84. **Nude Study** / 1938 / Seley Collection, **86**
85. **Two Clowns** / 1938 / Esther Gold Collection, **87**
86. **Clown with Red Wig** / 1938 / Private collection, **87**
87. **Clown with Hat** / 1939 / Private collection, **87**
88. **Study in Green and Gold** / 1939 / Liskin Collection, **88**
89. **Nude Back, Seated** / 1940 / Private collection, **88**
90. **Clown with Green Bow** / 1948 / Hughston Collection, **88**
91. **Thoughtful Youth** / 1949 / Collection: Cleveland
Museum of Art, **89**
92. **Sara in Slip** / 1949 / Collection: New Britain Museum of Art, **89**
93. **Lala** / 1950 / Kriendler Collection, **90**
94. **Pensive Youth** / 1953 / Private collection, **90**
95. **Susie in Tutu** / 1953 / Haskins Collection, **90**
96. **Nude in Half Shadow** / 1955 / Stolen, **91**
97. **Nude Resting** / 1955 / Collection: Syracuse University, **91**
98. **Italian Girl** / 1956 / Collection: Syracuse University, **92**
99. **Nude Kneeling on Chair** / 1957, **92**
100. **Ballerina Seated** / 1957, **92**
101. **Seated Ballerina** / 1958 / Collection: St. Lawrence
University, **93**
102. **1870 Costume with White Gloves** / 1958, **94**
103. **Half Nude** / 1958, **94**
104. **Half Nude with Arms Folded** / 1959 / Glick Collection, **95**
105. **Nude Kneeling** / 1961, **95**
106. **Ballerina Head** / 1961, **95**
107. **Ballerina in Gold Chair** / 1963 / Collection: Syracuse
University, **96**
108. **Nude Reading** / 1963 / Private collection, **96**
109. **Reclining Nude** / 1963 / Matt Collection, **96**
110. **Nude in Victorian Chair** / 1964 / Matt Collection, **97**
111. **Blond Primevera** / 1968, **97**

III. *Drawing*

112. **Cow and Calf** / 1925, **100**
113. **Lion Studies** / 1936, **100**
114. **Standing Nude** / 1938, **101**
115. **Shoreline with Boats (Puerto Rico)** / 1940, **101**
116. **Nude Back, Sitting** / 1941 / Collection: Syracuse University, **101**
117. **Performer Dressing** / 1941 / Collection: Syracuse
University, **102**

118. **Nude Back, Standing** / 1941 / Collection: Syracuse
University, **102**
119. **Nude in Repose** / 1941 / Collection: Syracuse University, **103**
120. **Head of a Man** / 1952 / Collection: Syracuse University, **103**
121. **Castello Saint Angelo** / 1953, **102**
122. **Head Study** / 1958, **103**
123. **Ballerina** / 1960, **103**
124. **Caroline Newhouse** / 1963 / Collection: Syracuse
University, **104**
125. **Seated Nude** / 1964, **104**
126. **Reclining Nude** / 1966, **105**

III. *The Still Life*

127. **Green Peppers** / 1939, **106**
128. **Fruit** / 1939, **107**
129. **Change of Life** / 1946 / 21 Club Collection, **107**
130. **Flowers in Glass Vase** / 1950 / Private collection, **107**
131. **Summer Flowers** / 1977, **107**

III. *The Landscape*

132. **Nürnberg** / 1928 / Johnson Collection, **109**
133. **Outside of Dinkelsbühl** / 1929 / Williams Collection, **109**
134. **Vermont Landscape** / 1936 / Private collection, **109**
135. **Peacham, Vermont** / 1937 / Private collection, **110**
136. **Monhegan Island** / 1939 / Private collection, **111**
137. **Puerto Rico** / 1940, **111**
138. **Wyoming Landscape** / 1948, **111**
139. **Stockade Lake, South Dakota** / 1948 / Edwards Collection, **111**
140. **Montecastello** / 1950 / Private collection, **112**
141. **Greek Island** / 1962 / Private collection, **113**
142. **Greek Island (Mikonos)** / 1962 / Private collection, **113**

III. *Prints and Monotypes*

143. **Man with a Cane** / 1929, **116**
144. **Bavarian with Newspaper** / 1929, **117**
145. **Wilhelm Funk** / 1929, **117**
146. **Houses in Nürnberg** / 1929, **117,**
147. **Munich, Englishe Garten** / 1929, **118**
148. **Landscape near Dinkelsbühl** / 1929, **118**
149. **Man with Bottle** / 1929, **118**
150. **City on a Rock (after Goya)** / 1932, **119**
151. **Sibyl (after Corot)** / 1932, **119**
152. **Self Portrait (El Greco)** / 1932, **119**
153. **Nude Undressing** / 1935 / Minikoff Collection, **120**
154. **Nude Undressing** / 1935 / Minikoff Collection, **120**
155. **Nude Undressing** / 1937, **121**
156. **Clown Talk** / 1939 / Private collection, **121**

III. *The Portrait*

157. **Head of a Woman** / 1923 / Private collection, **130**
158. **Bavarian Peasant in Sunshine** / 1924 / Warnecke Collection, **130**
159. **Queenie Smith** / 1925 / Private collection, **130**
160. **Miss Betty Hunner** / 1926 / Private collection, **131**
161. **Dr. Guy L. Hunner** / 1926 / Private collection, **131**
162. **Mother** / 1926, **131**
163. **Father** / 1926, **131**
164. **The Reverend L. M. Johnston** / 1927 / Johnston Collection, **132**
165. **Frank Alvah Parsons** / 1927 / Collection: Parsons School of Design, **132**
166. **Bavarian Peasant** / 1928, **132**
167. **Man with a Cane (the Poet)** / 1929, **133**
168. **Bavarian with Newspaper** / 1929 / Private collection, **134**
169. **Woman with Jug** / 1929 / Private collection, **134**
170. **The Gold Shawl** / 1929, **134**
171. **Girl in Costume (Susie)** / 1929, **135**
172. **Laurence Schmeckebier** / 1929 / Schmeckebier Collection, **136**
173. **Edwin Malone** / 1929 / Private collection, **136**
174. **President Martin Luther Brittain** / 1930 / Collection: Georgia Institute of Technology, **136**
175. **Professor Heneker (Uncle Heinie)** / 1930 / Stolen from Georgia Institute of Technology, **137**
176. **Negro Boy** / 1935 / Private collection, **138**
177. **Self Portrait** / 1939, **138**
178. **Gypsy Girl** / 1940 / Kriendler Collection, **138**
179. **Puerto Rican Boy** / 1940 / Kelbl Collection, **139**
180. **Blind Man, Puerto Rico** / 1940 / Private collection, **139**
181. **General John W. Moore** / 1947 / Collection: Virginia Military Institute, **139**
182. **The New Hat** / 1950, **140**
183. **Harrison Cady** / 1950, **140**
184. **Forget Me Not** / 1951, **140**
185. **Florentine Girl** / 1952 / Rayvid Collection, **141**
186. **Sardinian Girl** / 1952, **141**
187. **Jean** / 1956 / Collection: Columbus Museum of Arts and Sciences, **141**
188. **Jean Renoir** / 1956 / Renoir Collection, **142**
189. **Irwin Rothschild** / 1959 / Rothschild Collection, **142**
190. **The Foley Children** / 1960 / Foley Collection, **142**
191. **Miss Celia Gary** / 1960 / Feighner Collection, **143**
192. **Jack Passailaigue** / 1960 / Passailaigue Collection, **143**
193. **The Taylor Children** / 1965 / Taylor Collection, **143**
194. **Samuel J. Newhouse** / 1965 / Newhouse Collection, **144**
195. **D. Abbott Turner** / 1966 / Collection: Columbus Bank and Trust Co., **144**
196. **William T. Young** / 1967 / Young Collection, **144**
197. **Dr. Othell Hand** / 1971 / Hand Collection, **145**
198. **Mrs. George E. Lipscomb** / 1971 / Lipscomb Collection, **145**
199. **Colonel Blake Ragsdale Van Leer** / 1972 / Collection: Georgia Institute of Technology, **145**
200. **Mrs. Nathaniel Hardin** / 1973 / Hardin Collection, **145**
201. **Philip H. Alston, Jr.** / 1973 / Collection: University of Georgia, **146**
202. **Fitzgerald Hudson** / 1974 / Hawkins Collection, **146**
203. **J. Thomas Morgan, Jr.** / 1975 / Collection: Litho-Krome Co., **146**
204. **Arthur Torrey** / 1977 / Collection: St. Lawrence University, **147**
205. **Chief Justice Edward D. Re** / 1977 / Re Collection, **148**

ILLUSTRATIONS

Wedding photograph of the artist's parents, 1890, **4**
The twins, Henry and John, at six months, **4**
Henry, age four, **5**
Cover design for "The Caliper," 1919, **5**
Carnival watercolor, 1919, **6**
Knights in armor, Metropolitan Museum, 1919, **7**
Sketch of Harry B. Baker, 1921, **7**
Seated figure, 1921, **8**
Sketchbook exercise, 1921, **9**
Advertising design project, 1921, **10**
Wilhelm Funk's "HRH the Crown Princess of Bavaria," **10**
Charcoal studies, 1923, **11**
Hofbrau sketch, 1925, **12**
Hugo von Habermann's "Portrait in Gray and Pink," **14**
Gouache study, "The Executive," 1926, **15**
Portraits for the "Hall of Fame" project, 1927, **16**
Cover pastel for the Munich "Jugend," 1929, **18**
Flora Mir trademark, 1927, **20**
The artist and his parents, 1932, **21**
Caricature of the artist by William Auerbach Levy, **31**
Nordhausen sculpture, **99**
Analytical drawings for the "old masters" monotype series, **115**
Preliminary portrait studies, **125**
The artist with portrait of George Waldo Woodruff, 1964, **126**
Unveiling of former Secretary of State Dean Rusk's portrait, 1974, **129**

Index

"Admiral Arleigh Burke" (1961), plate, 54
Agnes Scott College, 152
Albers, Josef, 23
Allied Artists of America, 24; Gold Medal Award, 1951, plate, 42
Alston, Philip H., Jr., plate, 146
Alte Pinakothek, 7, 8, 17
American Abstract tradition, 24
"American" art, 21, 22, 24
"American Artist," 114 fn.
American College, 152
American Realists, 21
American Watercolor Society, 19, 22
Armory Show of 1913, 22, 24
Art Institute of Chicago, 19
Art Students League, 9
"Arthur Torrey" (1977), plate, 147
"Artist, The," 26
"Artists and Models," 14 fn.
Artists' Fellowship, 22
"Atlanta American," 21 fn.
Audubon Artists, 19, 22; award, 1947, plate, 39
"Aus Meiner Münchener Mappe," 11
"Autumn Flowers" (1958), plate, 49

"Baby Gwenn" (1930), 18, plate, 35
Baker, Harry B., 4, illus., 7
Balanchine, George, 68
"Balancing Act" (1936), plate, 81
"Ballerina" (1958), plate, 51
"Ballerina" (1960), plate, 103
"Ballerina Head" (1961), plate, 95
"Ballerina in Gold Chair" (1963), plate, 96
"Ballerina Resting" (1938), plate, 85
"Ballerina Seated" (1957), plate, 92
"Ballet Dancer (Eda)" (1938), plate, 85
Baltimore Institute of Art, 19
"Baltimore Sun," review, 15
Baracca, Francisco, 15
"Bareback Riders" (1936), plate, 80
"Bavarian Peasant" (1928), 17, plate, 132
"Bavarian Peasant in Sunshine" (1924), 13, plate, 130
"Bavarian with Newspaper" (1929), plate, 117
"Bavarian with Newspaper" (1929), 17, plate, 134
Beal, Gifford, 16, 18, 24, 69
Beckmann, Max, 7, 10
Bellows, George, 5 fn., 14, 19, 31
"Ben Hurt Hardaway III" (1967), plate, 56
Bernstein, Miriam, 19, 20
Bird, Mr. and Mrs. Ernest Stevenson, 127
Bird Library, 127
Blake, William, 114
Blanche, Arnold, 20, 22
"Blind Man, Puerto Rico" (1940), plate, 139
Bliss Family collection, 22
"Blond Primevera" (1968), plate, 97
Böcklin, Arnold, 6, 10
Boelcke, Oswald, 15
Bordoni, Irene, 13, plate, 19
"Boy in the Sun" (1923), 13, plate, 12
Braque, Georges, 31
Briggs, Walter, 9
Brittain, Professor Martin Luther, plate, 136
"Bronx Home News," 3
Burke, Admiral Arleigh, plate, 54
"Burlesque" (1937), plate, 81
"Burlesque Bump" (1935), plate, 75
"Burlesque Dancers" (1934), 116, plate, 75
"Burlesque Figure" (1934), plate, 75
Burress, General Withers A., plate, 44
Byrd, Richard, 15
"Byzantine Church, Aegina, Greece" (1962), plate, 55

Cady, Harrison, plate, 140
Calder, Alexander, 15, 69
"Caliper, The," 4, illus., 5
Camp Croft, 23
Carnival watercolor, illus., 6
"Caroline Newhouse" (1963), plate, 104
Carter, David G., 5 fn.
Carter, Ruth Hinman, 21
Caspari (Gallery), 7
"Castello Saint Angelo" (1953), plate, 102
Cezanne, Paul, 7, 115
Chagall, Marc, 69
Chamberlin, Clarence, 15
"Change of Life" (1946), 23, plate, 107
Chase, William Merritt, 5, 7, 14, 27, 114
"Chief Justice Edward D. Re" (1977), plate, 148
"Child in Garden" (1929), 21, plate, 28
Chrissoveloni Collection, 55
"Circus Folks" (1936), plate, 80
"Circus Friends" (1935), plate, 77
"Circus People" (1936), plate, 78
"City on a Rock (after Goya)" (1932), 115, plate, 119
"Clarisse" (1948), plate, 40
Cleveland Museum of Art, 152; collection, 89
Close, Chuck, 29
"Clown Making Up" (1938), plate, 37
"Clown Talk" (1939), 116, plate, 121
"Clown with Green Bow" (1938), plate, 37
"Clown with Green Bow" (1948), plate, 88
"Clown with Hat" (1939), 116, plate, 87
"Clown with Red Wig" (1938), plate, 87
"Clowns Resting" (1935), plate, 77
College of the City of New York, 152; collection, 48, 152
"Colonel Blake Ragsdale Van Leer" (1972), plate, 145
Columbus Bank and Trust Co. Collection, 144
Columbus College, 152
Columbus, Georgia, 27
Columbus Museum of Arts and Sciences, 128, 152; collection, 50, 141
Connor, William, Foundation, 152; collection, 85
Constable, John, 30
Corcoran Gallery, 19
Corinth, Lovis, 6
Cornell University, Herbert F. Johnson Museum of Art, 152
Corot, Jean Baptiste Camille, 115, plate, 119
Courbet, Gustave, 6, 10, 98, 122
"Cow and Calf" (1925), plate, 100
Cowles, Russell, 69
Criterion Theater, 15
Crocker, E.B., Art Gallery, 7 fn.
Currier, Frank, 7
Curry, John Steuart, 24

"D. Abbott Turner" (1966), plate, 144
Daguerre, Louis, 124
Dali, Salvador, 30
Darlington School, 152
da Vinci, Leo, 14
Davis, Stuart, 20
"Dean Annie Louise MacLeod" (1958), 53
Degas, Edgar, 10, 26, 68, 98, 114
Delacroix, Eugene, 24, 98
"Der Blaue Reiter," 7
Desind Collection, 62
"Deutsch-Amerika," 11 fn.
Diez, Wilhelm, von, 6
Digby W. Chandler Prize, plate, 40
Dix, Otto, 23
Doerner, Max, 8, 126
"Dr. Othell Hand" (1971), plate, 145
"Dr. Guy L. Hunner" (1926), 131
Drawing, 98-100
Dufy, Jean, 69
Duveneck, Frank, 7, 13, 14
"Dynamic Symmetry in Composition as Used by
    Artists," 5 fn.

Eakins, Thomas, 14, 99
Edwards Collection, 111
"Edwin Malone" (1929), plate, 136
"1870 Costume with Parasol" (1958), 52
"1870 Costume with White Gloves" (1958), plate,
    94
"1890 Costume Standing, Back" (1967), plate, 59
El Greco, 16, 115, plate, 119
Emory University, 152
Esther Gold Collection, 73, 87
Explorers' Club, 22
Expressionists, 13

"Father" (1926), plate, 131
Feighner Collection, 143
Ferargil Galleries, 69
Fifth Annual Conference on Art Education (1947),
    99
Figure painting, 67-69
Fiore, Frank, 4
First American Artists' Congress (1936), 20
Fitzgerald, Boylan, 26
"Fitzgerald Hudson" (1974), plate, 146
Flora Mir candy shops, 15, 19, 20; trademark,
    illus., 20
"Florentine Girl" (1952), plate, 141
"Flowers in Glass Vase" (1950), plate, 107
"Flying Trapeze" (1936), 116, plate, 79
"Flying Trapeze" (1936), plate, 81
Foley Children, plate, 142
Foley Collection, 57, 142
Fonck, René, 15
"Forget Me Not" (1951), 69, plate, 140
Fort Belvoir, 23
Foster, Gerald, 19
"Frank Alvah Parsons" (1927), 132
Frank, Waldo, 99
French "Art Noveau," 6 fn.
French modernism, 21
Fritz, Henry, 3
"Fruit" (1939), plate, 107
Funk, Lyle W., 9
Funk, Wilhelm Heinrich, 9, 11, 14, 17, 18; "HRH
    the Crown Princess of Bavaria," plate, 10

Gary, Miss Celia, plate, 143
Gauguin, Paul, 7
"General Withers A. Burress" (1952), plate, 44
"General John W. Moore" (1947), plate, 139
Georgia Institute of Technology, 152; collection,
    136, 137, 145
Giles, Howard, 4, 5, 5 fn.
"Girl in Costume (Lillian Bliss)" (1925), 15, plate,
    22
"Girl in Costume (Susie)" (1929), 17, plate, 135
"Girl in Peasant Costume" (1930), plate, 72
"Girl in Pinafore" (1956), 18, plate, 47
"Girl in White Shawl" (1923), 13, plate, 13
"Girl with Puffed Sleeves" (1934), plate, 74
"Girl with the Red Shawl" (1930), 18, plate, 73
Glackens, William, 114
Glaspalast (Munich), 6
Glenn Collection, 52
Glick Collection, 95
Globe Theater, 20
Gold, Esther, Collection, 73, 87
Goya, 25, 26, 31, 98, 115, plate, 119
Grand Central Gallery, 19, 25
Great Depression, 19, 20
"Greek Island" (1962), plate, 113
"Greek Island (Mikonos)" (1962), plate, 113
"Green Peppers" (1939), plate, 106
Gregoriev, Boris, 123
Gropius, Walter, 99
Grosz, George, 23
Gulbransson, Olaf, 8
Guynemer, Georges, 15
Gynne Lennon Award, 1974, plate, 58
"Gypsy Girl" (1940), 69, plate, 138

Habermann, Hugo Freeherr, von, 6, 8, 10, 13, 14;
    "Portrait in Gray and Pink," plate, 14
"Half Nude" (1935), plate, 76
"Half Nude" (1958), plate, 94
"Half Nude with Arms Folded" (1959), 95
"Hall of Fame," 15; portraits for, illus., 16
Halmi, Arthur, 123
Hals, Franz, 10, 13, 17, 26, 31, 115
Hambridge, Jay, 5, 5 fn.
"Hambridge Research," 5
Hampden, Walter, 5 fn.
Hand Collection, 145
Hand, Dr. Othell, plate, 145
Hanfstaengl (Gallery), 7
Hardaway Collection, 56
Hardin Collection, 145
Hardin, Mrs. Náthaniel, plate, 145
"Harrison Cady" (1950), plate, 140
Hartley, Jonathan Scott, 27
Haskins Collection, 90
Hawkins Collection, 146
Hayter, Stanley William, 99
"Head of a Man" (1952), plate, 103
"Head of a Woman" (1923), plate, 130
"Head of Woman" (1923), plate, 34
"Head Study" (1958), plate, 103
Hearn Collection, 26
Heneker, (Uncle Heinie), Professor, plate, 137
Henri, Robert, 5 fn., 14, 15, 16, 17, 21, 29, 31, 99
Heymann, 8
Higgins, Eugene, 114
High Museum of Art, 19, 21
"Hille Babbe," 115
"History of the Parsons School of Design, A,
    1896-1966," 4
Hitler, Adolph, 11, 23
Hodler, Ferdinand, 7
Hofer, Karl, 7
Hofmann, Hans, 8, 10, 24, 26, 31
Holty, Carl, 10
Homer, Winslow, 98
"Houses in Nürnberg" (1929), plate, 117

"HRH the Crown Princess of Bavaria," (Wilhelm
    Funk), plate, 11
Hudson, Fitzgerald, plate, 146
Huff Collection, 51
Hughston Collection, 88
Hunner, Dr. Guy L., plate, 131
Hunner, Miss Betty, plate, 131

"Indicator, The," 4
"Indonesian Ballerina" (1937), plate, 84
"Indonesian Ballerina (Durine Dieters)" (1937),
    plate, 85
"Injured Performer" (1935), plate, 76
Innes, George, 27, 30
Irving, Washington, 27
"Irwin Rothschild" (1959), plate, 142
"Italian Girl" (1956), plate, 92
Ivins, William M., Jr., 21

"J. Thomas Morgan, Jr." (1975), plate, 146
"Jack Passailaigue" (1960), plate, 143
"Jean" (1956), plate, 141
"Jean Renoir" (1956), plate, 142
Johansen, John C., 15
John, Augustus, 25
Johnson Collection, 109
Johnston Collection, 132
Johnston, The Reverend L. M., plate, 132
Jones, Marjorie F., 4
Joseph S. Isidor Prize, 1939, plate, 85
"Jugend," 6 fn., 12, 17, illus., 18
"Jugendstil," 6, 6 fn.

Kandinski, Wassily, 7
Karfiol, Bernard, 31, 69, 99
Kastellow, Alexander, 99
Kelbl Collection, 139
Kennedy, Senator Edward, illus., 129
Kent, Rockwell, 20
Kirchner, Ernst Ludwig, 7
Klee, Paul, 7, 10
Knappertsbusch, Hans, 9
Kokoschka, Oskar, 10, 25, 31
Kramer, Hilton, 29, 123
Kriendler Collection, 90, 138
Kroll, Leon, 5 fn., 31, 99
Kuhn, Walt, 24, 99

La Farge, John, 27
Lake Huntington, illus., 21
"Lala" (1950), plate, 90
"Landscape near Dinkelsbühl" (1929), 114, plate, 118
Landscape painting, 108
Landston, Tolbert, 114
"Laurence Schmeckebier" (1929), plate, 136
Leander, Madam, 13, plate, 14
Leibl, Wilhelm, 6, 10, 13
Le May, General Curtis, 23
Lenbach, Franz, von, 6, 10, 13
Lenbach Museum, 7
Levy, William Auerbach, 31
Leydendecker, J. C., 9, 14
Liebermann, Max, 6
Lindbergh, Charles, 15, illus., 16
"Lion Studies" (1936), plate, 100
Lipscomb Collection, 145
Lipscomb, Mrs. George, plate, 145
Liskin Collection, 88
Litho-Krome Co. Collection, 146
"Little Girl with Doll" (1929), 17, plate, 26
Long Island University, 152
Louis E. Seley Award, 1961, plate, 48
Lowenfeld, Viktor, 99
Luks, George, 14, 17, 21, 29, 31

Macbeth Gallery, 19
Macbeth, Robert, 19
MacDowell Colony Fellowships, 19
Macke, August, 7
MacLeod, Dean Annie Louise, 128, plate, 53
"Madam Leander" (1923), plate, 14
Malone, Edwin, 18, plate, 136
"Man with a Cane" (1929), 114, plate, 116
"Man with Bottle" (1929), plate, 118
"Man with a Straw Hat," 115
"Man with Red Beard" (1924), plate, 17
Manet, Edouard, 30
Marc, Franz, 7
Marées, Hans, von, 6
Marsh, Reginald, 29, 31
Massachusetts Institute of Technology, 23
Matt Collection, 84, 96
McCormick, William B., 21
Memorial Union Gallery (University of Wisconsin), 115
Mercer College, 152
Metropolitan Museum of Art, 19, 20, 115, 122; Medieval Hall, knights in armor, illus., 7
Metropolitan Opera, 20
Miller, Barse, 69
Milles, Carl, 25, 26
Millman Collection, 74
Minikoff Collection, 120
Mink Collection, 72

Mischa Lempert Prize, 1949, plate, 89
"Miss Irene Bordoni" (1925), 13, plate, 19
"Miss Celia Gary" (1960), plate, 143
"Miss Betty Hunner" (1926), plate, 131
"Miss Else Thieme" (1924), plate, 16
Mollier, Professor, 8
"Monhegan Island" (1939), plate, 111
Monotypes, 114-116
"Montecastello" (1950), plate, 112
Moore, Gen. John W., 27, 123, 128, plate, 139
Moran, Thomas, 27
Morgan, J. Thomas, Jr., plate, 146
Morris High School, 19
Morris, William, 6 fn.
"Mother" (1926), plate, 131
"Mother and Child" (1938), plate, 86
"Mrs. Nathaniel Hardin" (1973), plate, 145
"Mrs. George E. Lipscomb" (1971), plate, 145
Mumford, Louis, 20
Munch, Edvard, 7, 10, 25
"Munchener Neuste Nachrichten," 12
Munchener Sezession, 6, 6 fn.
Munich Academy of Fine Arts, 6, 9, 13, 14, 18
"Munich and American Realism in the 19th Century," 7 fn.
"Munich, Englishe Garten" (1929), plate, 118
Munich, artistic scene in 1920, 6-7
Munich Glaspalast, 9
Munich Künstlergenossenschaft, 7
Munich Kunstgewerbeschule, 8
"Munich Men," 7 fn.
Munich Putsch, 11
Museum of Modern Art, see Whitney Museum of Modern Art
"Musical Clowns" (1936), plate, 79

"Natalia" (1950), 69, plate, 42
"Natalia Half Nude" (1950), plate, 43
"Natalia Nude" (1950), plate, 43
National Academy of Design, 19, 22, 114
Navy Art Cooperation and Liaison Committee, 27
Navy Combat Art Program, 27
"Negro Boy" (1935), plate, 138
Nelson, C. G., 19
"Neuekünstlervereinigung," 7
Neu Pinakothek, 7
Neue Staatsgalerie, 7, 10
New Artists Federation, 7
New Britain Museum of Art, 152; collection, 77, 89
New Haven Paint and Clay Club Award, 1931, plate, 73
New School for Social Research, 24
New York City Ballet, 68
New York School Art League, 4, 20, 22
New York School of Fine and Applied Arts, 5, 127
New York School of Industrial Art, 19
"New York Times," 29, 123
Newhouse, Caroline, plate, 104
Newhouse Collection, 144
Newhouse, Samuel I., plate, 144
Nolde, Emil, 7
Nordhausen, A. Henry: Abstraction, 31; American West landscapes, 108; "The Art of Henry Nordhausen," 14; awards: 24, 39, 40, 42, 48, 58, 73, 77, 79, 83, 85, 89, 139, 150, 151; anatomy,

study of, 98-99; artistic maturity, 15-17; background, 3; birth, 3; "Change of Life," 23-24; caricature by Levy, illus., 31; circus painting, 23-24, 68-69; conversations on art, 30-32; drawing, 98-100; early life, 3-4; early portraits, 13; education in New York, 3-5, 24, in Munich, 8-11; exhibitions, 12, 14, 19, 21, 24, 69, 115, 128; expressionism, 31; fellowship, 16; Fifth Annual Conference on Art Education, 99; figure painting, 67-69; Flora Mir candy shops, 20; free-lance commercial work, 15; William Funk, 17-18; German landscapes, 108; "Hall of Fame," 15; Hans Hofmann, 26; landscape painting, 108; Manhattan, 28-29; marriage, 20; Monhegan Island paintings, 108; monotypes, 114-116; "The Monotypes of A. Henry Nordhausen," 114 fn.; Munich, 1922-1925, 6-13; Munich, 1928-1929, 17-18; Munich Putsch, 11; Munich work, 12-13; parents, illus., 4, 21; Peacham, Vermont, 108; photograph, age 4, illus., 5; photograph with John, illus., 4; portrait painting, 122-129; prints, 114-116; professional portraiture, 27-28; Puerto Rican landscapes, 108; realism, 20; return to New York, 1925, 13-15; return to New York, 1929, 18; Ringling Brothers-Barnum and Bailey Circus, 23-24; Salmagundi Club, 16, 27; scholarship, 4; still life, 106; struggle for artistic integrity, 21; study in Munich, 8-11; study in New York, 3-5; surrealism, 30; teaching during Depression, 19-20; trips abroad, 25; U.S. Navy assignment, 25; Vermont landscape, 108; World War II, 23
"Nude" (1924), plate, 70
"Nude" (1928), plate, 71
"Nude" (1929), plate, 71
"Nude Back, Seated" (1936), plate, 78
"Nude Back, Seated" (1940), plate, 38
"Nude Back, Seated" (1940), plate, 88
"Nude Back, Sitting" (1941), plate, 101
"Nude Back, Standing" (1941), plate, 102
"Nude Fixing Hair" (1936), plate, 78
"Nude in Half Shadow" (1955), plate, 91
"Nude in Repose" (1941), plate, 103
"Nude in Victorian Chair" (1964), plate, 97
"Nude Kneeling" (1961), plate, 95
"Nude Kneeling on Chair" (1957), plate, 92
"Nude on Mulberry Couch" (1947), plate, 39
"Nude on Purple Couch" (1965), plate, 55
"Nude Reading" (1963), plate, 96
"Nude Resting" (1955), 91
"Nude Study" (1938), plate, 86
"Nude Undressing" (1935), plate, 120
"Nude Undressing" (1937), plate, 121
"Nude with Hat" (1967), plate, 57
Nungesser, Charles, 15, illus., 16
"Nürnberg" (1928), plate, 109

"Okhee Chae" (1954), plate, 45
"Old Fashioned Blouse (Sera)" (1938), plate, 86
"Outside of Dinkelsbühl" (1929), plate, 109

Paris Salon of 1884, 122
Paris Société des Arts, 9
Parsons, Frank Alvah, 4, 16, 127, plate, 132
Parsons School of Design Collection, 132
Passailaigue Collection, 60, 143
Peacham, Vermont, 108
"Peacham, Vermont" (1937), plate, 110
Pearlstein, 29
Pechstein, Max, 7
Pennsylvania Academy, 19

"Pensive Youth" (1953), plate, 90
Pentagon, The, collection, 54
Pepsi-Cola "Paintings of the Year," 24; award, 1948, plate, 139
"Performer Dressing" (1941), plate, 102
"Philip H. Alston, Jr." (1973), plate, 146
Picasso, Pablo, 23, 31
Piloty, Karl, von, 6
Pollock, Jackson, 31
"Portrait in Gray and Pink" (Hugo von Habermann), plate, 14
"Portrait of a Lady," 17, illus., 18
"Portrait of a Man," 115
"Portrait of the Artist's Mother" (1950), plate, 41
Portrait painting, 122-129
Post, C.W., College, 152
Prendergast, Maurice, 114
"President Martin Luther Brittain" (1930), plate, 136
Print Collectors' "Newsletter," 114 fn.
Prints, 114-116
"Professor Heneker (Uncle Heinie)" (1930), plate, 137
"Professor Dean Rusk" (1974), plate, 64
"Puerto Rico" (1940), plate, 111
"Puerto Rican Boy" (1940), plate, 139

"Queenie Smith" (1925), plate, 130

Raleigh, H.P., 9
Ranger Fund Purchase Award, 1942, plate, 77
Raphael, 30, 122
Rayvid Collection, 74, 141
Re, Chief Justice Edward D., plate, 148
Re Collection, 148
"Ready to Go On" (1968), 60
"Reclining Nude" (1963), plate, 96
"Reclining Nude" (1966), plate, 105
"Red Headed Nude" (1938), plate, 36
Reinhardt Gallery, 122
Rembrandt, 10, 25, 30, 122
Renior, Auguste, 114
Renoir Collection, 142
Renoir, Jean, plate, 142
Renoir, Pierre A., 10, 26, 98
Rhode Island School of Design, Museum of Art, 5 fn.
Richtofen, Manfred, von, 15
Rickenbacker, Eddie, 15
Riley Collection, 80
Ringling Brothers-Barnum and Bailey Circus, 23-24
Rodin, Auguste, 98
Roerich Museum, Master Institute, 4, 19
Rogers Collection, 78
Rosa, Guido, 4
Ross, Denman, 5 fn.
Rothschild Collection, 142
Rothschild, Irwin, plate, 142
Rouault, Georges, 69
Rubens, Peter Paul, 10, 17, 26, 122, 126
Rusk, Dean, illus., 129, plate, 64
Ryder, Albert P., 27

St. Lawrence University, 152; collection, 93, 147
Salmagundi Club, 16, 19, 22, 27, 152; collection, 63
"Salmagundi" essays, 27
Sample, Paul, 19
"Samuel I. Newhouse" (1965), plate, 144
"Sara in Slip" (1949), plate, 89

"Sardinian Girl" (1952), 69, plate, 141
Sargent, John Singer, 16, 123; "Madame X," 122
"Saturday Evening Post," 122 fn.
Schackgalerie, 7
Schmeckebier, Laurence, 18; collection, 136; plate, 136
Schmidt-Rottluff, Karl, 7
Schockley, William, 23
"Seated Ballerina" (1957), plate, 48
"Seated Ballerina" (1958), plate, 93
"Seated Ballet Figure (the Red Rose)" (1970), plate, 61
"Seated Half Nude" (1935), plate, 76
"Seated Nude" (1937), plate, 83
"Seated Nude" (1964), plate, 104
"Seated Nude, Back" (1925), plate, 70
Seley Collection, 86
"Self Portrait" (1939), plate, 138
"Self Portrait" (1971), plate, 63
"Self Portrait (El Greco)" (1932), plate, 119
Shane, Flora and Jessie, 20
"Shoreline with Boats (Puerto Rico)" (1940), plate, 101
Shorter Collection, 85
Shorter College, 152
Shorter, Edward S., 128
"Sibyl (after Corot)" (1932), 115, plate, 119
"Simplicissimus," 8
Sketch Club, 27
Slevogt, Max, 6
Sloan, John, 31, 99
Smith, Queenie, 15, plate, 130
Society of American Artists, 7 fn.
Soyers, Moses and Raphael, 27, 31, 99
Speicher, Eugene, 31, 99
Springer Opera House, 152
Sproehnle, Katherine, 122
"Standing Nude" (1938), plate, 101
"Standing Nude, Back" (1937), plate, 82
"Standing Nude, Front" (1937), plate, 82
Sternberg, Harry, 99
Still life, 106
"Stockade Lake, South Dakota" (1948), plate, 111
Stuck, Franz, von, 6, 6 fn., 10
"Study in Green and Gold" (1939), plate, 88
Stuyvesant Technical High School, 3
"Summer Flowers" (1977), plate, 107
"Susanna and the Elders" (1930), 67, plate, 71
"Susie in Tutu" (1953), plate, 90
Syracuse University, 127, 128, 152; collection: 39, 53, 91, 92, 96, 101, 102, 103, 104

Taylor Children, plate, 143
Taylor Collection, 82, 143
Ted Krautsky Memorial Award, 1957, plate, 83
"Teddy" (1929), plate, 24
Thannhauser (Gallery), 7
"The Art of Henry Nordhausen," 14
"The Bathers" (1955), 46
"The Business of Portrait Painting," 122
"The Eight," 19, 29, 31
"The 1890 Costume" (1968), plate, 58
"The Executive" (1926), illus., 15
"The Foley Children" (1960), plate, 142
"The Gold Shawl" (1929), 17, plate, 134
"The Monotypes of A. Henry Nordhausen," 114 fn.
"The New Hat" (1950), plate, 140
"The Old Fashioned Blouse" (1934), plate, 74
The Pentagon, 152; collection, 54
"The Reverend L. M. Johnston" (1927), plate, 132
"The Taylor Children" (1965), plate, 143
Thieme, Else, 12, 13, plate, 16
"Thoughtful Youth" (1949), plate, 89
Three Arts Theater, 126, 152
Tiffany, Louis C., 27
Tiffany, Louis Comfort, Foundation, 16

Tintoretto, Jacopo Robusti, 98
Titian, 122
Torrey, Arthur, plate, 147
Trask, Spencer, Foundation, 19
Trübner, Wilhelm, 6 fn.
Turner Collection, 70
Turner, D. Abbott, plate, 144
Twentieth Air Force, 23
21 Club, 23; collection, 107
"Two Clowns" (1938), plate, 87
"Tying Her Ballet Slipper" (1958), plate, 50
"Tying Her Slipper" (1970), plate, 62

Uhde, Fritz, von, 6 fn.
"Uncle Heinie" (1930), 18, plate, 137
U.S. Embassy (Lisbon), 152
Universal Service, 21
University of Florida, 152
University of Georgia, 152; collection, 64, 146; illus., 129
University of North Carolina, 152
University of South Carolina, 152; collection, 77

Van Gogh, 7, 31
Van Leer, Colonel Blake Ragsdale, plate, 145
Velásquez, 17, 25, 26, 31
"Venus and the Devil" (1924), 67, plate, 70
"Vermont Landscape," 108
"Vermont Landscape" (1936), plate, 109
Virginia Military Institute, 152; collection, 44, 139
Vytlacil, Vaclav, 10

Wall Street Art Association Award, 1963, plate, 79
Walter, Bruno, 9
Warnecke Collection, 130
Watson, Ernest W., 114
Whistler, James Abbott McNeill, 6
White, Stanford, 27
Whitney Museum of American Art, 21, 99, 123
"Wilhelm Funk" (1929), plate, 117
William Connor Foundation, 152; collection, 85
Williams Collection, 58, 79, 86, 109
Williams, Ethel Chandler, 128, 151
"William T. Young" (1967), plate, 144
"Wings," 15
"Woman Reading" (1930), plate, 72
"Woman with Jug" (1929), 17, plate, 134
Woodruff Collection, 49
Woodruff, George Waldo, illus., 126
WPA art program, 19, 22
Wyeth, Andrew, 30
Wyeth, N.C., 9, 14
"Wyoming Landscape" (1948), plate, 111

Yashitoni Collection, 45
Young Collection, 144

Zerbe, Karl, 69
Zügel, Heinrich, von, 6
Zuloaga, Ignacio, 122-123, 124

THE ART OF A. HENRY
NORDHAUSEN

has been published in a first edition of three thousand copies. Designed by A. L. Morris, the book was composed in Palatino and Helvetica and printed by Courier Printing Company in Littleton, New Hampshire, on S N Text specially manufactured for this edition by Monadnock Paper Mills of Bennington, New Hampshire. The binding in James River Graphics' Scottek C and Kivar 9 was executed by New Hampshire Bindery in Concord, New Hampshire, and the color separations were made by Graphic Color Service of Waterville, Maine.

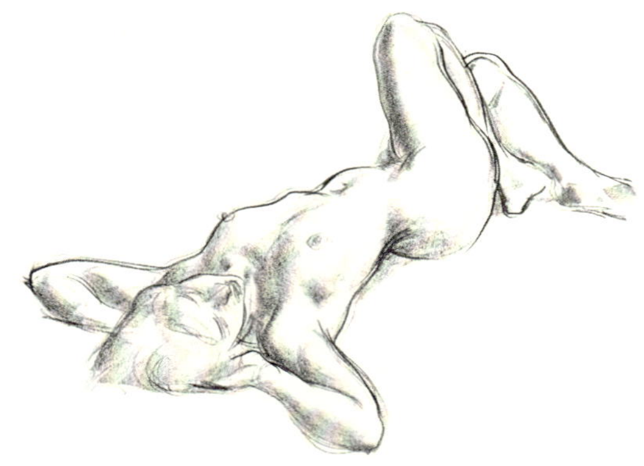

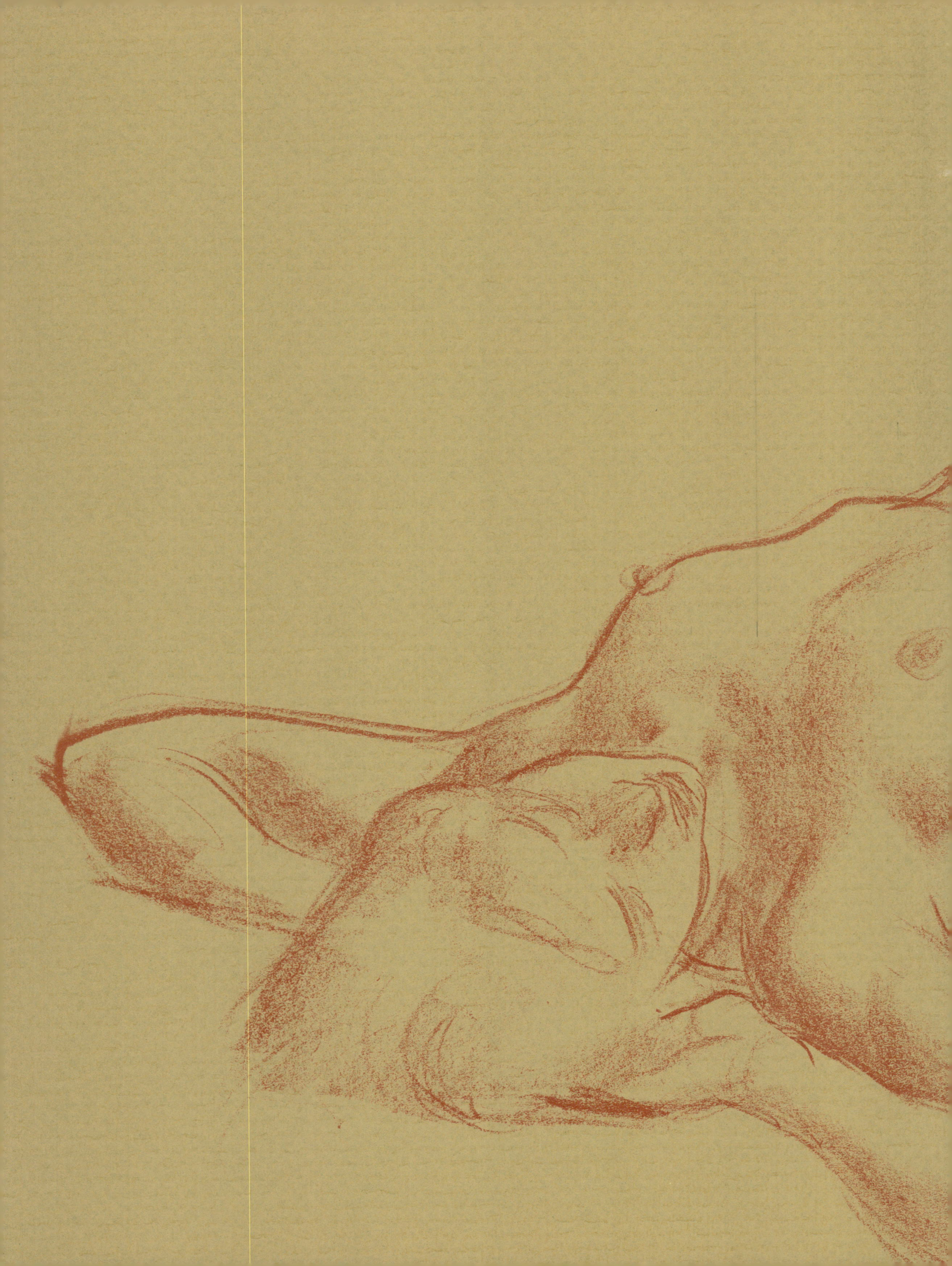